Beyond Multiple Choice:
Evaluating Alternatives
to Traditional Testing for Selection

Beyond Multiple Choice: Evaluating Alternatives to Traditional Testing for Selection

Edited by

Milton D. Hakel
Bowling Green State University

LEA LAWRENCE ERLBAUM ASSOCIATES, PUBLISHERS
1998   Mahwah, New Jersey   London

Lawrence Erlbaum Associates, Inc., Publishers
10 Industrial Avenue
Mahwah, NJ 07430

Library of Congress Cataloging in Publication Data

Beyond multiple choice : evaluating alternatives to traditional testing for selection / edited by Milton D. Hakel.
　　　p. cm.
Includes bibliographicical references and index
ISBN 0-8058-2053-1 (alk. paper)
1. Employment tests. I. Hakel, Milton D.
HF5549.5.E5B49 1997
153.9'4—dc21　　　　　　　　　　　97–8626
　　　　　　　　　　　　　　　　　　　CIP

Books published by Lawrence Erlbaum Associates are
printed on acid-free paper, and their bindings are chosen
for strength and durability.

Printed in the United States of America
10　9　8　7　6　5　4　3　2　1

Contents

Preface

Selection testing today has become identified in the public eye as "traditional testing"—paper-and-pencil multiple-choice ability tests. Surely there must be something better. There is also a high tide of concern about testing in the schools, with calls for reform reverberating in Congress, state legislatures, business circles, and parent–teacher associations around the country. Can't we do better as a nation?

These testing problems, evident in the early 1990s, set the stage for a conference held at Maumee Bay State Park, Ohio, in October 1994. For decades researchers have been investigating the measurement and prediction of individual differences in performance. The conference was held to take stock of the state of the art in selection testing, specifically to see what progress had been made on some perennial problems and to speculate about prospects for useful, new initiatives.

Robert Guion, Mary Tenopyr, David Kleinke, and Ann Marie Ryan joined me on the conference planning committee. We sought to bring together participants who could address the many diverse domains of selection-testing research and practice and who would do so without hype or partisanship. We wanted to cover both human resources and educational research and sought scholarly and critical appraisals supported by research evidence. The chapters in this volume are based on several papers presented at the conference. In some cases these chapters include substantial amounts of added detail and context beyond that delivered at the conference.

Support for the conference came from the Ohio Board of Regents' Eminent Scholar and Academic Challenge grants and from the Institute for Psychological Research and Application. The BGSU Psychology Foundation gave additional funding and will receive all royalties this book earns. I thank Lisa Friedel for her helping to organize the conference and Karen Ury for helping to prepare the indexes for this volume.

—*Milton D. Hakel*

1

Into the Great Beyond

Milton D. Hakel
Bowling Green State University

The Chinese were the first to have actually implemented a selection-testing system. Beginning in the second century BC, entry into the bureaucracy that governed China was limited to those who succeeded in passing a series of strict written examinations administered by the rulership and based on a thorough knowledge of the Chinese classics. In AD 669 Empress Wu Tse-t'ien ordered the tests to be organized, standardized, and administered systematically for political purposes, to control access to jobs. In 690 this empress became the only woman to rule China, as Emperor Wu Chao.

The Chinese examination system endured for over 20 centuries; it was efficient and favored the selection of the best candidates. The system operated effectively in periods of political unity, but in times of strife or dynastic change it tended to break down. The system had defects; there was undue stress on memorization, and wealthy candidates naturally enjoyed superior opportunities to acquire the education that would make success possible.

After the Mongols invaded China in 1210, the examination system languished because the Mongols lacked a proper administrative organization. Later the tests were revived:

> When the first doctoral examinations were organized in the Chinese style in 1315, quotas were reserved for different nationalities: Of a total of 300 appointments, a quarter were reserved for Mongols, a quarter for foreigners, a quarter for candidates from North China, and a quarter for southern Chinese. The operation was a parody of the Chinese competitions, for the Mongols and various foreigners

1

were uneducated and most of the families of literati lived in the lower Yangtze towns, in South China. (Gernet, 1982, p. 369)

Preparation for, and maintenance of, the examination system drained the energies of generations. Up to 12,000 examinees sat for a single examination, and grading took years, not just because all 12,000 essays had to be read but because the complete rank order of all examinees was reported. As the sole means of access to political honors and responsibilities, the examinations served to inculcate in those who sat for them the virtues of devotion and submission indispensable to the autocratic empire. Successful examinees or promotion candidates were indebted for their success to parents, to friends, and sometimes to those who had financed their studies and wagered on their success. The artificial character of the tests was apparent, particularly after the inclusion of the "composition in eight parts, a sterile, empty stylistic exercise" (Gernet, 1982, p. 505; see also Bodde, 1981).

Testing technology has evolved since the Chinese instituted written examinations for the selection of civil servants. The most visible change is that scoring has become objective, in the sense that there are clear, simple rules to follow to determine whether the answer marked as correct by the test taker is the same as the answer designated as correct by the test constructor. Invention of test-scoring equipment has permitted rapid and efficient collection and processing of answers to test questions, and the spread of networked personal computers promises further efficiencies. But although contemporary selection tests have been improved in many ways, some problems apparent in the Chinese experience continue to confront us today.

In 1917, the Army Alpha test was created to assist in the classification of military recruits. It ushered in the era of traditional testing—objectively scored, mass administered, paper-and-pencil ability tests. The Alpha was put into service in September 1917, and by the end of World War I in November 1918, 1,700,000 men had taken it.

Reading Robert M. Yerkes' account of the development and use of the Alpha (Yerkes, 1921) always leaves me awestruck. Based on laboratory prototypes and a limited amount of field experience, the designers of the Alpha pioneered approaches to every strategic and tactical testing issue we fight about today. In just over 4 months, a major social technology emerged full blown. Today's tests are less speedily developed, but in nearly every respect they are recognized as linear descendants of the Alpha.

The Army Alpha was the first widely used test, and thus it was the first that could be widely misused. The designers and implementers of the Alpha made some interesting choices, one of which was to assign letter grades to levels of mental ability. The Alpha was scored by adding points to yield a total score, which could range from zero to 212. Letter grades (A to D–) were assigned to score ranges and then used for personnel decisions. Some 8,000 recruits with D– grades (raw scores of 0 to 14) were discharged immediately for "mental inferiority," and 10,000 with grades of D (raw scores of 15 to 24) were assigned to heavy labor battalions. On the high end, those with grades of A, awarded for scores of 135 or above, were sent to officer candidate school. Current officers were required to take the Alpha, and those who failed to get a grade of A were stripped of their commissions and served out the war as enlisted men. Inevitably some mistakes were made—some of the demoted officers must have had satisfactory job performance records. And for those classified as D–, no one appeared to be aware of the operation of chance in responding to test questions, so those with scores of 14 or below literally lucked out of the service, because of and in spite of the label attached to them.

Being cognizant of the need to investigate validity, the Alpha's designers did so as part of the test development process. Besides correlating Alpha scores with individually administered tests such as the Stanford Binet ($r = .87$) and Doll's translation of the Binet scales ($r = .81$), the designers looked for evidence of discriminant validity. They sought to create a measure of native mental ability, one not too influenced by schooling. Although the convergent validity correlations were gratifyingly high, discriminant validity turned out to be disappointing because the observed correlation of .73 between Alpha scores and years of schooling was substantially higher than desired.

In the years since 1917, multiple choice testing has become widespread in employee selection and even more widespread in education. Not surprisingly, there have been many critiques of testing; indeed, we are once again in a period of heightened scrutiny. Debate about testing got a big boost from Steven Jay Gould's *The Mismeasure of Man* (1981), and F. Allan Hanson's *Testing Testing: Social Consequences of the Examined Life* (1993). Even the general public took notice of testing issues on the publication of *The Bell Curve*, by Richard J. Hernnstein and Charles Murray (1994). The protest aroused by this book has quieted down, supplanted lately by a fight over the legal standing of affirmative action. In November 1996, California voters adopted Proposition 209, a citizen initiative that makes it illegal for the state to exercise any form of preference based on gender or ethnicity in state contracts. This fight promises to be interesting, with some African Americans recognizing the costs of affirmative action (for example, Steele [1990] examined self-doubt and victimization) and journalists entering into the fray (Zelnick, 1996). *Fairness* is not so easily given an operational definition as is *merit*, and giving merit a widely accepted operational definition is contentious enough in its own right.

In 1993, the American Psychological Association, the National Council on Measurement in Education, and the American Educational Research Association convened a committee to prepare a revised edition of the Standards for Educational and Psychological Tests. In 1994, the National Academy of Sciences appointed a board on testing and assessment to advise the public on policy issues about test use. An earlier Academy report had noted:

The diminished prospects of the average American give the debate about testing an especially sharp edge. Because they are visible instruments of the process of allocating economic opportunity, tests are seen as creating winners and losers. What is not as readily appreciated, perhaps, is the inevitability of making choices: whether by tests or some other mechanism, selection must take place. (Wigdor and Garner, 1982, p. 205).

Loud calls for reform in education have been heard for more than a decade. Criticism of multiple-choice testing has been most concentrated, and alternatives vigorously investigated, in the field of education. Because constructing a correct response differs substantially from recognizing one in a list of potential responses, portfolios and "authentic" performance assessments are attracting considerable attention. The Educational Testing Service now includes objectified scoring of constructed responses for some of the examinations it conducts.

Education is not the only venue in which alternatives to multiple-choice testing of cognitive ability have been and are being investigated. Industrial and organizational psychologists work in many settings that require innovation beyond multiple-choice ability testing, and biographical data forms, structured interviews, work simulations, personality inventories, assessment centers, and other techniques continue to receive research attention. Regardless of the venue in which they work, researchers are always looking for improved techniques for making, by some means or other, inevitable choices.

These days people are far more cognizant of varieties of error and other issues in test use. Title VII of the Civil Rights Act of 1964 and subsequent judicial decisions have made it abundantly clear that merit is to be the basis for making selection decisions. The net effect of living with Title VII for over 30 years has been to reinforce the use of appropriate and improved procedures for making personnel decisions. This fact is clearest in the concept of job relatedness, which was codified in *Griggs v. Duke Power* (1971). Selecting people based on their ability to do the job is a simple and compelling notion fully consistent the ideal of fairness, embodying the principle of merit.

But by what operational means should merit be measured? The due process and equal protection clauses of the Constitution provide the basis for the commonly accepted idea that all people similarly situated be treated alike, both in the privileges conferred and in the liabilities imposed. This idea is embedded in equal employment opportunity law, and there is continuing controversy about two questions: Who is "similarly situated?" Who requires "equal protection?"

On the surface, selection based on traditional testing seems to satisfy the concept of fairness. Unlike many alternatives to traditional testing, tests are color blind. All test takers are treated exquisitely alike, without regard to race, ethnic origin, sex, age, religion, or other irrelevant considerations. The problem, however, is that test scores, by their specificity, narrowness, and appearance of precision, may inhibit the introduction of other information relevant to the employment decision. Test scores typically reflect only one or a few dimensions of individual differences. The "whole person" is not measured well by a single test score, and yet the "whole person" is hired for the job.

Hence we face the search for alternatives to traditional testing for selection and see the need to go beyond multiple choice. Let us investigate the great beyond.

REFERENCES

Bodde, D. (1981). *Essays on Chinese civilization*. Princeton, NJ: Princeton University Press.

Gernet, J. (1982). *A history of Chinese civilization*. New York: Cambridge University Press.

Gould, S. J. (1981). *The mismeasure of man*. New York: Norton.

Hanson, F. A. (1993). *Testing testing: Social consequences of the examined life*. Berkeley, CA: University of California Press.

Herrnstein, R. J. & Murray, C. (1994). *The bell curve*. New York: Free Press.

Steele, S. (1990). *The content of our character: A new vision of race in America*. New York: St. Martin's Press.

Wigdor, A. K. & Garner, W. R. (Eds.). (1982). *Ability testing: Uses, consequences, and controversies*. Washington, DC: National Academy Press.

Willie Griggs et al. v. Duke Power Company. U. S. 424 (1971).

Yerkes, Robert M. (1921). *Psychological examining in the United States Army*. Washington, DC: Government Printing Office.

Zelnick, B. (1996). *Backfire: A reporter's look at affirmative action*. Washington, DC: Regnery.

2

Jumping the Gun at the Starting Gate: When Fads Become Trends and Trends Become Traditions

Robert M. Guion
Bowling Green State University

The title, and its horse-race metaphor, are incomplete.[1] Like winning horses, psychometric traditions are not immediately traditions; they must win many competitions against many competitors. Psychometric traditions begin when someone comes out of the starting gate doing something remarkable. At that point no one knows whether the "doing" will become a tradition; it is merely remarkable. It may have been done before, but it may be remarkable this time because it is done so well—or so outrageously. It may be remarkable because it is something new—a new activity, a new idea, a new criticism. Others notice, remark, and copy it. Copycats are usually unable to have their own new thoughts, but they are in love with the idea that being different from tradition is the same as being creative. A bevy of copycats can turn remarkable somethings into fads. Cheering faddists do not help horses run faster or improve ideas. Thoughtful people, those who score high on Factor V (of the Big Five personality factors) , notice the remarkable something, see some merit in it, perhaps modify it, adopt it, and use it with good (if not remarkable) effect.

---

[1] This chapter has been based on the keynote address to the conference, Beyond Multiple Choice: Evaluating Alternatives to Traditional Testing for Selection, Bowling Green State University, Maumee Bay State Park, Ohio, October 25–26, 1994.

These people start a fashion. With enough followers, the fashionable something becomes a trend. Trends are exciting—perhaps not as exciting as a horse race, but stimulating, nevertheless. A trend is mysterious; people never know whether it will win or fade out. A trend can move up a bit, then fall back, and become mere folderol, the habit of the also-rans who are not quite with-it.[2] A trend can lose ground if a competing trend runs better, or a sudden infusion of adrenaline can push it to the head of the pack. A trend that wins on many tracks becomes a tradition, but if an alternative is remarkable enough long enough, what was once traditional can become passé.

The psychometric tradition is the standardized, multiple choice, cognitive ability test with standard instructions, items, time limits, and scoring. This tradition has been a winner for a long time. It has won against oral trade tests, miscellaneous projective instruments, and ratings; it has raced on tracks in both employment and educational testing. It wins on grounds of reliability and predictive validity. To continue the silly metaphor, it is out of Otis by Yerkes.[3] This trend was well under way—with people like E. F. Wonderlic, Joseph Tiffin, C. H. Lawshe, and Jay Otis in employment testing—when International Business Machines (IBM) provided the infusion of adrenaline known as the test-scoring machine. With this invention, other contenders—essay tests, short-answer forms, arrangement items, matching items—were effectively out of the race. Multiple choice became the tradition.

The multiple choice test became traditional in an easier age. Neither Lee Cronbach nor Sam Messick had yet been invented; now they are both winners. Cronbach's (1971) remarkable idea was that validity resides in the inferences drawn from scores; Messick's (1989) was that the consequences of measurement help to define this validity. Without these inventions, we could talk without embarrassment about the "validity of a *test*," and, moreover, we could use a single coefficient to describe it. If something undesirable happened—a student got a low score or was denied admission to the school of choice and therefore suffered a loss of self-esteem, or a job candidate who really could have done the job was rejected—it was not the fault of the valid test. Nor was it the fault of the test if teachers looked at the test items to decide what to teach or if personnel managers looked only at test scores without a glance at an applicant's achievements in similar jobs. When validity generalization came along, it confirmed that traditional tests were great, and it sent the challengers to the stables. (Some of them are back on the track, however.)

We really need to consider the challenges of alternatives. The tradition is aged; it is not so fast out of the gate anymore. It can be strengthened, but we must be open to new ideas. A half-dozen problems supply reasons.

---

[2] The allusion to Dunnette (1966) is quite apt.

[3] According to an oral history told by E. E. Ghiselli, Arthur Otis was working on a dissertation when he and his dissertation were drafted in World War I; the kinds of test items he was working on were multiple-choice items that became the basis for the Army Alpha tests. Yerkes had earlier used a multiple-choice format in studying animal behavior, albeit not with paper and pencil.

First, traditional testing for selection is based on large sample criterion-related validation. *Large* means many more cases than the word did in the pre-employment-opportunity-era; for any single job, the prospects for adequate samples seem to be dimming as time passes.

Second, we have to redefine standardization and what it does for measurement. Traditional testing called for standardization of procedures and items and for the standardization provided by homogeneous research samples; directly or indirectly, testing offered reliable, internally consistent assessment, linear regression, and top-down selection. Now, instead of standard sets of items, different people get different items on adaptive tests. Research samples are increasingly heterogeneous, and sometimes include many people who are uncomfortable with standard English. We have no clue how to maintain standardization while accommodating people who are disabled. Unidimensional tests and homogeneous samples make monotonic regression interpretable and top-down selection the optimal selection paradigm. But content-oriented test components may be uncorrelated and lack internal consistency; because we can no longer be sure that either scores or predictions can be interpreted unambiguously, arguments favoring strict top-down selection are diluted. Moreover, top-down selection is based on norm-referenced thinking, and we sometimes move, surreptitiously, to a domain-referenced mode of thinking about predicted performance: We want to choose people who are not only better than other candidates but who are objectively *good*.

Third, the criterion problem, never easy, has grown worse. Performance criteria were simpler when job design meant job simplification. Now many jobs are neither simple nor static. Workers are expected to be able to shift from assignment to assignment, or from task to task, as needs arise. Change is a major fact of life, yet we rarely use *response to change* as a criterion.

Fourth, new times may call for new constructs. Factor analysis was, and remains, a remarkable tool, but some of us were unduly enthusiastic about it. With it we sliced cognitive function into ever-thinner slices. I believe, as I read Carroll's (1993) encyclopedic review of its results, that it gave us important insights into the ways people think. I do not, however, believe it is the only path to truth; other paths may offer more complex and more useful constructs for predicting behavior in practical settings. Among constructs to think about developing, consider "street smarts," the kind of intelligence, distinguished from academic aptitude, considered essential to coping successfully with life's vicissitudes. Efforts to use traditional tests to measure something called *practical intelligence* or *social intelligence* have been with us for decades without achieving much success. If such constructs need to be defined and assessed, it may take some truly remarkable new ideas to do so.

Fifth, the problem of bias does not go away. It does not lie in mean differences in the scores of people in different subgroups. I think it lies in the occasional enormity of the discrepancy between the sizes of mean differences on the test and those on the criterion. It is commonplace, in Black–White comparisons, to find the mean criterion difference to be about half the size of the mean predictor difference. I have been told that the discrepancy is artifactual, but I think it is either stubborn or naive to believe that mean test differences two or more times the mean criterion differences are merely regression oddities. It is, of course, equally stubborn and naive to believe that the discrepancy is due only to demographic bias. Look again at the assumption of within-group homogeneity on variables that tests are not measuring. Suppose people differ in the cleverness of their test-taking strategies, and that some strategies are more common in one group than in the other. That supposition could account for much of the mean difference in test scores. If the strategies are specifically associated with multiple-choice items, then we must either teach people how to take such tests or find alternatives where strategies are not correlated with group membership. New alternatives may help solve this aspect of the bias problem. Facing the problem head on, working to solve it in traditional testing, may also provide a solution—without providing new and unknown corollary problems.

Sixth, those touting alternatives to traditional testing claim that traditional multiple-choice tests are superficial measures of the wrong things. Those who say that traditional tests are necessarily superficial simply have not seen multiple-choice tests as those used by architectural registration boards. Alternative, constructed response projects can be useful and in fact, they have been introduced into architectural tests. But superficial tests emerge from superficial thinking in establishing test specifications and developing items, not from an inherent superficiality in the form.

People will continue to measure the wrong things as long as they fail to define what they want to measure. This fact is not a matter of assessment method; construct validation is the basis of validity. Most of us, traditionalists and modernists alike, now agree that validity is a unitary concept; that qualifying adjectives—like content, criterion related, convergent, or consequential—merely confuse matters. Nearly all of us know and agree that the essential issue in validation is to collect evidence bearing on how well the scores reflect the meaning of an intended, underlying construct. What we seem not to have considered is how to evaluate the *measurement* of a construct we have never bothered to *define*. In personnel testing, we say that we try to predict performance, but only quite recently have efforts to define *performance* been explicated in any detail (e.g., Campbell, McCloy, Oppler, & Sager, 1993). The constructs of individual differences can be defined by factor analysis, by theory, by organizational values, or simply by thinking clearly about something deemed worth measuring. These constructs must be defined, by one method or another. Only with a fairly good notion of a construct can we begin to apply the reasonably well-known rules for evaluating whether that construct can be validly inferred from the scores.

Clearly, we have good reason to invent, examine, evaluate, and perhaps to adopt some alternative models of testing and assessment. Less clear is whether evaluation can keep the pace set by invention and hullabaloo. Several challengers have been contending for the floral horseshoe. Some contenders do little more than nip the heels of the champion and suggest that it be put out to pasture or be sent to the psychometric equivalent of the glue factory. At a recent conference, one speaker attributed virtually all of society's ills (with the possible exception of drought) to the existence and use of multiple-choice tests.

Not all alternatives are alternative ways to assess. One alternative is not to assess at all. Employment testing has been treated with disdain by many organizational psychologists for at least 3 decades, but they have anointed no contenders for a new psychometric tradition. They are simply not interested. The idea of assessing individual differences and predicting performance levels has seemed old fashioned to them, not worthy of their interest. For them, the appealing alternative to traditional tests is to put them away and not replace them. This idea does not enthrall most testers, but it is a challenger and merits consideration.

Those of us who *are* interested have seen, and even run, a few contenders of our own. We have, all along, used work samples, noncognitive tests, biodata, interviews, and new technologies as selection procedures. They have not yet been competitive on the grounds of reliability and validity. We have had assessment centers, which collectively seem a true contender to many of us; these have not won the race, and may just be trends, or mere folderol.

What are the alternatives to tradition? What are the passing fads, or the seriously challenging trends? One set of alternatives is methodological, the vast array of constructed, relatively unconstrained response formats, ranging from short answers through essays to portfolios. Another is a collection of new constructs being proposed. Others include different media, taking advantage of the opportunities posed by the electronic revolution. We should also consider the combinations of constructs and media that can permit alternative ways to assess neglected noncognitive characteristics.

Let me comment on just one challenger. It is an old loser reincarnated, the constructed response item that we used to call free response. It has now become a major challenger by the simple expedient of its advocates' declaring it superior to the multiple-choice format. Declaration without evidence is one form of jumping the gun. I am perfectly willing to agree that a good constructed response item is better than a poor multiple choice item. I am not willing to agree that a constructed response item is *necessarily* better, regardless of construct or the purpose of assessment. In part, my reluctance is based on the belief that different purposes may be better served by different methods. In greater part, however, because Cronbach and Messick *have* been invented, my reluctance lies in uncertainty about consequences of constructed responses that add unwanted, systematic sources of variance to the scores and obscure the nature of valid inferences.

Consider an example given by Snow (1993). A traditional multiple-choice mathematics test was modified merely by requiring a constructed response—a computation—before indicating a choice from the multiple options. The consequence was a substantial test anxiety component, especially evident in low scores. The traditional multiple choice form had a slight, apparently trivial, negative relation between number of right answers and test anxiety; adding that one little requirement—to construct an approximate correct answer before choosing a response option—turned the slope of this regression to a sharp negative one, as illustrated in Fig. 2.1. High-scoring test takers had less anxiety with the test when they had to construct a response before choosing an option, but low-scoring test takers had a great deal of anxiety about constructing a response.

If the purpose of the test is to identify and somehow reward those who have the highest levels of the mathematics skills being tested, then the constructed response version is preferable because its scores at high levels are less contaminated by test anxiety and therefore more valid. If the purpose is to screen out those deficient in computational skills, that is, to deny a reward or an opportunity, then one consequence of adding the constructed response requirement is to deny this opportunity to some candidates who, were it not for their added test anxiety, would have done reasonably well on the test. *Touting constructed responses as the ideal replacement for the traditional winner is a prime example of jumping the gun at the starting gate*—of evaluating an alternative without collecting the evaluative evidence. Please note that in this example, not every low score can be attributed to the contaminating effect of test anxiety. Some test takers with low scores simply were not any good at the computations required. *But we know only the scores; we do not know which ones truly do not deserve the reward and which ones are denied it because of the invalidating contamination in scores.*

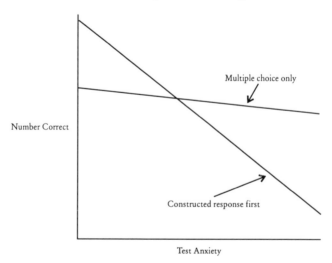

FIG. 2.1. Interaction of test score and test anxiety when a constructed response is (or is not) required before answering multiple-choice math items.

We hear a great deal these days—although less than a couple of years ago—about *authentic* performance assessment. The term grows from genuine needs in education. The psychometric problem is not so much a problem of prediction as one of description and diagnosis: What can students do after instruction that they could not do before, or could not have done as well? What were they supposed to learn how to do—but did not? These questions are serious and important; they deal with both school and individual effectiveness. Unfortunately, the cheering spectators do not distinguish between prediction and description; they apply the same judgments to methods of assessment regardless of purpose, and, worse, they want their judgments of the *best* form of assessment to be used in hiring decisions as well as in the schools. Their rhetoric claims that traditional tests are inherently bad, that the problems can be solved only by new approaches to assessment (which, in usually undefined ways, is somehow different from testing).

Perhaps the ultimate in constructed response assessment is the portfolio concept, not a particularly new idea. Art schools and employers of commercial artists, for example, have asked candidates for their portfolios for years. Such portfolios may not be quite the same as those being proposed and sometimes used in statewide educational assessment programs. In assessing candidates for admission to schools, for employment, for promotion, or for possible additional training, the portfolio concept can be classed as a remarkable something; it may not yet be a fad, but talking about it is. Developing a portfolio consists of a person's collecting samples of what he or she has done: recordings (including videotapes) of performances, paintings, essays, short stories, ad layouts, or records of processes that led to special achievements. These items are considered products or signs of creative thought or skill. Unreliability is a problem with portfolios, but not the one that bothers me most. Nor is deliberate dishonesty, when a portfolio includes another's work. What bothers me most is that the assessee chooses both the stimulus and the response portions of the assessment. That is, a stimulus—a sunset, an assignment, a conversation overheard by chance, a personal fear—occurred, possibly uniquely, to the assessee, who then responded in a personal way. At a later date, for assessment purposes, the assessee, using his or her own idiosyncratic judgment, collects the *best* paintings, or essays, or whatever.[4] The potentially invalidating problem is that the construct the assessee has vaguely in mind when collecting his or her own best work may not match the construct held by the judges who rate it.

For instance, my current extraprofessional interest is blowing glass. If I were a judge evaluating handblown bowls, for example, I would look for evidence of control of the hot glass, shown either by symmetry or by pronounced, clearly planned asymmetries. But one of the best artists in the studio where I work

---

[4] In educational assessments, a teacher may help students assemble their portfolios. This supervision may change, but by no means eliminate, the idiosyncratic component of portfolio assembly.

said, "If you want symmetry, go to Kmart." In collecting pieces for his portfolio, he would set aside his symmetrical pieces and offer those that were a bit out of round, or had one side a bit higher than the other. He considered symmetry boring. If I were the rater, my ratings would not match his because we do not use the same ideas of excellence. My construct would be a narrow view of craftsmanship (the *narrow* indicates appreciation if not acceptance of his view); his construct would be one of *interest*. The constructs, the products, and the rules used for evaluating portfolios are not standardized. Some people see this fact as a virtue. I do not.

The last few years have been rich in remarkable ideas in testing and in assessment. The last few decades, and especially the last 2 or 3, have been equally rich in prescriptions, or standards, for evaluating assessment procedures. Should some of the fads turn into trends? Should some of the trends become new traditions? My answer: Let the better horse win!

If the challengers are truly contenders for taking the championship away from traditional testing, if comparisons are to be fairly made, then the contenders and the champion should all be running around the same track and following the same track rules. Most of us agree with this. I have heard no proponents of change say that their notions for improved assessment should be evaluated by different evaluative prescriptions or standards, although some seem to behave as if they thought so—and one recent article argued that assessments need not be reliable to be valid (Moss, 1994). (Suggestions made in the article would, however, improve the reliability of judgments about constructed responses.)

Perhaps most of us would also agree that there are different races defined by different purposes and that different trends win on different tracks. Different assessment methods may be *best* for different purposes. The purpose of reaching a go–no-go decision about somebody is distinctly different from the purpose of identifying each person's relative strengths and weaknesses. The purpose of predicting a future performance construct from the aptitude or ability construct at hand is distinctly different from the purpose of defining how close a person comes to mastery of the domain defined by the construct at hand. The purpose of measuring one construct, say a general mental ability, is distinctly different from the purpose of measuring a completely different construct, say explosive upper body strength. If two or more different methods of assessment are to be compared, debated, and evaluated, they should be compared, debated, and evaluated for the same purposes. It is plain silly, although the idea surfaces in employment testing literature, to say that work samples for assessing existing job skills are better than aptitude tests for predicting future achievement. Similar silliness permeates the educational testing literature, and deflects attention from considering the real merits of alternative approaches to assessment for a given purpose.

Alternatives need to be considered, carefully and thoughtfully. It is equally silly to reject alternatives out of hand, for any purpose, without considering data that may be presented. If the various alternatives compete on the same track, for the same purposes, and according to the same rules of evaluation, let the better horse win.

But if an alternative should win and become a new tradition, I would still have a further concern. I fear the loss of excitement as a new idea proves itself through the efforts of those who rode it to victory, only to become the method of choice among inept, careless mediocrities who do not understand it and its use. Then what was once an exciting new idea becomes merely a routine, dull, unimaginative set of procedures for superficial measurement of the wrong things.

Our deliberations may make such an outcome less likely, if we heed this poetic advice (Wherry, 1975, p. 16):

Gentlemen, Choose Your Models

Models are fine and statistics are dandy
But don't choose too quickly just 'cause they're handy
Stick to a model that's been through the mill
Don't try something new just for the thrill
A new shiny model is full of allure
But making it work is no sinecure

REFERENCES

Campbell, J. P., McCloy, R. A., Oppler, S. H., & Sager, C. E. (1993). A theory of performance. In N. Schmitt & W. C. Borman (Eds.), *Personnel selection in organizations* (pp. 35–70). San Francisco: Jossey-Bass.

Carroll, J. B. (1993). *Human cognitive abilities: A survey of factor-analytic studies.* Cambridge, England: Cambridge University Press.

Cronbach, L. J. (1971). Test validation. In R. L. Thorndike (Ed.), *Educational measurement* (2nd ed.), (pp. 443–507). Washington, DC: American Council on Education.

Dunnette, M. D. (1966). Fads, fashions, and folderol in psychology. *American Psychologist, 21,* 343–352.

Messick, S. (1989). Validity. In R. L. Linn (Ed.), *Educational measurement* (3rd ed.), (pp. 13–103). New York: Macmillan–American Council on Education.

Moss, P. A. (1994). Can there be validity without reliability? *Educational Researcher, 23,* 5–12.

Snow, R. E. (1993). Construct validity and constructed-response tests. In R. E. Bennett & W. C. Ward (Eds.), *Construction versus choice in cognitive measurement: Issues in constructed response, performance testing, and portfolio assessment* (pp. 45–60). Hillsdale, NJ: Lawrence Erlbaum Associates.

Wherry, R. J., Sr. (1975). Underprediction from overfitting: 45 years of shrinkage. *Personnel Psychology, 28,* 1–18.

3

Measure Me Not:
The Test Taker's New Bill of Rights

Mary L. Tenopyr
AT&T Corporation

One of the most common responses to test misuse has been to set up standards or guidelines to control test development, research, and use. This approach has been followed by professional associations, government agencies, and legislatures. The emphasis on alternatives to testing became a major issue in psychology with the publication of the 1970 U.S. Equal Employment Opportunity Commission (EEOC) guidelines that covered validation and use of employee selection procedures. This document introduced a requirement for employers to show that there were no suitable alternatives to a valid test having disparate impact on a group protected by the Civil Rights Act of 1964.

Although published data are sparse, most employers seem to have abandoned testing after publication of the guidelines and their subsequent favorable treatment by the U.S. Supreme Court in its decision of *Griggs v. Duke Power* (1971). Although later decisions by the Court have placed on the complaining party the responsibility to show suitable alternatives, employment testing seems to have greatly diminished since the 1960s.

The guidelines and standards have, however, had a positive effect by stimulating considerable research on the validity and generalizability of test validity. The results of this research have generally supported testing and have shown that most federal guidelines on testing are too restrictive and should be revised.

Nevertheless, changing social climate, affected largely by philosophical and political views in the field of education, has shifted emphasis from debates about whether test results yield accurate information and are useful for making predictions about future behavior to the effects of such results on people. In fact, the paper-pencil multiple-choice test is currently under so much attack that some believe that its opponents support an alternative of no testing at all. Although there are several current threats to testing, three deserve special attention: new emphases on rights of test takers, the movement toward performance-based assessment, and the attempt to redefine validity in terms of testing consequences.

TEST TAKERS' RIGHTS

In the 1970s, "Truth in Testing" bills were introduced in the U. S. Congress and in state legislatures. The proposed legislation required that an examinee, after being tested, be given a copy of the test with the correct answers. Opposition to this approach was swift and organized. Constantly revising tests made obsolescent through disclosure of items was an economic and practical impossibility for all but the largest testing organizations. Consequently, federal Truth in Testing legislation would have eliminated most paper–pencil testing in the country. The State of New York, however, enacted similar legislation that pertains only to educational tests used for decisions, such as determining college admissions.

With the new emphasis on test takers' rights, various documents bearing titles such as "The Test Takers' Bill of Rights" have been prepared or are in various stages of development, largely by those in the education community. Some of these statements of rights are reasonable and balance the needs of test takers and test users, and, as guidance, they can serve a useful social purpose. A pressing problem, however, is the planned inclusion of a chapter on test takers' rights in *Standards for Educational and Psychological Testing*, being prepared by the American Educational Research Association, the American Psychological Association, and the National Council of Measurement in Education. There is a strong probability that the standards will be endorsed by the courts in civil rights litigation. The rights of test takers may, thus, become legally enforceable.

The notion of expanded test takers' rights has also appeared in a widely distributed draft document of a booklet of learning principles, developed by a large consortium of educational and psychological associations. One principle in this booklet has claimed that the students should be involved in negotiating how assessment is done and what standards are applied.

PERFORMANCE-BASED ASSESSMENT

Also from the field of education has come the emphasis on performance-based assessment. This highly promoted movement involves measuring devices that are hailed as alternatives to the multiple-choice tests. *Performance-based assess-*

ment is a term applied to the use of an assortment of measuring tools such as work samples, portfolio evaluations, interviews on problem-solving styles, and other methods not in the paper-pencil domain. The consortium of educational associations' draft set of learning principles circulating among those in the field of education contained the statement that assessments should be based on authentic and meaningful tasks. The compilers of this booklet have compounded measurement problems by specifying both students' right to negotiate measurement standards and the types of measurement that must be done. Performance-based assessments have even been written into major federal laws.

With enough expertise, time, and economic support, adequate performance-based assessment systems can obviously be developed (Baker, O'Neil, & Linn, 1993). Furthermore, performance on some tasks is apparently easier to assess than it is on other tasks. For example, considerable effort has been directed toward assessing writing performance, but assessing performance in subjects like science, where equipment and other physical material must be used is more difficult. Science tests that have been developed often involve, for reasons of economics, inexpensive materials that do not survive many reusings, and most of these tests must be administered individually. Another problem with some of these tests, such as one involving classifying real seashells, is that it is impossible to develop parallel alternate forms.

Mathematics tests present further difficulties. The performance-assessment movement has emphasized mental processes used, not correct answers obtained. In one widely distributed mathematics test without correct answers, a person completes the test and is then interviewed about the types of thought used to obtain the answers.

Measuring process to the neglect of product is problematic. First, in real life, correct answers and usable products are sought in almost every employment situation. By measuring process, educators can well give students an unrealistic view of the requirements life will expect from them. Second, no agreed-on set of constructs informs the evaluation of processes used in solving problems. The discipline of education, like the field of psychology, appears all too willing to apply the labels *construct* or *process* to entities for which the literature does not justify labels. The notion of a universal set of constructs upon which all or even just some psychologists agree, however, appears to be far fetched. Furthermore, were there such a set of constructs, teaching evaluators to recognize the extent and degree of the constructs' use would be an arduous task. Thus, to make subjective judgments about mental processes used in performance-based assessments causes genuine construct validity problems. Reliability is also a matter of concern. Inter-rater agreement on ratings involving ill-defined and ill-observed constructs is likely to be lacking.

Portfolio evaluations present yet other impediments. Standardization of the portfolio content is a difficult task, and there may be questions about who actually did the work in a portfolio. For these reasons, some businesses have been shunning portfolio evaluation and moving to formal work-sample testing for jobs such as public relations writer. Furthermore, scoring of portfolios is difficult and hinders the obtaining of satisfactory reliability more than any other form of performance assessment. The mere cost of scoring with multiple raters is extremely high. Also, in the education area, the quality of a portfolio for a child from a middle-class home is likely to be higher than that of a portfolio for a child from a less-afffluent home.

Some explicit assumptions underlie the actions of those in the performance-assessment movement, who have claimed that traditional measurement drives the wrong learning behaviors and that the tenets of traditional measurement are not important. In education circles, *reliability* and *validity* have become code words for multiple-choice tests.

Some interesting implicit assumptions are also associated with the arguments of those who promote performance-based assessment. These people have stated that by changing to performance assessment, educators can maintain high standards that everyone can meet. The obvious contradiction in this notion appears to escape many observers. Also implicit in the performance-assessment position is the idea that such assessments result in less predictive bias relative to race, nationality, and gender than do traditional tests. When assessments are properly developed and reliably scored, they will undoubtedly have many of the attributes of traditional tests, including adverse effects on selected groups. Any present indications that smaller disparate effects on groups are associated with performance assessments than are associated with multiple-choice tests result from the poor measurement qualities of many assessment systems that have been developed.

Manageability and cost are not the least considerations in determining the viability of performance assessment. Already these two factors are causing some leaders in education to reconsider widespread adoption of large performance-assessment systems, and multiple-choice tests can be predicted to return to favor in education, particularly for purposes of accountability. In the meantime, however, performance-assessment advocates can influence professional standards so much that they weaken paper-pencil tests, a particular concern because federal regulations on testing have not been revised for many years and in civil rights litigation the courts may rely on newer professional standards.

VALIDITY AND CONSEQUENCES

Consequential validity is a term being casually discussed in the educational community as if it had some agreed-on meaning. A literature search indicates that the term is frequently used without definition or referencing in publications. Messick (1975) has long been discussing the role of values in measurement. In recent years Messick (1989) has refined his views and has spoken directly about consequences. In his view, if adverse consequences for a group are a function of irrelevant sources of test or criterion variance, the issue is test invalidity. But, if group differences reflect valid properties of the construct for which measurement is desired, the issue is then test validity.

If it can safely be judged that any adverse consequences of test use can be attributed to properties of the construct being tapped, then the issue is one of social policy. Thus, consequences of test use are but one piece of evidence in making judgments about construct validity, and adverse consequences can either support or detract from construct validity.

Messick, significantly, has never advocated using the term *consequential validity*. Those who would redefine validity on the basis of consequences of test use have apparently misunderstood his thinking. Furthermore, in view of the current national debates about affirmative action, people can significantly disagree about when a consequence of testing is "adverse." What one person or group believes is adverse, another person or group may think of as salutary. Social policy judgments are involved throughout the testing process, and they should be recognized as such.

Creating a new category of validity called consequential validity flies in the face of science. Redefining validity to include the effects of test use may appear to be a noble goal for some, but it is a complete corruption of the concept of validity because it mixes social policy considerations with scientific ones. Although values are taken into account to some extent throughout any testing process, to create a special category of validity only for the purpose of accommodating values lacks any scientific credibility.

SUMMARY

An alternative to testing is no testing at all. Various philosophical and social concerns, largely in the field of education, have lent impetus to at least three developments that may cause traditional paper–pencil testing to be abandoned. The rights of test takers are receiving new consideration, and "Bills of Rights" have been written or are being prepared. Performance-based assessments are being written, to the exclusion of multiple choice tests, in federal laws, despite the great difficulties in both theoretical and practical areas with this type of assessment. Furthermore, for social reasons, some people are intent on inventing a new type of validity that rests on the social consequences of measurement.

REFERENCES

American Educational Research Association, American Psychological Association, & National Council on Measurement in Education (1985). *Standards for educational and psychological testing*. Washington, DC: American Psychological Association.

Baker, E. L., O'Neil, H. F., Jr., & Linn, R. L. (1993). Policy and validity prospects for performance-based assessment. *American Psychologist, 48*, 1210–1218.

Messick, S. (1975). The standard problem: Meaning and values in measurement and evaluation. *American Psychologist, 30*, 955–966.

Messick, S. (1989). Validity. In Linn, R. L. (Ed.). *Educational measurement* (3rd ed.), (pp. 13–103). New York: American Council on Measurement in Education.

Willie Griggs et al. v. Duke Power Company. U.S. 424 (1971).

4

Innovations in Computer-Based Ability Testing: Promise, Problems, and Perils

James R. McBride
Human Resources Research Organization (HumRRO)

In the early days of the personal computer (PC) industry, the Apple Computer, Incorporated company had a marketing department position with the job title *Evangelist*. An Apple evangelist was a professional true believer, whose paid mission was to spread the gospel of personal computing, especially personal computing with Apple computers. I have never worked for any computer company, but for 10 years or more, I too was something of an evangelist, spreading the gospel of computer-based ability testing. My evangelistic efforts were sufficiently unsuccessful that I had to supplement my income doing things like designing paper and pencil tests, and even dabbling in biodata (Snell, Stokes, Sands, & McBride, 1993).

Despite what I regarded as my evangelistic failures, in the past several years, computer-administered testing has suddenly been accepted on a large scale in the United States. The Graduate Record Examinations (GREs) are now available in a computerized adaptive format. The largest licensure testing program in the United States—the Nurse Certification and Licensing Examination (NCLEX)— is now administered entirely by computer. Many states now use computer-administered examinations to license vehicle drivers and insurance agents. Computerized versions of two principal college entrance examinations—the Scholastic Aptitude Test (SAT) and the American College Test

23

(ACT)—are in preparation in earnest. Last but certainly not least, the U.S. Department of Defense has begun to convert its enlistment selection testing program from paper and pencil to computerized adaptive testing. All these innovations have happened despite my ineptitude from the pulpit. (My own daughter, Chrissy, called me from college to ask for money to take the GRE before its conversion to computerized administration—another evangelical failure.)

To foster the growth of computer-based testing, I had to stop preaching its merits. In this chapter, I take a somewhat contrarian position. In the face of the burgeoning use of computers to give ability tests, I want to sound a warning about some perils and pitfalls of automated testing. Admittedly, this is a little dishonest on my part: I am a shameless advocate of computerized testing and would rather develop computerized testing systems than do anything else. Nonetheless, I point out some recent problems, many of which I never anticipated in my years of evangelism. Think of this as advice to the unwary.

The approach to this chapter has four steps. First, I outline some reasons we personnel research people must be interested in computer-administered selection tests. Second, I enumerate some important applications of computer-administered selection tests in the United States. Third, I recount some anecdotes that illustrate some research into problems and issues that have come up since we began to use computerized testing for personnel selection. Fourth, I discuss an unusual research project that has to do with computer-administered testing, the 1997 Profile of American Youth.

THE PROMISE OF COMPUTERIZED TESTING

Computerized testing is attractive (to some of us) for a variety of reasons. The first is administrative efficiency: The same computer that administered the tests can score them, print out individual and group score reports, and keep detailed records of everything that happens. Anyone interested in the "paperless personnel office" ought to find computerized testing attractive.

The second reason is psychometric efficiency, which applies especially to computerized *adaptive* tests, that offer users the option of shorter tests (without sacrificing measurement precision) or improved precision (without lengthening the tests). This reason may sound mundane, but a number of significant testing programs have moved or are moving to adaptive testing.

The third attractive feature of computer-administered tests is their obvious potential to expand the content of tests, to include such features as audible (rather than written) directions and interactive video. Perhaps the best example is the potential use of multimedia technology as a base for a new generation of tests. McHenry and Schmitt (1994) published an excellent overview of the opportunities (and challenges) in this area. Ashworth and McHenry (1993) reported on a specific instance of multimedia technology.

The fourth reason for interest in computerized testing is scientific: Surely we can exploit the computer as a medium to measure facets of cognitive ability that cannot be measured with traditional paper-and-pencil multiple-choice tests or to measure traditional abilities in ways that have greater fidelity to the underlying cognitive processes. The work of Pat Kyllonen at the U. S. Air Force's Armstrong Laboratory is an example of how computers can be used to define and measure new ability constructs (Kyllonen, 1994, gives a very interesting approach to this area). In England, Sidney Irvine and his colleagues at the University of Plymouth (Irvine, Dann, & Anderson, 1990) have been both creative and productive in applying some of Kyllonen's ideas. At the other extreme—the use of computers to improve measurement of traditional ability constructs—is the development of a computerized version of the venerable French Kit of Reference Tests (French, Ekstrom, & Price, 1963); Ekstrom and Bejar (1990) introduced this new application. Together, these four aspects of computerized testing add up to a substantial promise.

RECENT EXAMPLES OF COMPUTER-BASED SELECTION AND CLASSIFICATION TESTING

In the United States, some computer-based personnel selection testing programs have been launched in the past several years. The more noteworthy examples can be classified in two broad categories, which I use to differentiate some of these programs from others. The first category consists of existing selection tests converted from the printed medium to computer. The second category is composed of selection tests that have been developed specifically for computer administration.

A phenomenon serving to facilitate the introduction of computerized testing has been the rise of commercially operated computer-based testing centers around the United States. At least three companies and more than 500 testing centers deliver clients' computer-based tests and training programs. The largest of these companies is Sylvan Learning Systems; their 240 SylvanTechnology Centers have delivered the GREs and other tests for more than 100 private-sector and government organizations. The Sylvan centers, and their competitors, have made it possible for a widely dispersed organization to introduce computer-based tests without any need to buy, operate, or maintain its own test administration computers.

Selection Tests Converted from Print to Computer

Major U.S. organizations have introduced, or are developing, computer-administered versions of selection tests that they have been using for years. In some cases, the computer-administered versions have been adaptive; in others, the tests have remained conventional, and the computer has merely served to "turn the page" for examinees. Four such organizations that use computerized tests are the U.S. Department of Defense, the Department of Labor, AT&T Corporation, and the Procter & Gamble Company.

U.S. Department of Defense

The U.S. Department of Defense, after almost 2 decades of research, has begun to replace printed versions of the Armed Services Vocational Aptitude Battery (ASVAB), their enlisted personnel selection test battery, with CAT-ASVAB, in a computerized adaptive version (Sands, Waters, & McBride, in press). Nationwide implementation of CAT-ASVAB is now in progress; computerized personnel selection tests will ultimately be in use in all 65 U.S. military entrance processing stations.

U.S. Department of Labor

The General Aptitude Test Battery (GATB) is a battery of tests used by the U.S. Employment Service (USES) for more than 50 years. Recently, the USES prepared computer-administered versions of six GATB tests (Tannenbaum, 1995). The traditional printed versions of all six tests are well-known to be speeded to some extent: Some combine both speed and power and others are mostly speed measures. Test speededness was one subject of a critique of GATB by the National Academy of Sciences; development of the computerized version is part of the USES response to the critique. In the computerized version of the GATB, three of the six cognitive ability tests are adaptive (and therefore "pure" power tests); the other three retain their speeded natures. The developers will conduct a pilot test of computer-administered GATB in the near future.

Procter & Gamble Company

Procter & Gamble company has been a leader among U.S. companies in the use of personnel selection testing for selecting office workers, factory workers, and even entry-level management and technical personnel. Despite the demonstrable value of personnel selection and classification testing, many companies in the United States have been reluctant to use tests, largely because of concerns about litigation. A few companies, not deterred by such concerns, have made selection tests an important component of their hiring procedures. One such company is Procter & Gamble, where selection tests have played an especially important role because the company fills almost all job vacancies by promotion from within. It hires selectively and knows that future senior managers and executives will come from current entry-level ranks. To assist in this, the company has long used printed tests of cognitive abilities, and of background experiences as well, to select entry-level managers. Recently, Procter & Gamble introduced a computerized adaptive version of the cognitive test battery they use in selecting entry-level managers (Mattimore, 1996).

AT&T Corporation

As reported by Kehoe, Kingston, and McCormick (1993), AT&T Corporation has been among the most reluctant to consider the use of computer-administered tests. The primary reason for this has been concern about costs: the costs of computer equipment, the cost of developing computer software to administer tests, the cost of maintaining computer equipment and software, and the cost of validity research to justify the use of new, computer-based tests. With the exception of typing and data-entry tests, AT&T has long avoided developing any computer-administered tests. The company changed this position, however, when automation of other personnel management activities brought computers into personnel offices; as a result, the equipment for computerized test administration became available without significant capital outlay for testing itself.

AT&T chose to develop computer-administered versions of some printed cognitive ability tests they used for personnel selection. The rationale was that because the printed tests demonstrated validity for selection, there was no strong reason to develop new tests; but computerizing the tests did offer to improve administrative efficiency, increase test scheduling flexibility, and automate test data entry and record keeping.

AT&T's computer-based personnel selection testing program is still in the research and development stage; it is not yet operational.

Selection Tests Developed Specifically for Computer Administration

Even more exciting than the spread of computer-delivered and adaptive tests are the major innovations being introduced in testing technology. Corporations including IBM Corporation, Ford Motor Company, Allstate Insurance Company, and Bell Atlantic Corporation have developed personnel tests designed specifically for computers, and the Department of Defense has also been a player in this game.

IBM Corporation

One of the best examples of innovative test design is a multimedia testing system for selecting manufacturing plant employees, developed by IBM Corporation (Dyer, Desmarais, & Midkiff, 1993; Masi & Desmarais, 1996). The IBM system uses computer-controlled, interactive video to deliver a battery of 10 tests that represent a combination of traditional measures, job preview, and job simulation. The concept is imaginative, even daring, and the execution is excellent.

The most obvious innovation of the IBM tests is that the entire test battery is delivered in a multimedia format, using a computer and an interactive laser disk. The tests include a narrated interactive video, viewed on the computer screen, that gives job applicants an orientation to a simulated manufacturing company (a lot like IBM) and explains that applicants will be assessed on a number of skills related to the simulated company's business. All the directions for the tests are part of an overarching scenario delivered in the form of interactive video. This idea alone is a significant innovation: It completely replaces the usual practice in which a test administrator gives oral instructions and examinees read printed directions for each test.

Another innovation has been the variety of approaches to testing that the battery included. As Dyer et al. (1993) explained, there were three different test formats in the battery: traditional tests, video-based tests, and interactive computer-based simulations. Even the traditional tests, of course, were computer administered; they included tests of mathematics, reading, vocabulary, table and graph interpretation, and background information (biodata). The computer simulations included measures of variables rarely included in selection tests, such as resistance to boredom, attention to detail, and dual task processing. Each video-based test presented a series of scenes, such as realistic workplace situations, and required the applicants to interpret what is happening and to select an appropriate response. Included among the video-based tests were tests of situational judgment, troubleshooting ability, and on-the-job learning ability.

Ford Motor Company

The Ford Motor Company developed a battery of eight computer-administered tests for use in selecting secretarial personnel. The tests were specifically designed to be computer administered, and reflected the central role computer use has assumed in the work of Ford's secretaries. As Schmitt, Gilliland, Landis, and Devine (1993) described the test development, the eight tests were constructed to represent actual secretarial work identified by means of an analysis of secretarial jobs at Ford. In addition to traditional secretarial activities such as typing, note taking, letter preparation, and the like, the job analysis identified more modern functions, including working with computer files and using computer databases, spreadsheets, and electronic communication systems.

Schmitt et al. (1993) wanted their test battery to include measures of the ability to perform the computer functions just listed, but did not want their tests to limit high scores to applicants with experience in any particular computer or software applications. Hence, they decided to develop a software package specifically for the computerized test.

Bell Atlantic Corporation

Several years ago, Bell Atlantic Corporation developed the Universal Test Battery (UTB), a computer-administered battery of 10 tests administered to virtually all applicants for nonmanagement jobs throughout the company. The UTB has been administered in Bell Atlantic personnel offices throughout the

Middle Atlantic states. In cases where testing was infrequent, computers were carried in for the occasion and carried out again once testing was finished. Portable computers have been used for this purpose and, because Bell Atlantic wanted to ensure that test administration conditions were the same everywhere, they used portable computers to administer all their UTB tests. In fact, they use just one portable computer model; this has created an unexpected problem, discussed in a later section.

RESEARCH, PROBLEMS, AND ISSUES

Computerized testing shows promise along several dimensions: It can help eliminate a lot of paper from the process of assessment—test booklets, answer-sheets, score reports, even personnel folders. It can reduce testing time or make time available for measuring additional attributes. It can measure in ways that cannot be done via paper and pencil. And it seems to have the potential to redefine ability measurement by assessing cognitive processes instead of their products.

Good news aside, no innovation is introduced without attendant problems or difficulties. There have been several "generations" of computer-administered selection and classification tests. Some problems were encountered and resolved early on, only to be replaced by new problems.

The First Generation: Cost

The first-generation worries of computer-administered tests were largely financial. Computer equipment was so costly that it clearly could not compete with paper and pencil on the basis of cost effectiveness. Software development was frightfully expensive. And perhaps most expensive of all was a cost that has not yet materialized, as far as I know: the forecast cost of the litigation that might ensue as soon as an organization introduced computer-administered testing.

As an example of the cost problem, take the case of the U.S. Department of Defense's CAT-ASVAB system. By 1986, research had shown it to be an efficient, technically acceptable alternative to the printed ASVAB for selection and classification. Ten years later, CAT-ASVAB was only then being implemented in the United States. A principal reason for the long delay between demonstrated effectiveness and full-scale operational use has been the cost of the system. In 1988, an economic analysis showed that CAT-ASVAB would be more expensive than printed ASVAB, without substantial offsetting benefits; at that time, the equipment cost alone was estimated to be somewhere between $25 million and $50 million. Just 8 years later, the estimated cost of equipment for the 65 military entrance processing stations with CAT-ASVAB was less than $3 million; a new economic analysis showed that CAT-ASVAB would benefit recruiting and enlistment processing efficiency enough to outweigh these small costs.

With the possible exception of equipment cost, other potential financial issues are still factors to be reckoned with. In my experience, the first-generation problems were largely appreciated in advance, and the concern and fear they engendered probably accounted for the slow pace of implementing computerized selection testing in the United States. The second- and third-generation problems were less well anticipated.

The Second Generation: Problems in Converting Printed Tests to Computer Administration

In my taxonomy, the second-generation problems have accompanied the process of converting an operational testing program from the traditional printed medium to computer administration. The first potential problem was obvious and usually dealt with in advance: possible changes in what the tests measure and in the psychometric characteristics of test score scales, referred to as *construct equivalence* and *scale equivalence*, respectively. The computerized version of my reliable, valid, and trusted old test battery might not measure exactly the same ability attributes that the printed version measured. Even if it did, the scores might not be comparable; scores on the computer version might be systematically higher or lower, or distributed differently, than paper and pencil test scores. These are real issues. (For a thorough review of them, see Mazzeo & Harvey, 1988, Mead & Drasgow, 1993, and Wise & Plake, 1989). Dealing with them requires research that can be costly: a construct equivalence study and an equating or scale calibration study. The larger problem is that the construct equivalence study may find differences: In some cases, the computerized versions of tests may indeed turn out to measure something a little or a lot different from the paper version.

As an example of this, take the AT&T research (Kehoe, Kingston, & McCormick., 1993) on converting their selection and classification tests to computer, which I mentioned earlier. As AT&T planned to do nothing more than duplicate existing tests on the computer, the research related to computer-based testing had a narrow focus: to demonstrate the equivalence of the computerized tests to their paper and pencil counterparts. Equivalence could be demonstrated simply by obtaining the correlation between scores from the printed tests and from computer versions of the same tests; if the correlations were nearly 1.00 (after correcting for attenuation from unreliability), the matter was settled. If the corrected correlations were substantially less than 1.00, further analysis would be needed.

Although this explanation sounds simple, it was complicated by several things. For one, some of the existing AT&T tests were speed tests; either the psychometric characteristics or the construct composition, or both, of speed tests have repeatedly been found to change when they are converted to computer administration (Greaud & Greene, 1986; Mead & Drasgow, 1993). This change may be an inevitable consequence of differences between computer and print in the way the test items are displayed and in the psychomotor features of the way examinees respond to them. In any event, differences between computer and print versions of power tests are usually small or even negligible; but the opposite is true of speed tests. AT&T decided to design the computer versions of its speed test in such a way as to mimic as closely as possible all the salient features of the printed version, including presentation format and response selection task. The company hoped that using a mouse pointer, rather than a keyboard, as the response device would make the perceptual and motor aspects of answer–selection and answer–marking task similar to printed tests. But AT&T also anticipated that examinees would perform faster on computer-administered speed tests.

AT&T's research is still in progress, as far as I know, so I cannot summarize its outcome. I can give a related example from my own experience: After developing a computerized adaptive version of the Differential Aptitude Tests (DAT), we (McBride, Corpe, & Wing, 1987) found that one of the eight tests correlated just .35 with its paper and pencil counterpart. The covariance structures of the two versions of the battery were virtually identical (Henly, Klebe, McBride, & Cudeck, 1990) except for the one test, a measure of clerical speed and the only speeded test in the battery. In hindsight, it was obvious that an examinee's task was different in the electronic medium: The psychomotor task of marking the answer sheet was absent in the computer version and this aspect affected speed. We also found that the computerized version of the speed test was correlated with general cognitive ability, something that was untrue of the paper and pencil version. Somehow, a paper and pencil measure of clerical speed had become a computer-administered measure of g. The lesson was obvious: Proceed with caution in converting selection tests from paper and pencil to computer administration.

Assuming the conversion is successful, it is still necessary to be wary of scale differences. The computerized adaptive version of the military's ASVAB provides two cases in point. As with the DAT, the problem was with the only speeded tests in the battery, one a measure of coding speed, the other a measure of speed in simple arithmetic operations. Both these ASVAB tests have been shown to measure the same ability variables regardless of the administration medium, but the computer version turned out to be much "easier": On these speeded tests, almost every item is answered correctly; the number of items reached in the time limits virtually determines the score. Greaud and Green (1986) showed that if time limits were the same in both media, scores were much higher on the computerized than on the printed version, and the distributions of the computer-based test scores were highly skewed. The two authors suggested a different approach to scoring the computer version: a rate score, rather than the number of correct answers. Their suggestion was adopted; speeded test scores of the CAT-ASVAB battery are based on timed response rates—the average number of seconds per correct answer. Thus, a change of metric accompanied the change of administration medium. This change necessitated an equating study—relatively expensive, but something that should probably have been done in any case. The lesson here is to be prepared for differences across media, not only in score levels, but also in the shape of score distributions.

Assume that a company has implemented a computer-based selection testing system and used it satisfactorily for a while. Does this situation solve all problems? Not necessarily. What happens when, a few years into the program, more computers are needed, either to expand or to replace worn-out equipment? The computers now is use are no longer available in the marketplace. Even if the manufacturer is still in business, your make and model is no longer being manufactured; the computers you bought today are not the same ones you bought even 3 years ago. Will this make a difference in the company's testing program? Regrettably, it could, and if the tests are highly speeded, it probably does.

This failure can occur because the processors in today's computers are many times faster than the ones of just a few years ago; disk access also is considerably faster. As a concrete example, in early 1996, I replaced a computer purchased in 1990; a benchmark comparison of the old and new computers showed that the new one processed more than 100 times faster than the old one, and got data from mass storage more efficiently as well. Both factors could make a difference in test scores if tests are closely timed. Other things could make a difference as well. For example, new computers may have a somewhat different keyboard layout, which could affect the speed of response. An updated video display might improve the legibility of displayed text and the resolution of displayed graphics and figures—and thus might affect scores.

This problem is not imaginary in selection testing: another instructive example is the CAT-ASVAB. After the battery had been used in a few sites for test and evaluation purposes for 2 years and approved for nationwide implementation, the Hewlett-Packard computers that had supported the 5 years of CAT-ASVAB research were no longer available. CAT-ASVAB software had to converted to PC-compatible equipment and from the UNIX operating system to Microsoft's DOS. The new computers bore surprisingly little physical resemblance to the old ones—to say nothing of differences below the surface. Because it is a conscientious organization, the U.S. Department of Defense commissioned a research study of "hardware effects." There were indeed significant differences between test scores obtained using the old and the new computers (Segall, in press). Notably, all the significant differences were in the two speeded tests; the nine adaptive power tests had no problems.

Bell Atlantic encountered a similar problem with the portable computers used to administer the UTB. As I mentioned earlier, out of concern for standardized testing conditions, the company used a single computer model for test administration and had purchased hundreds of these portable computers when the UTB was introduced. After a fairly short time, the computers began wearing out, probably because they were moved frequently among test administration sites. When Bell Atlantic sought to replace the worn-out computers with new ones, they could not find any; the manufacturer by now was making much more technically advanced computers, but no more of Bell Atlantic's chosen variety. The same concern about standardization that led the company to select a single type of computer for all testing also led Bell Atlantic to question whether administering the UTB on a newer computer model would produce test scores equivalent to those of the old model.

To address this question, Bell Atlantic commissioned HumRRO to study the problem from three perspectives: those of a computer systems engineer, a human factors engineer, and a psychometrician (McBride, Wall, Parsons, & Gribben, 1995). The central questions to be addressed from all three perspectives were: Are the computers available today materially different from the ones Bell Atlantic is already using? If so, are the differences likely to affect UTB test scores?

The 1995 computer systems analysis found that no portable computer currently manufactured had performance or display characteristics similar to the 5-year-old model on which Bell Atlantic had standardized. Our analysis indicated that virtually all new personal computers were superior to Bell Atlantic's current model in all characteristics related to processing speed, disk storage access, and transfer rates. In addition, new portable computer displays were somewhat superior in terms of display luminance contrast, and all cathode-ray tubes displays were vastly superior.

The human factors review led to the opinion that because of these differences, "human processing time" was one of the most important variables likely to influence test scores when the battery was moved to another computer. Simply put, if some characteristics of the new computer had the effect of increasing the processing time available to examinees in the elapsed time limits for each test, scores on that test were likely to increase. Both human factors characteristics and computer performance characteristics might cause the scores to increase. Examples of salient human factors characteristics include display size, luminance contrast, response key size and spacing, keyboard position, and distance from the display. Examples of salient computer performance characteristics include processor speed, video display speed, disk access speed, and data transfer rate.

The implication of all of this analysis is that using a new computer to administer the UTB would almost certainly increase the time available to examinees to read, process, and respond to test items, even though the test's time limits do not change. When test time limits were held constant, faster computer processing speed made more time available for "human processing" of the test items and could result in increased test scores, but only to the extent that each UTB test was speeded. If all examinees finished every item on a test, we would not expect more available processing time to have any effect on scores. If substantial numbers of examinees failed to complete all the items in a test, however, scores might increase when enough additional processing time became available on a new computer.

Our psychometric analyses focused on the possible impact of a new computer platform on UTB test scores. The thrust of these analyses was to: evaluate the extent to which each of the power tests is speeded; determine the relative contribution of speed and cognitive abilities to each of the UTB timed power tests; and estimate what would happen to UTB test scores if additional time became available to examinees as a result of improved computer performance. We found that examinees' speed was a significant factor in the scores on seven of the UTB's nine cognitive ability tests, even though only one was acknowledged to be a speed test. We then used computer performance measurements from our engineering analyses, in conjunction with data from the psychometric analyses, to estimate the magnitude of test score differences likely to occur if a certain computer model were to replace the current one. The expected increase in raw scores varied from very small to very large indeed.

How should such results be interpreted? Very simply, test scores can be expected to be higher if the computers used for test administration are even the least advanced of today'scommercially available computers. These results have similar implications for any computer-based testing program in which some tests have an appreciable speed component.

The common thread that runs through these cautionary tales about problems in converting a printed selection test to the computer is that all the problems I have noted have to do with *speeded* selection tests.

The Third Generation: Problems in Developing Innovative Tests of Abilities

So far, I have written about problems that arise when converting successful paper and pencil tests to the computerized medium. The third generation of problems accompany innovation in ability measurement by computer. Probably the most appealing thing about computerized testing is the potential of using the medium to remedy some shortcomings of printed tests and to develop new measures that could not be delivered in the printed medium. Some regard this potential as the most promising use of computers in testing, but with the promise goes a significant element of risk.

Perhaps the largest risk is that our reach may exceed our grasp: Our ambitions for using the computerized testing medium to break new ground may exceed the limits imposed by the state of the arts. The *arts* in this case encompass not only computer and video technology, but also scientific understanding of human abilities and cognitive processing. There are at least two kinds of problems involve here: *validity* and *incremental validity*.

The *validity* problem arises because we may not fully understand what an innovative, computer-based selection test measures. Preferably, the development of such tests starts with not only a good idea but also a sound basis in psychological theory. In practice, what seems like a good idea may lack theo-retical foundation; a new test development project may proceed on the basis of the "gee-whiz" factor, only to fall short when it comes time to assess reliability, construct validity, and predictive utility of the innovative measure.

The *incremental validity* problem is a different animal (with a brief history): Perhaps dissatisfied with a set of conventional ability measures, we might try to develop one or more new measures that we expect to improve on existing multiple-choice tests, which seem to measure general cognitive ability and little else. We might base the development on a solid theory and on sound test development practices. And we might expect the new measures to have greater fidelity to certain ability constructs, to add reliable variance to the existing battery, and to contribute significantly to predictive power. The proof is in the pudding, though; to assess the value of our new measures, we have to show a competitive advantage over the traditional tests.

The U.S. military attempted to demonstrate the incremental value of a new set of measures with a battery of innovative, computer-administered tests called Enhanced Computer Administered Testing (ECAT). ECAT(Alderton, Wolfe, & Larson, 1997) was intended to supplement the ASVAB by adding measures of psychomotor abilities and cognitive processes to the academically oriented content of the latter battery. ECAT tests' validity for predicting military training and job performance was evaluated in a substantial study (Wolfe, Alderton, Larson, & Held, 1993) that compared ECAT and ASVAB validity. The study looked at the validity of the old and the innovative tests for predicting training performance (as indicated by grades and performance measures) in 18 job specialties in the Army, Navy, and Air Force. In each case, the study compared the validity of the new test against that of current selection proce-dures; these selection procedures vary as to the specific ASVAB tests they include. The good news was that the innovative tests demonstrated substantial zero-order validity. The bad news was twofold: With the exception of a few job specialties, the ECAT tests in combination had little incremental validity over the full battery of ASVAB tests—the median increment was .012 corrected multiple correlation points (Pass, 1993); the study also found the same or better incremental validity in the ASVAB tests that were not included in the job-spe-cific selection procedures (Wolfe et al., 1993). A possible explanation of the minuscule incremental validity of the ECAT battery is that, despite its consid-erable differences from the tests in the ASVAB, it simply augmented the crystallized intelligence measures of the ASVAB with fluid intelligence meas-ures (Alderton & Larson, 1994).

To summarize this *incremental validity* problem, it may be difficult to show that an innovative selection test is appreciably superior to a satisfactory tradi-tional test, in terms of statistical relations to personnel performance. For this reason, it is probably much easier to justify the use of an innovative test in situations where no test has been used before or where the incumbent test has not been satisfactory.

THE PROFILE OF AMERICAN YOUTH

Not to conclude this paper on a pessimistic note, I have saved for last a brief summary of a research project of great interest to me. (I confess I have a minor role in it, but that is not what makes it interesting.) Other research projects that I have summarized here have been designed to resolve technical or scientific questions. A U.S. Department of Defense project, the 1997 Profile of American Youth (1997 Profile), has a different purpose, one with few if any counterparts in selection and classification testing research.

The 1997 Profile is technically a test norming project. Its objective is to develop current norms for the ASVAB tests; a test's norms are simply tables of the distribution of test scores in a specific reference group of examinees. What is unique about the 1997 Profile is that the examinee reference group is the population of U. S. youths of military age. The distribution of test scores, then, is tantamount to an inventory of intellectual abilities in the population from which the U.S. military selects applicants for enlistment. This inventory is extremely useful for military manpower planning: Because the norms describe what proportion of military-age youths scores above or below a specific score on any ASVAB test or test composite, manpower planners know how many military-eligible young people meet a specific selection or classification criterion. Consequently, if there comes a proposal to raise the qualifying score for enlistment in the Armed Services, the data from the 1997 Profile can inform manpower managers what proportion of the population becomes ineligible as a result. Combine these data with census data, and the managers know how *many* individuals nationwide qualify at the new score. Combine this information with data from other sources, such as enlistment propensity data, and the managers can estimate the impact of the higher qualifying score on the cost of meeting current recruiting goals. Data from the 1997 Profile also have direct implications for the use of test scores for personnel classification—assignment of individuals to specific military technical specialties—which for the most part is done before an individual enlists in the Armed Forces. For example, if the qualifying scores for assignment to training as electronics technicians are increased while the recruiting goals remain the same, it would be more difficult to meet recruiting goals for other highly selective occupations. The "inventory" data from the 1997 Profile will allow manpower planners to anticipate the impact of such a decision and to make whatever adjustments are necessary to avoid disrupting the manpower system as a whole.

How will the 1997 Profile data be collected? Obviously, there are two broad alternatives. One alternatve—to test the entire military-eligible population—sounds impossible, but it happened once: In 1945, with a world war in progress, virtually the entire population of military-eligible males was tested—millions of men. Getting their cooperation was easier than it would be today because they were already in uniform.

The other alternative is to draw a representative sample, test the sample members, and estimate the population norms using the techniques of survey sampling statistics. This approach is taken in the 1997 Profile: A multistage area probability sample of households will be drawn; the households will be canvassed to enumerate and list military-eligible youths living in them; and these youths will be enticed to take the ASVAB tests. To accomplish this, the Department of Defense is working with the U.S. Bureau of Labor Statistics (BLS). BLS periodically conducts national longitudinal surveys to study various aspects of the U.S. labor market. BLS planned a national longitudinal survey of youth to begin in 1997; the Department of Defense will underwrite some of the costs of the survey in exchange for an opportunity to administer its ASVAB tests to many military-eligible members of the survey sample households. BLS is happy to cooperate, because it wanted to measure intellectual abilities in its sample; the ASVAB will serve this purpose well.

Time and space do not permit me to provide much detail of the 1997 Profile of American Youth. Let me summarize by saying that the tests were to be administered in the summer of 1997, to 18,600 people. There were to be three samples: 6,000 military-age youths, 6,600 BLS survey sample members in three secondary school grades, and 6,000 younger BLS survey sample members, ages 12 to 14.

Two of the most interesting aspects of the 1997 Profile, to me at least, are these: First, the tests include the ASVAB itself, as well as a vocational interest inventory recently developed by the Department of Defense; consequently, the 1997 Profile inventoried not only vocationally relevant mental abilities, but also vocational interests. Second, all the tests used in the 1997 Profile were administered by computer, in particular, the computerized adaptive version of AS-VAB, the first instance in which nationwide test norms have been developed using computerized adaptive tests.

CONCLUSION

Two conclusions can be drawn about my discussion in this chapter. One point is that many of the largest organizations in the United States are using, or are in the advanced stages of developing, computer-administered tests for personnel selection and classification: The examples I gave included IBM, Ford, Procter & Gamble, AT&T, Bell Atlantic, and the Department of Defense. The second point is that such development by large organizations has proceeded slowly and cautiously, in part because despite their great appeal and substantial promise, there are problems in the development and use of computer-based selection tests. These problems are: Computer-based tests can be expensive to develop and implement (and perhaps to defend); and adaptations of successful printed tests to computer administration can be difficult, because the computerized versions may not measure what the printed tests measure or may have significantly different test score distributions. Finally, developing innovative tests designed specifically for computerized administration has its own problems: the tests may not measure what they are intended to measure, and even if they do, it may not be worth the effort, in terms of gains in personnel selection and classification.

This summary is pessimistic enough to disqualify me from further employment as an evangelist in the cause of computer-based selection testing. I hope, though, that the things I am cautioning about do not deter anyone from developing and using computer-based selection tests. If these statements seem contradictory, let me explain by saying that the field of computer-based selection testing is sufficiently well developed today to avoid risk. If we are attentive to the lessons others have learned in this field—summarized incompletely and all too briefly in this chapter—we can develop computerized test applications successfully without having to experience many problems ourselves.

REFERENCES

Alderton, D. L., & Larson, G. E. (1994). Dimensions of ability: Diminishing returns? In M. G. Rumsey, C. B. Walker, & J. H. Harris (Eds.), *Personnel Selection and Classification* (137–144). Hillsdale, NJ: Lawrence Erlbaum Associates.

Alderton, D. L., Wolfe, J. H., & Larson, G. E. (1997). ECAT. *Military Psychology 9*(1), 5–38.

Ashworth, S. D., & McHenry, J. J. (1993, April). *Developing a multimedia in-basket: Lessons learned.* Paper presented at the eighth annual conference of the Society for Industrial and Organizational Psychology, San Francisco, CA.

Dyer, P. J., Desmarais, L. B., & Midkiff, K. R. (1993, April). *Multimedia employment testing in IBM: Preliminary results from employees.* Paper presented at the eighth annual conference of the Society for Industrial and Organizational Psychology, San Francisco, CA.

Ekstrom, R. B., & Bejar, I. I. (1990, August). *Computer-based assessment of cognition: The ETS factor kit.* Paper presented at the 105th annual convention of the American Psychological Association.

French, J. W., Ekstrom, R. B., & Price, L. A. (1963). *Kit of reference tests for cognitive factors.* Princeton, NJ: Educational Testing Service.

Greaud, V. A., & Green, B. F. (1986). Equivalence of conventional and computer presentation of speed tests. *Applied Psychological Measurement, 10,* 23–34.

Henly, S. J., Klebe, K. J., McBride, J. R., & Cudeck, R. (1990). Adaptive and conventional versions of the DAT: The first complete test comparison. *Applied Psychological Measurement, 13,* 463–471.

Irvine, S. H., Dann, P. L., & Anderson, J. D. (1990). Towards a theory of algorithm-determined cognitive test construction. *British Journal of Psychology, 81,* 173–195.

Kehoe, J. F., Kingston, N. M., & McCormick, D. J. (1993, April). *Practical considerations for low cost computerized testing.* Paper presented at the eighth annual conference of the Society for Industrial and Organizational Psychology, San Francisco, CA.

Kyllonen, P. C. (1994). Cognitive abilities testing: An agenda for the 1990s. In M. G. Rumsey, C. B. Walker, & J. H. Harris (Eds.). *Personnel selection and classification* (pp. 103–126). Hillsdale, NJ: Lawrence Erlbaum Associates.

Masi, D. L., & Desmarais, L. B. (1996, April). *Multimedia mania: Is the illusion real?* Paper presented at the 11th annual conference of the Society for Industrial and Organizational Psychology, San Diego, CA.

Mattimore, L. K. (1996, April). *Comprehensive global selection at Procter & Gamble.* Paper presented in at the 11th annual conference of the Society for Industrial and Organizational Psychology, San Diego, CA.

Mazzeo, J., & Harvey, A.L. (1988). *The equivalence of scores from automated and conventional educational and psychological tests: A review of the literature* (College Board Report No. 88-8). New York: College Entrance Examination Board.

McBride, J. R., Corpe, V. V., & Wing, H. (1987). *Equating the computerized adaptive edition of the differential aptitude tests.* Paper presented at the 102nd annual convention of the American Psychological Association, New York, NY.

McBride, J. R., Wall, T., Parsons, H. M., & Gribben, M. (1995). *Computer transportability study,* (Final Report FR-WATSD-95-04 to Bell Atlantic Network Services, Inc.). Alexandria, VA: Human Resources Research Organization.

McHenry, J. J., & Schmitt, N. (1994). *Multimedia testing.* In M. G. Rumsey, C. B. Walker, & J. H. Harris (Eds.), *Personnel Selection and Classification.* Hillsdale, NJ: Lawrence Erlbaum Associates.

Mead, A. D., & Drasgow. F. (1993). Equivalence of computerized and paper-and-pencil cognitive ability tests: A meta-analysis. *Psychological Bulletin, 114*(3), 449–458.

Pass, J. J. (1993). *Validity of experimental computerized tests for predicting training achievement.* Briefing for the Manpower Accession Policy Working Group ASVAB Review Technical Committee, San Antonio, TX.

Sands, W. A., Waters, B. K., & McBride, J. R. (in press). *Computerized adaptive testing:From inquiry to operation.* Washington, DC: American Psychological Association.

Schmitt, N., Gilliland, S. W., Landis, R. S., & DeVine, D. (1993). Computer-based testing applied to selection of secretarial applicants. *Personnel Psychology, 46,* 149–165.

Segall, D.O. (in press). *The psychometric comparability of computer hardware.* In W. A. Sands, B. K. Waters, & J. R. McBride (Eds.), *Computerized adaptive testing: From inquiry to operation.* (pp. 219–226). Washington, DC: American Psychological Association.

Snell, A. F., Stokes, G. S., Sands, M. M., and McBride, J. R. (1993). Adolescent life experiences as predictors of occupational attainment. *Journal of Applied Psychology, 79*(1), 131–141.

Tannenbaum, H. P. (1995). *The development of the Computerized General Aptitude Test Battery (CAT-GATB)* (Draft Report). New York: Eastern Assessment Research and Development Center, New York State Department of Labor.

Wise, S. L., & Plake, B.S. (1989). Research on the effects of administering tests via computers. *Educational Measurement: Issues and Practice, 8,* 5–10.

Wolfe, J. H., Alderton, D. L., Larson, G. E., & Held, J. D. (1993). *Incremental validity of Enhanced Computer Administered Testing (ECAT)* (NPRDC TR-93-[Draft]). San Diego, CA: Navy Personnel Research and Development Center.

5

Testing Medium, Validity, and Test Performance

James L. Outtz
Outtz and Associates

Researchers have studied the validity of psychological tests, particularly employment tests, for many years, (Ghiselli, 1966). Evidence of validity is essential to establishing the utility of an employment selection device. The purpose of this chapter is to explore the relations among the characteristics of a test, test performance, and validity.

The term *test* is used here in the broadest sense to mean any standardized procedure designed to improve selection decisions. For convenience, test characteristics are placed under the broad label of *testing medium*. A *medium* is defined as an object or vehicle through which something is conveyed or transmitted. *Testing medium* refers to the characteristics that make a test different from other tests. The testing medium includes such things as the type of item (e. g., multiple choice or free response); test instructions (i.e., penalty for guessing); the mode in which test content is presented (e.g., written or oral); the type of response required; and the method of scoring. Testing medium focuses on the characteristics of a test rather than on the trait or traits that the test is designed to measure.

People have long known that the way in which a construct is measured can alter the measurement itself, a phenomenon called *method variance* (Meier, 1994). Nevertheless, little research has been devoted to the effects of testing medium on test performance generally or on the test performance of specific subgroups (e.g., racial and ethnic minorities). Most of the published literature on test characteristics has focused on the effects of various paper and pencil formats on performance and, to a lesser degree, on validity.

TRADITIONAL TEST FORMATS
AND TEST PERFORMANCE

Cronbach (1941) demonstrated that the type of item used on a test can influence test performance in ways that are unrelated to the construct the test is intended to measure. In his study, Cronbach used two different sets of instructions to convert 22 multiple-choice items into multiple true–false items. The 22 test items contained a total of 110 choices, of which 55 were correct or true. The subjects, college students in a general psychology course, were given one of two sets of instructions.

Under one set of instructions, students were told that most questions had more than one correct answer and they were directed to mark every choice that they believed to be correct. The students were also told that they would be penalized if they marked an incorrect choice as correct. Under the second set of instructions, students were told to evaluate every answer and to mark it correct or incorrect. These students were also told that they would be penalized for marking an incorrect choice as correct, but they were advised to guess if they had at least partial knowledge of the correct answers.

Cronbach (1941) found that the students who were required to mark every response as true or false tended to mark more responses true than did students who were required to mark only the responses they thought were correct. He concluded that a personality trait, which he labeled "acquiescence," accounted for the difference in the way the two groups responded. He defined acquiescence as a subject's tendency to mark a statement true, when the subject lacked sufficient information to determine the correct answer. He concluded that a tendency toward acquiescence would be associated with a high score on true–false tests if more than half of the items were keyed *true* and with a low score if less than half were keyed *true*.

In a follow-up study, Cronbach (1942) obtained results that corroborated his earlier finding. When answering true–false questions, subjects tended to mark an item true when guessing. On the basis of these results, he concluded that acquiescence was independent of the knowledge or ability the test was designed to measure. Cronbach also found that acquiescence was not controlled even with penalty-for-guessing instructions. Subjects still guessed when penalty-for-guessing instructions were given. The penalty-for-guessing instructions might simply have added personality factors such as risk taking or submissiveness to directions to test scores and as a result might have reduced validity.

Traub and Fisher (1977) compared the performance of eighth-grade students on mathematical reasoning and verbal comprehension tests that presented the same test items in three response formats. The formats were traditional multiple choice; nonstandard multiple choice, in which subjects were instructed to identify as many incorrect answers to each question as possible; and constructed (free) response. Special keys were constructed for the free-response format to ensure reliability.

Factor analysis of the test results indicated that the tests of mathematical reasoning were equivalent regardless of format, but performance on the tests of verbal comprehension was influenced by format. The free-response format for the verbal comprehension tests appeared to measure *different* abilities from the other formats. Measures were also taken of the relations among test performance, the ability to follow directions, memory, and the propensity to engage in risk-taking behavior. The results of the factor analysis of these variables were inconclusive. Traub and Fisher (1977) concluded that different formats may produce measures of different abilities, at least where tests of verbal comprehension are concerned.

Ward, Frederiksen, and Carlson (1980) developed both a machine-scorable and a free-response version of four tests designed to measure the problem-solving ability of undergraduate psychology students. The tests were constructed so that there was no single right or wrong answer to each question. Under the free-response format, students were required to write down short answers. The machine-scorable format required the students to choose several answers from a list provided. Factor analysis of the scores indicated that the two versions of the test could not be considered equivalent.

Thissen, Wainer, and Wang (1994) used a research design similar to Ward et al. (1980) to study the relations between the free-response and multiple-choice items on achievement tests in computer science and chemistry. Factor analysis of the scores indicated that although the factor structure of the tests was similar, the free-response items on both tests were measuring something different from the element measured by the multiple-choice items.

Ward (1982) administered three forms of verbal aptitude tests—antonyms, sentence completion, and verbal analogies—in four formats and assessed the effects on test performance. The four formats were conventional multiple choice and three formats that required the subjects to produce rather than recognize the correct answers. The results indicated that response format did not make a difference for sentence completion and antonym items but there was a difference between the multiple free-response formats and the multiple-choice format for verbal analogy items.

Boyle (1984) studied the effects of three answer sheet formats for subtests of the General Aptitude Test Battery. All the answer sheets were machine scorable and designed for use with optical scanning machines, but they differed in the type of mark the test subject was required to make: darkening the circle below the letter for the correct answer; darkening the space between two parallel lines; or darkening the area in a rectangle.

Boyle found a significant interaction between subtest and answer sheet format. Performance on speeded subtests was significantly lower when the darken-the-circle format was used. Apparently, darkening a circle took more time than marking the answer in the other formats and resulted in completion of fewer items on the speeded subtests. Conscientiousness might also have been a factor in Boyle's results. Some subjects, by making an effort to follow the instructions to the letter and by staying completely inside each circle and darkening it completely, might have needed considerably more time to answer each item than did more careless subjects.

TRADITIONAL TEST CHARACTERISTICS AND SUBGROUP PERFORMANCE

Several studies have indicated that specific test characteristics affect the performance of subgroups in different ways. Using subtests designed to measure verbal, quantitative, or analytical ability, Scheuneman (1987) tested 16 hypotheses about test item variations that would result in different test performance for African American and White examinees on the Graduate Record Examination (GRE). Variations of the test items included presenting vocabulary items in or out of context; requiring subjects to make an inference to determine the correct answer versus not having such a requirement; and constructing items on the basis of abstract versus concrete information.

Ten of Scheuneman's 16 hypotheses were supported in that there were interactions between group membership and the version of the item used, but the complexity of the interactions indicated that factors other that those hypothesized contributed to the findings. One unexpected finding was that some changes in item format had a greater effect on the performance of Whites than of African Americans. In each instance, the difference in the performance of the 2 groups became larger as a result of the manipulation. Scheuneman concluded that the results of his study provided more questions than answers about factors that affect test performance differentially by race. This finding is troubling because the test characteristics manipulated by Scheuneman were limited to the traditional paper and pencil format.

Breland, Danos, Kahn, Kubota, and Bonner (1994) studied the effect of multiple-choice and free-response items on the performance of male and female examinees on advanced placement examinations in history. The free-response items were scored on several criteria including English usage, number of words written, number of main points given, supporting evidence for the points made, and factual errors. The results indicated a significant difference in favor of males on the multiple-choice items but a nonsignificant difference on the free-response items. Breland et al. concluded that the most reasonable explanation for the gender differences was that the two formats measured different skills, both of which were important in the study of history. Here again, a change in the paper and pencil format produced significant differences in performance for specific subgroups.

NONTRADITIONAL TESTS AND TEST PERFORMANCE

Test-characteristic studies that went beyond mere changes in paper and pencil format also showed differential effects by subgroup. One such characteristic is the context in which a test is presented. Carraher, Carraher, and Schliemann (1985) presented mathematics items to children working in markets in the streets of Brazil. The mathematics items were presented in three different formats: oral questioning, simple arithmetic testing, and arithmetic word problems.

In the first format, children were tested on the street by interviewers posing as customers. During the course of interacting with each child, the interviewer asked successive questions about potential or actual purchases and obtained a verbal response. At the end of the interaction, the child was asked to take part in a second interview later, at the same place or at the child's home. The second interview was held approximately 1 week later.

During the second interview, the child was given a formal arithmetic test in which he or she was presented arithmetic problems modeled after the initial interview questions. Two variations of the formal math test were presented. In one variation, the problems were presented as straightforward mathematical operations ($105 + 105 = ?$). The second variation consisted of word problems in which the mathematical operation was presented in context (John purchased two apples. Each apple cost X. How much did John pay altogether?).

The results showed that 98% of the problems presented during the street interviews were correctly solved. In contrast, 73% of the problems presented in context on the formal arithmetic test were solved correctly, and only 38% of the mathematical operations presented without context on the test were solved correctly. The informal tests involved the oral presentation of test material and an oral response by the subject. This context was the same as that in which the children carried out mathematical operations on a day-to-day basis. Performance in this context was superior to that in which similar problems were presented with limited context or in a context-free format, even though the problems involved the same operations.

NONTRADITIONAL TEST CHARACTERISTICS
AND SUBGROUP PERFORMANCE

In recent years, researchers in the field of industrial and organizational psychology have explored the possibility that testing medium, broadly defined beyond the limits of the paper and pencil format, may affect the test performance of members of specific racial and ethnic groups. The impetus for this research has no doubt been the desire to find alternatives to traditional employment selection devices such as cognitive ability tests. Cognitive ability tests tend to produce differences as large as 1 standard deviation between minority and nonminority applicants (Gottfredson, 1986). Therefore, cognitive ability tests are thought to have substantial adverse impact against minority applicants.

The concept of adverse impact originated in the Uniform Guidelines on Employee Selection Procedures (1978). According to the Uniform Guidelines, a test or selection procedure has adverse impact if test scores of applicants who are members of a protected class are (statistically) significantly lower than those of nonminority applicants, or if the selection rate for such applicants is less than 80% of the selection rate for nonminority applicants. If either condition exits, an employer must provide validity evidence to substantiate the appropriateness of the test.

The Uniform Guidelines also provide that even with evidence of validity, use of a test may be unlawful if there is an alternative test with equal validity and less adverse impact. This "equal validity but less adverse impact" provision of the Uniform Guidelines has to some extent fueled recent research aimed at identifying alternatives to traditional selection devices such as cognitive ability tests.

In a comprehensive review of the literature, Reilly and Chao (1982) attempted to identify alternatives to cognitive ability tests. Eight categories of selection procedures were evaluated: biographical information, employment interviews, peer evaluations, self-assessments, reference checks, academic performance measures, expert judgment, and projective techniques. A selection device was considered a suitable alternative if there was evidence of validity equal to that of cognitive ability tests and evidence of less adverse impact. Reilly and Chao concluded that the data then available offered no clear indication that any of the categories met these criteria. None of the alternatives appeared promising and only two, the situational interview and self-assessment, deserved further study.

In the years following the Reilly and Chao (1982) literature review, researchers and practitioners were motivated to try new selection approaches—not only because of the legal environment, but also because the demographics of the applicant population were changing. The number of minorities and women in any given applicant pool grew steadily between 1980 and 1990 (Carnevale & Stone, 1995). Over a decade after the first review of the literature, Reilly and Warech (1994) revisited the question of alternatives to cognitive ability tests. This time, they found four alternatives that met the criteria of having equal validity and less adverse impact than did cognitive ability tests (i.e., the alternatives produced smaller differences between racial groups). The alternatives were trainability tests, work samples, assessment centers, and biodata.

Trainability tests involve the presentation of training information derived from a job analysis. Subsequent assessment of learning can be based on a paper and pencil test, but it usually involves performance tests.

Work samples are simulations of actual job content or samples of tasks directly relevant to the job. Robertson and Kandola (1982) classified work samples into the following four categories:

Psychomotor: This involves behavior such as manipulating objects, typing, or using a power tool.

Individual situational decision making: Here applicants are expected to make decisions similar to those required on the job. The test might include a specific exercise such as an in-basket, or it might present the applicant with hypothetical situations and ask how he or she would respond.

Job-related information: This category includes paper and pencil job knowledge tests designed to measure the applicants' information about a job.

Group discussions-decision making: Included in this category are exercises such as leaderless group discussion.

Assessment centers usually consist of a combination of exercises including an in-basket, group fact-finding exercise, role play, and oral presentation.

Biodata or biographical information instruments are self-report measures designed to identify applicants' experiences and activities that are predictive of future job performance. These measures are not designed to assess ability per se and therefore differ considerably from the other predictors in format and type of response allowed.

All four test alternatives go beyond the usual paper and pencil format common to cognitive ability tests. Three of the four—trainability tests, work samples, and assessment centers—usually involve standardized sampling of work behaviors that closely approximate the actual job. These three also have a cognitive component. Biodata is the only self-report measure among the four alternatives, and in this regard it would appear to differ most from cognitive ability tests in terms of test characteristics.

The four alternatives Reilly and Warech (1994) identified as having less adverse impact than cognitive ability tests illustrate that test characteristics beyond the traditional pen and pencil format may be significant factors in subgroup performance.

Wigdor and Green (1991) compared the performance of African American and nonminority military personnel on work sample measures, paper and pencil job knowledge tests, and tests of cognitive ability. The results indicated that differences in the performance of the 2 groups were much greater on the job knowledge and cognitive ability tests than on the work samples.

Some researchers have expanded the study of test characteristics to include audiovisual technology as a medium with which to present test content (Curtis, Gracin, & Scott, 1994; Dyer, Desmarais, & Masi, 1994; Outtz, 1993). McHenry and Schmitt (1994) coined the term *multimedia tests* to describe tests presented through the use of audiovisual technology. These tests are basically measures that rely on audio and video technology to present test instructions, test items, or both.

Curtis et al. (1994) reported the results of four validity studies in which multimedia tests were compared with biodata and traditional cognitive ability tests for validity and adverse impact. The results showed that biodata and multimedia assessment measures were as valid as the cognitive ability tests yet produced less adverse impact. Unfortunately, their research design did not permit the researchers to determine whether adverse impact was reduced because different constructs were measured or a different medium was used to measure the constructs. This is an important question that must be addressed in future research.

Dyer et al. (1994) compared two multimedia tests with traditional tests designed to measure reading comprehension, basic arithmetic skills, and the ability to read tables and graphs. Their findings indicated that several possible combinations of predictors yielded equivalent validity. They found also that different predictor combinations yielded different results in terms of adverse impact. Moreover, individual predictors produced unexpected, and seemingly inexplicable, performance differences among African Americans, Hispanics, Asians, and Whites. The patterns of adverse impact were different for each racial group. As an example, the multimedia tests produced smaller differences between African Americans and Whites than did the traditional tests of tables and graphs, arithmetic, and reading comprehension. On the other hand, the multimedia tests produced larger differences between Asians and Whites than they did between African Americans and Whites. The data showed that the Asians in the study scored below African Americans on four of the five tests administered. The researchers found this to be quite unusual, because the typical pattern of differences is that Asians score at a level on equal to and in some instances exceeding that of Whites. This result suggests that the Asian sample might simply have been atypical; the results might reflect difficulty with the English language for the Asian sample rather than anything else.

One finding emerging from research that compares the validity and adverse impact of various predictors is that tests with equivalent validity can vary considerably in adverse impact—as the studies described show. The question is why this phenomenon occurs rather than whether it occurs.

TESTING MEDIUM AND METHOD VARIANCE

The primary objective of many researchers and practitioners in the employment area has been to find predictors or selection procedures that do not have adverse impact; such tests would meet a real need for employers (i. e., they would offer protection from legal challenge). This objective is unfortunate, because the implications for the science of measurement greatly exceed the practical value of simply satisfying a legal mandate. If different test characteristics interact with demographic and experiential factors to influence test performance, the important questions are how and why. Which test characteristics affect the test performance of which groups in what ways? These may seem like novel questions, but they are not.

Systematic variance in test scores attributable to test characteristics may be considered *method variance* (Meier, 1994). The same phenomenon defined in terms of traits would be considered *response sets*. Cronbach (1946) defined as a response set any tendency of a person to respond differently to an item than the person would respond if the item were presented in a different form. As an example, when subjects are allowed to omit test items, some omitted more than did others who had equal knowledge (Cronbach, 1946). That is, despite having equal knowledge, their scores differed because of traits such as acquiescence, risk taking, or a tendency to emphasize accuracy rather than speed. Cronbach proposed that, because response sets are consistent, they may raise test reliability. Response sets lower construct validity, but they may raise or lower predictive validity depending on the relation between the response set and the criterion (Cronbach, 1946).

The research on test validity and adverse impact (Reilly & Warech, 1994; see also Curtis et al., 1994; Dyer et al., 1994) seems to indicate that method variance (or response sets) may interact with subgroup membership. Therefore, it may be as useful to focus on test characteristics as it is on traits in attempting to understand differences in subgroup performance. Test characteristics are more readily controlled and manipulated for experimental purposes, and it may be easier to objectively classify tests than test takers. Finally, classifying tests on the basis of test characteristics may help clarify whether differences in test performance across subgroups are due to measurement of different constructs or due to measurement of the same construct in different ways.

One approach to studying the effects of test characteristics would be to classify tests according to specific test characteristics and to assess subgroup differences in performance in and between classifications. For example, tests might be classified according to testing medium. The test itself is the medium through which information is conveyed to a test taker in an attempt to elicit behavior that is indicative of an ability or attribute. Unfortunately, little attention has been given to differences between tests (particularly employment tests) when they are viewed strictly from the standpoint of testing medium. If testing medium is related to the concept of adverse impact, do tests of equal predictive validity presented through different media produce different levels of adverse impact?

Does the medium (including test directions, test content, response medium, and scoring method) in which a test is presented affect test performance differently for different subgroups without affecting predictive validity? Guion (1965) indirectly called attention to this issue more than 30 years ago when he noted that test developers must often grapple with the question of whether complex abilities can be predicted from knowledge or ability level in a simpler content area (e.g., whether social ability can be assessed adequately by testing the ability to think verbally). Guion noted that most testing in applied psychology rests on the assumption that this question can be answered in the affirmative, but this assumption may not be correct.

Stone, Stone, and Gueutal (1990), for example, showed that questionnaires (instruments that may be even less cognitively demanding than paper and pencil tests) place greater cognitive demands, in terms of reading ability, on respondents do than other types of measures. This increased reading demand can produce unintended results, such as decreased reliability for subjects with low reading ability, and lowered performance for such groups regardless of the construct that is intended to be measured. Research such as that by Stone et al. (1990) has questioned whether certain characteristics of traditional paper and pencil employment tests (e.g., test instructions, item format, and response medium) significantly affect test performance between subgroups in ways unrelated to the construct(s) the tests are intended to measure.

One benefit of focusing on the relations between test characteristics and test performance is the possibility of identifying classes or patterns of characteristics that might provide additional evidence of the construct(s) being measured. It might also be possible to learn more about why tests with equivalent predictive validity produce significantly different (in both practical and statistical terms) levels of performance between subgroups. What would such a classification system look like? How might we begin to organize tests solely on the basis of test characteristics or testing medium? A good starting point would be the work of Vernon (1962) and Cattell and Warburton (1967).

In looking at sources of variance in educational tests, Vernon (1962) proposed four sources of variance that could be classified (for the purposes of this discussion) as characteristics of the test: the form of test material presented—verbal, symbolic, visual or performance—where these factors are not intended to be relevant to the purpose of the test; the type of presentation—verbal, visual or oral; difficulty level and speediness, which may alter factor content; and response type—multiple choice, short answer.

A more comprehensive classification system was provided by Cattell and Warburton (1967). They proposed a system based on three dimensions: the test instructions, the material test or the characteristics of the test items (i.e., written versus performance, etc.), and the manner in which test behavior is scored. According to Cattell and Warburton, a useful taxonomy could be constructed based solely on the objective operational features of tests categorized in terms of these three dimensions.

In attempting to actually categorize tests, Cattell and Warburton soon realized that the dimensions were not independent: They could not determine the number of possible test designs simply by determining the number of possible combinations of the three dimensions. Certain instructions, for example, were incompatible with certain test items, and certain item types were incompatible with certain methods of scoring, and so on.

Instructed-Stimulus Situation

Because the instructions essentially define stimulus material, Cattell and Warburton proposed that these dimensions be combined to form what they called the "instructed situation" (Cattell & Warburton, 1967). The instructed situation determines the type of response to which a scoring method is applied. The researchers hypothesized that tests can be classified based on the dimensions of the stimulus-instruction situation (which includes the type of response required) and the method of scoring applied to the response.

The following test characteristics were proposed by Cattell and Warburton (1967) in the instructed-stimulus situation dimension (symbolized by the letter I):

I (1). *Tests requiring reaction from the subject*: Cattell and Warburton pointed out that for most tests the subject must react to a stimulus rather than inhibit a reaction. In some instances, however, the correct approach is to inhibit any response (i.e., role-play situations designed to test self-control).

I (2). *Restricted or unrestricted response*: In tests where a reaction is elicited, the subject's response may be restricted or the subject may not be restricted in any way with regard to the allowed mode of response. Cattell and Warburton suggested that unrestricted reaction is seldom allowed. The subject is usually given a choice of some implicit or explicit restrictions (i.e., choose only the best answer).

I (3). *Inventive or selective response:* This factor refers to whether the subject must produce a response or select a response from those provided.

I (4). *Single or multiple responses*: Is the subject instructed to provide a single response, or can multiple responses be provided?

I (5). *Items are ordered versus unordered*: Cattell and Warburton suggested that some tests require items to be answered in a particular order (e.g., individual IQ tests) or to be addressed independent of each other. This approach can be contrasted with a test in which a global response to the totality of a problem is required (e.g., Indicate how to handle a situation that occurs at work; Describe how to troubleshoot a malfunctioning piece of equipment).

I (6). *Homogeneous versus patterned response*: If the subject is required to make the same kind of response for each item (e.g., choose the best answer), it is said to be homogeneous. Tests that have distinct parts with changes of response form are said to be patterned. A multiple-choice test would be homogeneous, whereas an assessment center might be patterned or heterogeneous.

I (7). *Self-directed versus controlled performance*: This factor refers to whether the subject is instructed to work within time and quality constraints (i.e., as fast or as accurately as possible). Obviously subjects can be instructed to work at their own "natural" pace and to determine for themselves whether to emphasize speed or accuracy or both, as would be the case with many hands-on performance tests.

I (8). *Concluding reaction versus reacting to a reaction*: The subject may be instructed to react to each test stimulus and to move on, or to react to his or her reaction to the stimulus. As an example of the latter, Cattell and Warburton suggested that a subject may be instructed to evaluate his or her reaction to a test stimulus, memorize it, or associate it with another stimulus.

I (9). *Immediate meaning or referent meaning*: A test can make reference to other situations or information outside the test itself, or such referents can be minimal. When reference is made to situations outside the test, differences in familiarity with the referents play a limited role in determining test perform-ance.

I (10). *Itemized or global presentation*: A test can consist of several items or one global problem situation. This factor differs from *I* (5) in that the emphasis here is on the global nature of the stimulus and not the subject's response to it.

I (11). *Nature of the psychological decision made in the response*: A subject may be instructed to make a cognitive judgment as to what is most correct or to give an affective response reflecting likes or dislikes, irritation, or fear.

Cattell and Warburton proposed two additional characteristics with regard to the instructed-stimulus situation: *I* (12)—variations in motives for accepting the test situation and *I* (13)—variations in perceived freedom to leave the testing situation. These factors, however, appear to be personality traits rather than test characteristics.

The characteristics that Cattell and Warburton classified under instructed-stimulus–situation factors are quite extensive. The work of Vernon (1962) and others (Dyer et al., 1994; McHenry & Schmitt, 1994; Reilly & Warech, 1994) has suggested additional factors, *I* (14) through *I* (17) for the sake of consis-tency:

I (14). *Medium used to present the test*: Test instructions and, more particu-larly, test items can be presented in several media including oral, written, visual (video tape, slides, and photographs), or any combination of these. Each medium or combination of media may facilitate or hinder a subject's ability to grasp the test structure, the test items, or both and to determine the appropriate response(s). For example, oral test items use somewhat different abilities to process the information than does written material. Listening skills become paramount, and subjects can rely on their oral vocabulary and ability to recog-nize the meaning of words spoken in context. If members of different racial, cultural, or ethnic groups place different emphasis on processing information presented orally, then the use of an oral medium for the instructed-stimulus situation might affect these groups differently.

I (15). *The medium with which the subject responds*: Subjects can be instructed to respond to a test item orally (as in a structured interview), through the use of written statements (as in completing an employment application), by darkening a circle on an answer sheet, or by carrying out an overt behavior (as in the case of a hands-on work sample test). As an example, a subject's performance on a typing test may depend on whether he or she must answer multiple-choice items about typing, tell how to perform specific typing tasks, write a one-page summary describing how a typing task should be accomplished, or actually sit in front of a typewriter and type. This example is an oversimplification, but clearly the greater fidelity between the response medium and the medium or media that accurately reflect(s) the construct the test is designed to measure, the more likely it is that the test has construct validity.

I (16). *Context-based or context-free items*: Test items can parallel real-world problems or situations in terms of the context in which they are embedded. Items can also can be presented in a formal, context-free form.

I (17). *Freedom to guess or a penalty for guessing*: As discussed earlier, the presence of "do-not-guess" instructions can introduce personality factors such as acquiescence and risk taking into the testing situation regardless of the purpose of the test.

Method of Scoring

Cattell and Warburton (1967) also proposed five factors on which a test might be classified in terms of method of scoring. These factors, designated by the letter *S*, include:

S (1). *Objective versus self-evaluative*: Is the subject told what he or she is scored on and then scored on this basis, or is the subject scored on factors unknown to him or her? Practically all standardized ability tests fall into the former category, but personality inventories and biodata blanks probably fall into the latter category. This factor may determine the face validity of a test.

S (2). *Overt behavior or physiological response*: Does the test measure only overt behavior or does it also measure the subject's physiological reaction to the test stimulus? This factor may distinguish tests of mental ability from tests of physical agility or medical examinations.

S (3). *Dimensions of one possible response or classification among a variety of responses*: Some tests are scored so that one dimension of the subject's response, errors, for instance, is the focus of measurement. Other tests are scored so that the number of responses that fall in different categories is the basis of measurement. Cattell and Warburton suggested a picture interpretation test as an example of the latter.

S (4). *Total quantity of responses or the fraction meeting some prescribed criterion*: Is the subject's score the sum of the correct answers, or is it based on the percentage of answers, that meet a particular threshold in terms of correctness? As an example, when scoring an assessment center exercise, responses can be placed in three categories: best, good, and average. The exercise can be scored on the basis of the total number of appropriate responses or on the basis of the percentage of responses in the *best* category.

S (5). *Single homogeneous score versus patterned relational score.* A test can be scored based on all the items, or it can be scored on the basis of a pattern of answers associated with different groups of items. Again, using an assessment center exercise as an example, it is possible to score an exercise based on all the appropriate responses taken together or on the basis of a pattern of appropriate answers that fall in a particular dimension, such as planning and organizing or interpersonal skills.

Cattell and Warburton's work and the published literature on subgroup performance have provided a good starting point for possibly classifying tests based on test characteristics. The utility of such a taxonomy lies in the possibility of using it to develop a framework for understanding the relations among test characteristics, test validity, and test performance. If the taxonomy makes sense, it can help us understand how test characteristics affect test performance, which test characteristics interact with subgroup membership, and which test characteristics affect predictive validity and how they do so.

It would certainly seem appropriate on the basis of the research to date, to speculate about which test characteristics tend to minimize subgroup differences. Table 5.1 is one example of the way tests might be classified based on test characteristics, validity, and performance differences when two racial groups, African Americans and Whites, are considered.

It would be presumptuous to propose at this point that definitive relations have been identified among subgroup differences, specific test characteristics and validity. The research does appear to support educated speculation, however.

SUMMARY

Testing medium refers to the test characteristics that distinguish one test from another. A relatively small number of test characteristics (primarily related to the paper and pencil format) have been the subject of research for many years. The effects of other test characteristics, such as the medium and context in which test information is presented, have hardly been studied at all. Test medium can affect the performance of particular subgroups in different ways. A taxonomy of tests based on test characteristics may prove useful for understanding how the characteristics of tests affect test performance as well as validity. Moreover, greater understanding of the influences of test characteristics on test performance can help clarify the construct or constructs a test measures. Far too little attention has been given to the properties of the test itself as a contributor to our understanding of psychological measurement.

TABLE 5.1
Test Classification with High and Low Subgroup Differences

Subgroup differences	Test Characteristics	Examples of Employment Tests	Validity[a]
High	I(3) Selective response	Cognitive ability tests or written job knowledge tests	.10–.49
	I(4) Single response		
	I(7) Controlled performance		
	I(9) Referent meaning		
	I(10) Itemized presentation		
	I(11) Cognitive judgment		.35–.61
	I(14) Written test stimulus		
	I(15) Written response		
	I(16) Context-free items		
	I(17) Penalty for guessing		
Low	I(3) Inventive response	Structured oral interview or trainability tests or assessment centers or multimedia tests or work samples	.13–.25
	I(4) Multiple responses		
	I(7) Self-directed performance		
	I(9) No referent meaning		.29–.39
	I(10) Global problem		
	I(11) Affective response		.22 –.43
	I(14) Oral/visual test stimulus		
	I(15) Oral response		.20–.28
	I(16) Context-based items		
	I(17) Freedom to guess		.28–.40

[a]Based on uncorrected validity coefficients reported by Curtis et al., 1994; Dyer et al., 1994; McDaniel, Whetzel, Schmidt, & Mauers, 1994; Reilly & Warech, 1994; Wigdor & Green, 1991.

REFERENCES

Boyle, S. (1984). The effect of variations in answer-sheet format on aptitude test performance. *Journal of Occupational Psychology, 57*, 323–326.

Breland, H. M., Danos, D. O., Kahn, H. D., Kubota, M. Y., & Bonner, M. W. (1994). Performance versus objective testing and gender: An exploratory study of an advanced placement history examination. *Journal of Educational Measurement, 31* (4), 275–293.

Carnevale, A. P., & Stone, S. C. (1995). *The American mosaic: An in-depth report on the future of diversity at work.* New York: McGraw-Hill.

Carraher, T. N., Carraher, V., & Schliemann, A. O. (1985). Mathematics in the streets and in the schools. *British Journal of Developmental Psychology*, *3*, 21–29.

Cattell, R. B., & Warburton, F. W. (1967). *Objective personality and motivation tests: A theoretical introduction and practical compendium*. Urbana, IL: University of Chicago Press.

Cronbach, L. J. (1941). An experimental comparison of the multiple true-false and multiple-choice tests. *Journal of Educational Psychology*, *32*, 533–543.

Cronbach, L. J. (1942). Studies of acquiescence as a factor in the true-false test. *Journal of Educational Psychology*, *33*, 401–415.

Cronbach, L. J. (1946). Response sets and test validity. *Educational and Psychological Measurement*, *6* (4), 475–493.

Curtis, J. R., Gracin, L., & Scott, J. (1994, April). *Non-traditional measures for selecting a diverse workforce: A review of four validation studies*. Paper presented at the ninth annual meeting of the Society for Industrial and Organizational Psychology, Inc., Nashville, TN.

Dyer, P., Desmarais, L., & Masi, D. (1994, April). *Multimedia approaches to testing: An aid to workforce diversity?* Paper presented at the ninth annual meeting of the Society for Industrial and Organizational Psychology, Inc., Nashville, TN.

Ghiselli, E. (1966). *The validity of occupational aptitude tests*. New York: Wiley.

Gottfredson, L. S. (1986). The g factor in employment. [Special issue]. *Journal of Vocational Behavior*, *29*(3).

Guion, B. (1965). *Personnel testing*. New York: McGraw-Hill.

McDaniel, M. A., Whetzel, D. L., Schmidt, F. L., & Mauers, S. (1994). The validity of employment interviews: A comprehensive review and meta-analysis. *Journal of Applied Psychology*, *79*, 599–616.

McHenry, J., & Schmitt, N. (1994). Multimedia testing. In M. Rumsey, G. Walker, & J. Harris (Eds.), *Personnel selection and classification* (pp. 193–232). Hillsdale, NJ: Lawrence Erlbaum Associates.

Meier, S. (1994). *The chronic crisis in psychological measurement and assessment: A historical survey*. New York: Academic Press.

Outtz, J. (1993). Multimedia employment tests reduce adverse impact and improve validity. *Employment Testing, Law and Public Policy*, *2*(11), 177–192.

Reilly, R., & Chao, G. (1982). Validity and fairness of some alternative selection procedures. *Personnel Psychology*, *35*(1), 1–62.

Reilly, R., & Warech, M. (1994). The validity and fairness of alternatives to cognitive tests. In H. Wing & B. Gifford (Eds.), *Policy issues in employment testing* (pp. 131–224). Boston: Kluwer.

Robertson, I. T. & Kandola, R. S. (1982). Work sample tests: Validity, adverse impact, and applicant reaction. *Journal of Occupational Psychology*, *55*, 171–183.

Scheuneman, J. D. (1987). An experimental, exploratory study of causes of bias in test items. *Journal of Educational Measurement*, *24*(2), 97–118.

Stone, E. F., Stone, D. L., & Gueutal, H. G. (1990). Influence of cognitive ability on responses to questionnaire measures: Measurement precision and missing response problems. *Journal of Applied Psychology*, *75*(4), 418–427.

Thissen, D., Wainer, H., & Wang, X. -B. (1994). Are tests comprising both multiple-choice and free-response items necessarily less unidimensional than multiple-choice tests? An analysis of two tests. *Journal of Educational Measurement*, *31*(2), 113–123.

Traub, R. E., & Fisher, C. W. (1977). On the equivalence of constructed-response and multiple-choice tests. *Applied Psychological Measurement*, *1*(3), 355–369.

Uniform guidelines on employee selection procedures. (1978). *Federal Register*, *43*, 38290–38315.

Vernon, P. E. (1962). The determinants of reading comprehension. *Educational and Psychological Measurement*, *22*(2), 269–286.

Ward, W. C. (1982). A comparison of free-response and multiple-choice forms of verbal aptitude tests. *Applied Psychological Measurement*, *6*(1), 1–11.

Ward, W. C., Frederiksen, N., & Carlson, S. B. (1980). Construct validity of free-response and machine-scorable forms of a test. *Journal of Educational Measurement, 17* (1), 11–29.

Wigdor, A. K., & Green, B. F., Jr. (Eds.). (1991). *Performance assessment for the workplace* (Vol. I). Washington, DC: National Academy Press.

6

Alternative Modes of Assessment, Uniform Standards of Validity

Samuel J. Messick
Educational Testing Service

When people speak of alternatives to traditional testing nowadays, they are really referring to alternatives to standardized paper-and-pencil multiple-choice testing. In particular, the critical concern is with alternatives to the multiple-choice format because of possible constraints on the kinds of thinking and higher-order cognitive processing that can be assessed by multiple-choice tests (N. Frederiksen, 1984). The issues of standardization and paper-and-pencil delivery are not as salient, because alternatives to paper-and-pencil presentation, such as by means of interviewer or computer, have only subtle measurement implications as long as what is presented are still multiple-choice items. The measurement implications of the delivery mode are important but are highly dependent on the assessment mode. Nor is it the case that the alternative modes of assessment should be unstandardized, although the conditions that are controlled may differ from those of traditional testing (Messick, 1993). Hence it is alternatives to multiple choice that are my main concern here.

The defining feature of a multiple choice item is that the respondent must select an answer from among a set of options. The obvious alternative to multiple-choice testing requires the respondent to construct the answer de novo. This constructed response alternative has led to a resurgence of interest in performance assessment, which, though long a staple of industrial and military applications, is becoming increasingly popular in educational settings, especially in connection with standards-based education reform.

59

Because performance assessments appear to be noticeably different from traditional testing, the question arises as to whether the same standards of validity should apply to them as opposed to specialized validity standards (Linn, Baker, & Dunbar, 1991; Messick, 1994; Moss, 1992). Because of the developing consensus that validity is a unified concept (American Psychological Association, 1985; Messick, 1989), the preference would appear to favor uniform validity standards for all educational and psychological assessments, including performance assessments. Indeed, in this chapter I attempt to justify this position in terms of a comprehensive view of construct validity. First, however, I must examine varied perspectives on the meaning of performance assessment, because different conceptions have distinctly different implications for validation.

ASSESSMENT OF PERFORMANCE
OR OF CONSTRUCTS?

First I consider some variable properties of performance assessments in contradistinction to multiple choice. Next, I examine the tension between task-driven and construct-driven performance assessment in terms of whether the performance is to serve as the target or the vehicle of the assessment. Then I highlight the two major sources of test invalidity, which provide a basis for determining what *authenticity* and *directness* of performance assessment mean in validity terms.

Conceptions of Performance Assessment

In essence, a performance assessment requires a respondent to execute a task or process and to bring it to completion (Wiggins, 1993). That is, the examinee performs, creates, or produces something over a sufficient time period to permit evaluation of the process, the product, or both. This idea is in contradistinction to the impoverished trace or scorable record resulting when a test taker merely marks a correct or preferred option on an answer sheet as in a multiple-choice test, a process that does not reflect the amount or kind of thinking or effort underlying the choice of option.

Indeed, with respect to task processing, the boundary between multiple-choice tests and performance assessments is fuzzy: Some respondents on many multiple-choice items and most respondents on difficult multiple-choice items execute the solution process as a means of selecting the appropriate option (Traub, 1993). A critical distinction between the two types of tests is that the selected option in multiple choice can be appraised for correctness or goodness with respect only to a single criterion. There is no record, as in the typical performance assessment, of an extended process or product that can be scored for multiple aspects of quality.

A further complication is that the contrast between multiple-choice items and open-ended performance tasks is not a dichotomy, but a continuum representing different degrees of structure versus openness in the allowable responses. This continuum is variously described as ranging from multiple choice to examinee-constructed products or presentations (Bennett, 1993), for example, or from multiple choice to demonstrations and portfolios (Snow, 1993). Successive intervening stages include items requiring reordering or rearranging, substitution or correction, simple completion or cloze procedures, short essays or complex completions, problem exercises or proofs, teach-back procedures, and long essays.

A wide array of structured item formats falls toward the multiple choice end of the continuum. For example, Wesman (1971) described three varieties of short-answer form, five varieties of alternate choice form, two of matching form, and eight of multiple choice, including those allowing more than one right answer. In addition, he discussed three types of context-dependent item sets (the pictorial form, the interlinear form, and the interpretive exercise), to which a fourth type (the problem-solving scenario) has been added (Haladyna, 1992). Thus, contingent sets of structured items can be developed to tap complex aspects of task functioning, such as problem-solving processes and strategies (Ebel, 1984) as well as stylistic learning preferences (Heath, 1964). Contrary to popular misconceptions, structured item formats are not limited to the measurement of fact retrieval: They are also used effectively to assess knowledge application, evaluation skills, and problem-solving proficiencies. Multiple-choice or forced-choice techniques have also been applied in the measurement of social attitudes, personal needs and motives, vocational interests, aesthetic preferences, and human values (Messick, 1979).

At intermediate levels of the continuum are several formats, one example being multiple-choice items that require a respondent to give reasons why the chosen option is correct and possibly why each of the unchosen options is incorrect. Another instance is a multiple rating format in which each of several options is judged for quality against complex standards (Scriven, 1994). Specifically, a respondent might be asked to read a passage for the main idea and then to rate each of four sentences—say, by marking boxes labeled A to F—for the quality and completeness with which each captures the main idea. An added requirement might be that if none of the statements receives a grade of B or better, the respondent should write an A-quality main idea sentence of his or her own.

It should be noted that this continuum refers to response form, representing various degrees of structure or constraint imposed on examinees' responses. Another, at least partly independent, continuum refers to stimulus form that represents various degrees of structure in the questions or problems presented. These two continua are clearly separable in the structured-stimulus direction because highly structured problems can be presented in either multiple-choice or open-ended formats. The question is the degree to which the two continua are also separable in the unstructured-stimulus direction. In this regard, it is necessary to explore the possibility of retaining the efficiency of structured or partly structured responses while relaxing the degree of structure in the problems posed. As an instance, patient-management problems might be presented with multiple choice or key-list options at each decision point. The intent would be to create more realistic, less well-structured problems—perhaps even ill-structured problems—having structured or semistructured response formats.

Apart from multiple choice, the remainder of the response continuum is referred to as involving "constructed responses." However, not all constructed responses, notably those involving rearranging, substitution, and simple completion, are properly considered to be performance assessments because they do not yield a scorable record of an extended process or product. Prototypical performance assessments are more common toward the unstructured end of the response continuum and include such exemplars as portfolios of products collected over time, exhibits or displays of knowledge and skill, open-ended tasks with no single correct approach or answer, hands-on experimentation, and work samples. The openness with respect to response possibilities enables examinees to exhibit skills that are difficult to tap in the predefined structures of multiple choice, such as shaping or restructuring a problem, defining and operationalizing variables, manipulating conditions, and developing alternative problem approaches.

Evaluations of performance on such open-ended tasks usually rely on an assessor's professional judgment, and some proponents view such subjectivity of scoring to be the hallmark of performance assessment (e. g., J. R. Frederiksen & Collins, 1989; Stiggins, 1991). This view, however, appears too restrictive: Some performance tasks can be objectively scored, and some scoring judgments are amenable to expert-system computer algorithms (Bejar, 1991; Sebrechts, Bennett, & Rock, 1991).

A more appropriate hallmark of educational performance assessments is their nearly universal focus on higher-order thinking and problem-solving skills. According to Baker, O'Neil, and Linn (1993), "Virtually all proponents of performance-based assessment intend it to measure aspects of higher-order thinking processes" (p. 1211). Indeed, performance assessments in education frequently attempt to tap the complex structuring of multiple skills and knowledge, including basic as well as higher-order skills, embedded in realistic or otherwise rich problem contexts that require extended or demanding forms of reasoning and judgment. In this regard, Wiggins (1993) viewed "authentic" performance assessments as tapping understanding or as applying good judgment in adapting knowledge to fashion performances effectively and creatively.

This mention of *authentic* assessments broaches a further distinction. Just as performance assessments are a more open-ended subset of constructed responses, so-called authentic assessments are a more realistic subset of performance assessments. In particular, authentic assessments pose engaging and worthy problems (usually involving multistage tasks) in realistic settings or close simulations so that tasks and processes, as well as available time and resources, parallel those in the real world. The assessment challenge of complex performance tasks in general and authentic tasks in particular revolves around issues of scoring, interpretation, and generalizable import of key aspects of the complex performance, especially if the task is not completed successfully.

Performance assessment, may begin by clarifying the nature of the higher-order competencies or other constructs to be assessed and then selecting or constructing tasks that would optimally reveal the competencies. Contrariwise, starting with an important task that is worthy of mastery in its own right, a researcher can ask what competencies or other constructs this task reveals. This contrast embodies a tension in performance assessment between construct-centered and task-centered approaches (Messick, 1994). What is critical in performance assessment, however, is not what is operative in the task performance but what is captured in the test score and interpretation. Hence, the validity of the construct interpretation needs to be addressed sooner or later in either approach, as does the nature of convergent and discriminant evidence needed to sustain this validity.

Construct-Driven Versus Task-Driven Performance Assessment

The task-centered approach to performance assessment begins by identifying a worthy task and then determining what constructs can be scored and how. Often the mastery of such a worthy task functions as the target of the assessment in its own right, as opposed to serving as a vehicle for the assessment of knowledge, skills, or other constructs. This process might occur, for example, in an arts contest, an Olympic figure-skating competition, or a science fair. In such cases, replicability and generalizability are not at issue. All that counts is the quality of the performance or product submitted for evaluation, and the validation focus is on the judgment of quality. But in this usage of performance assessment as target, inferences are not to be made about the competencies or other attributes of the performers, that is, inferences from observed behavior to constructs such as knowledge and skill underlying this behavior. The latter type of inference requires convergent and discriminant evidence for support.

Large-scale educational projects such as dissertations are often treated as targets in this manner, by crediting the complex accomplishment as meeting established standards with no requirement of predictiveness or domain generalizability (Baker et al., 1993). Action implications of such complex assessments usually presume, however, with little or no specific evidence, that there is a global prediction of future success, that the knowledge and skills exhibited in the assessment will enable the student to accomplish a range of similar or related tasks in broader settings. In contrast, such presumptions should be buttressed by empirical evidence in the performance assessment of competencies or other constructs—that is, whenever the performance is the vehicle, not the target of assessment. A major form of this evidence bears on generalizability and transfer which represent critical aspects of construct validity. In effect, the meaning of the construct is tied to the range of tasks and situations that it generalizes and transfers to.

The task-centered approach to performance assessment is in danger of tailoring scoring criteria and rubrics to properties of the task and of representing any educed constructs in task-dependent ways that might limit generalizability. In contrast, the nature of the constructs in the construct-centered approach guides the selection or construction of relevant tasks as well as the rational development of construct-based scoring criteria and rubrics. Focusing on constructs also alerts researchers to the possibility of construct-irrelevant variance that might distort the task performance, its scoring, or both (Messick, 1994). The task-centered approach is not completely devoid of constructs, of course; task selection is often influenced by implicit construct notions or informal theories of learning and performance. The key issue is the extent to which the constructs guide scoring and interpretation and are explicitly linked to evidence supporting the interpretation as well as discounting plausible rival interpretations.

Sources of Invalidity

Construct-irrelevant variance is one of the two major threats to validity, the other being construct under-representation. A fundamental feature of construct validity is *construct representation,* whereby researchers attempt to identify through cognitive-process analysis or research on personality and motivation the theoretical mechanisms underlying task performance, primarily by decomposing the task into requisite component processes and assembling them into a functional model or process theory (Embretson, 1983; Wiley, 1991). Relying heavily on the cognitive psychology of information processing, construct representation refers to the relative dependence of task responses on the processes, strategies, and knowledge (including metacognitive or self-knowledge) that are implicated in task performance.

In the threat to validity known as construct under-representation, the assessment is too narrow and fails to include important dimensions or facets of the construct. In the threat to validity known as construct-irrelevant variance, the assessment is too broad and contains excess reliable variance that is irrelevant to the interpreted construct. Both threats are operative in all assessment. Hence a primary validation concern is the extent to which the same assessment might under-represent the focal construct while contaminating the scores with construct-irrelevant variance.

The concept of construct-irrelevant variance is important in all educational and psychological measurement, including performance assessments, especially in richly contextualized assessments and authentic simulations of real-world tasks: "Paradoxically, the complexity of context is made manageable by contextual clues" (Wiggins, 1993, p. 208). And it matters whether the contextual clues that are responded to are construct-relevant or represent construct-irrelevant difficulty.

What constitutes construct-irrelevant variance is a tricky and contentious issue, however (Messick, 1994). This observation is especially true of performance assessments, which typically invoke constructs that are higher order and complex in the sense of subsuming or organizing multiple processes. For example, skill in communicating mathematical ideas might well be considered irrelevant variance in the assessment of mathematical knowledge (although not necessarily vice versa). But both communication skill and mathematical knowledge are considered relevant parts of the higher order construct of mathematical power according to the content standards developed by the National Council of Teachers of Mathematics. It all depends on how compelling the evidence and arguments are that the particular source of variance is a relevant part of the focal construct as opposed to affording a plausible rival hypothesis to account for the observed performance regularities and relationships with other variables.

Authenticity and Directness as Validity Standards

Two terms that appear frequently, usually in tandem, in the literature of performance assessment are *authentic* and *direct* assessment. The terms are most often used in connection with assessments involving realistic simulations or criterion samples. If authenticity and directness are important to consider when evaluating the implications of assessment, they constitute tacit validity standards. What do the labels *authentic* and *direct* mean in validity terms?

The major measurement concern of authenticity is that nothing important has been left out of the assessment of the focal construct (Messick, 1994). This idea is tantamount to the familiar validity standard of minimal construct under-representation. However, although authenticity implies minimal construct under-representation, the reverse does not hold: Minimal construct under-representation does not necessarily imply the close simulation of real-world problems and resources typically associated with authenticity in the current educational literature on performance assessment. In any event, convergent and discriminant evidence is needed to appraise the extent to which the ostensibly authentic tasks represent (or under-represent) the constructs they are interpreted to assess.

The major measurement concern of directness is that nothing irrelevant that distorts or interferes with construct assessment has been added. This concept is tantamount to the familiar validity standard of minimal construct-irrelevant variance (Messick, 1994). Incidentally, the term *direct assessment* is a misnomer because it always promises too much. In education and psychology, "All measurements are indirect in one sense or another" (Guilford, 1936, p. 3). Measurement always involves, even if only tacitly, intervening processes of judgment, comparison, or inference.

UNIFORM VALIDITY STANDARDS

Although on the surface there appear to be several differences between performance assessments and traditional multiple-choice testing, the inferences
drawn from such alternative modes of assessment, as well as their action
implications, are fundamentally similar. "There is no absolute distinction between performance tests and other classes of tests" (Fitzpatrick & Morrison,
1971, p. 238). This fact implies that the same standards of validity should be
applied to performance assessments as to all educational and psychological
assessments, because what is to be validated is not the test or observation device
as such but rather the inferences derived from test scores or other indicators
(Cronbach, 1971)—inferences about score meaning or interpretation and about
the implications for action that the interpretation entails. In essence, then, test
validation is empirical evaluation of the meaning and consequences of measurement.

Perennial Validity Questions

To evaluate the meaning and consequences of measurement is no small order,
however, and requires attention to a number of persistent validity questions,
such as:

- Are measurement specialists looking at the right things in the right
  balance?
- Has anything important been left out?
- Does the way of looking introduce sources of invalidity or irrelevant
  variance that bias the scores or judgments?
- Does the way of scoring reflect the manner in which domain processes
  combine to produce effects and is the score structure consistent with the
  structure of the domain about which inferences are to be drawn or
  predictions made?
- What evidence is there that the scores mean what they are interpreted to
  mean, in particular, reflections of personal attributes having plausible
  implications for educational, personnel, or therapeutic action?
- Are there plausible rival interpretations of score meaning or alternative
  implications for action, and, if so, by what evidence and arguments are
  they discounted?
- Are the judgments or scores reliable, and are their properties and relationships generalizable across the contents and contexts of use as well as
  across pertinent population groups?
- Are the value implications of score interpretations empirically grounded,
  especially if pejorative in tone, and are they commensurate with the
  score's trait implications?

- Do the scores have utility for the proposed purposes in the applied settings?
- Are the scores applied fairly for these purposes?
- Are the short- and long-term consequences of score interpretation and use supportive of the general testing aims and are there any adverse side effects?

Which, if any, of these questions is unnecessary to address in justifying score interpretation and use? Which, if any, can be forgone in validating the interpretation and use of performance assessments or other alternative modes of assessment? The general thrust of such questions is to seek evidence and arguments to discount the two major threats to construct validity—construct under-representation and construct-irrelevant variance—as well as to evaluate the action implications of score meaning.

Aspects of Construct Validity

Such questions are inherent in the notion of validity as a unified concept. Unified validity does not imply answering only one overarching validity question or even several questions separately or one at a time. Rather, it implies an integration of multiple supplementary forms of convergent and discriminant evidence to answer an interdependent set of questions. To make this point explicit, it is illuminating to differentiate unified validity into several distinct aspects to underscore issues and nuances that might otherwise be downplayed or overlooked, such as the social consequences of performance assessments or the role of score meaning in applied use.

In particular, six distinguishable aspects of construct validity are highlighted as a means of addressing central issues implicit in the notion of validity as a unified concept—content, substantive, structural, generalizability, external, and consequential aspects of construct validity. In effect, these six aspects function as general validity criteria or standards for all educational and psychological measurement (Messick, 1989). They are briefly characterized as follows:

- The content aspect of construct validity includes evidence of content relevance, representativeness, and technical quality (Lennon, 1956; Messick, 1989).
- The substantive aspect refers to theoretical rationales for the observed consistencies in test responses, including process models of task performance (Embretson, 1983), along with empirical evidence that the theoretical processes are actually engaged by respondents in the assessment tasks.
- The structural aspect appraises the fidelity of the scoring structure to the structure of the construct domain at issue (Loevinger, 1957).
- The generalizability aspect examines the extent to which score properties and interpretations generalize to and across population groups, settings,

and tasks (Cook & Campbell, 1979; Shulman, 1970), including validity generalization of test-criterion relationships (Hunter, Schmidt, & Jackson, 1982).

- The external aspect includes convergent and discriminant evidence from multitrait-multimethod comparisons (Campbell & Fiske, 1959), as well as evidence of criterion relevance and applied utility (Cronbach & Gleser, 1965).

- The consequential aspect appraises the value implications of score interpretation as a basis for action as well as the actual and potential consequences of test use, especially in regard to sources of invalidity related to issues of bias, fairness, and distributive justice (Messick, 1980, 1989).

A key issue for the content aspect of construct validity is the specification of the boundaries of the construct domain to be assessed—that is, determining the knowledge, skills, and other attributes to be revealed by the assessment tasks. The boundaries and structure of the construct domain can be addressed by means of job analysis, task analysis, curriculum analysis, and especially domain theory, or scientific inquiry into the nature of the domain processes and the ways in which they combine to produce effects or outcomes. A major goal of domain theory is to understand the construct-relevant sources of task difficulty, which then serves as a guide to the rational development and scoring of performance tasks. At whatever stage of its development, then, domain theory is a primary basis for specifying the boundaries and structure of the construct to be assessed.

It is not sufficient, however, merely to select tasks that are relevant to the construct domain. In addition, the assessment should assemble tasks that are representative of the domain in some sense. The intent is to ensure that all important parts of the construct domain are covered, a process usually described as selecting tasks that sample domain processes in terms of their functional importance. Both the content relevance and representativeness of assessment tasks are traditionally appraised by expert professional judgment, documentation of which serves to address the content aspect of construct validity.

The substantive aspect of construct validity emphasizes two important points: One is the need for tasks providing appropriate sampling of domain processes in addition to traditional coverage of domain content; the other is the need to move beyond traditional professional judgment of content to accrue empirical evidence that the ostensibly sampled processes are actually engaged by respondents in task performance. Thus, the substantive aspect adds to the content aspect of construct validity the need for empirical evidence of response consistencies or performance regularities reflective of domain processes (Embretson, 1983; Loevinger, 1957; Messick, 1989).

According to the structural aspect of construct validity, scoring models should be rationally consistent with what is known about the structural relations inherent in behavioral manifestations of the construct in question (Loevinger, 1957; Peak, 1953). That is, the theory of the construct domain should guide not only the selection or construction of relevant assessment tasks, but also the rational development of construct-based scoring criteria and rubrics. Ideally, the manner in which behavioral instances are combined to produce a score should rest on knowledge of how the processes underlying these behaviors combine dynamically to produce effects. Thus, the internal structure of the assessment (i. e., interrelations among the scored aspects of task and subtask performance) should be consistent with what is known about the internal structure of the construct domain (Messick, 1989).

   The concern that a performance assessment should provide representative coverage of the content and processes of the construct domain is meant to insure that the score interpretation not be limited to the sample of assessed tasks but be generalizable to the construct domain more broadly. Evidence of such generalizability depends on the degree of correlation of the assessed tasks with other tasks representing the construct or aspects of the construct. This issue of generalizability of score inferences across tasks and contexts goes to the very heart of score meaning. Indeed, setting the boundaries of score meaning is precisely what generalizability evidence is meant to address.

   The emphasis here is on generalizability in two senses, namely, as it bears on reliability and on transfer. Generalizability as reliability refers to the consistency of performance across the raters, occasions, and tasks of a particular assessment, which might be quite limited in scope. For example, we have all been concerned that some assessments with a narrow set of tasks might attain higher reliability in the form of cross-task consistency, but at the expense of construct validity. In contrast, generalizability as transfer requires consistency of performance across tasks that are representative of the broader construct domain. That is, transfer refers to the range of tasks that performance on the assessed tasks facilitates the learning of or, more generally, is predictive of (Ferguson, 1956). Thus, generalizability as transfer depends not only on generalizability theory but also on construct theory. In essence, then, generalizability evidence is an aspect of construct validity because it establishes boundaries on the meaning of the construct scores.

   But because of the extensive time required for the typical performance task, there is a conflict in performance assessment between time-intensive depth of examination and the breadth of domain coverage needed for generalizability of construct interpretation. This conflict between depth and breadth of coverage is often viewed as entailing a trade-off between validity and reliability (or generalizability). It might better be depicted as a trade-off between the valid description of the specifics of a complex task performance and the power of construct interpretation. In any event, such a conflict signals a design problem that needs to be carefully negotiated in performance assessment (Wiggins, 1993).

The external aspect of construct validity refers to the extent to which the assessment scores' relations with other measures and nonassessment behaviors reflect the expected high, low, and interactive relations implicit in the theory of the construct being assessed. Thus, the meaning of the scores is substantiated externally by appraising the degree to which empirical relations with other measures, or the lack thereof, are consistent with this meaning. That is, the constructs represented in the assessment should rationally account for the external pattern of correlations.

Of special importance among these external relationships are those between the assessment scores and criterion measures pertinent to selection, placement, licensure, program evaluation, or other accountability purposes in applied settings. Once again, the construct theory points to the relevance of potential relations between the assessment scores and criterion measures, and empirical evidence of such links attests to the utility of the scores for the applied purpose.

The consequential aspect of construct validity includes evidence and rationales for evaluating the intended and unintended consequences of score interpretation and use in both the short and long term, especially those consequences associated with bias in scoring and interpretation or with unfairness in test use. But this form of evidence should not be viewed in isolation as a separate type of validity, say, of "consequential validity." Rather, because the values served in the intended and unintended outcomes of test interpretation and use both derive from and contribute to the meaning of the test scores, appraisal of social consequences of the testing is also seen to be subsumed as an aspect of construct validity (Messick, 1980).

The primary measurement concern with respect to adverse consequences is that any negative impact on individuals or groups should not derive from any source of test invalidity such as construct under-representation or construct-irrelevant variance (Messick, 1989). That is, low scores should not occur because the assessment is missing something relevant to the focal construct that, if present, would have permitted the affected individuals to display their competence. Moreover, low scores should not occur because the measurement contains something irrelevant that interferes with the affected persons' demonstration of competence. In contrast, if adverse consequences are associated with valid measurement, the primary concern is one of social policy that weighs these adverse consequences against potential benefits in deciding whether to use the test or alternative modes of assessment.

From the discussion thus far, it should be clear that *test validity cannot rely on any one of the supplementary forms of evidence* just discussed. But neither does *validity require any one form*, as long as there is defensible convergent and discriminant evidence supporting score meaning. To the extent that some form of evidence cannot be developed—as when criterion-related studies must be forgone because of small sample sizes, unreliable or contaminated criteria, and highly restricted score ranges—heightened emphasis can be placed on other evidence, especially on the construct validity of the predictor tests and the relevance of the construct to the criterion domain (Guion, 1976; Messick, 1989). What is required is a compelling argument that the available evidence justifies the test interpretation and use, even though some pertinent evidence had to be forgone. Hence, validity becomes a unified concept and the unifying force is the meaningfulness or trustworthy interpretability of the test scores and their action implications, namely, construct validity.

Validity As Integrative Summary

The six aspects of construct validity apply to all educational and psychological measurement, including performance assessments or other alternative assessment modes. Taken together, they provide a way of addressing the multiple and interrelated validity questions that need to be answered to justify score interpretation and use. In previous writings I have maintained that it is "the relation between the evidence and the inferences drawn that should determine the validation focus" (Messick, 1989, p. 16). This relation is embodied in theoretical rationales or persuasive arguments that the obtained evidence both supports the preferred inferences and undercuts plausible rival inferences. From this perspective, as Cronbach (1988) concluded, validation is evaluation argument. That is, as stipulated earlier, validation is empirical evaluation of the meaning and consequences of measurement. The term *empirical evaluation* is meant to convey that the validation process is scientific as well as rhetorical and requires both evidence and argument.

By focusing on the argument or rationale employed to support the assumptions and inferences invoked in the score-based interpretations and actions of a particular test use, researchers can prioritize the forms of validity evidence needed in terms of the important points in the argument that require justification or support (Kane, 1992; Shepard, 1993). Helpful as this arguement-based view of validity may be, problems still remain in setting priorities for needed evidence because the argument may be incomplete or off target, not all the assumptions may be addressed, and the need to discount alternative arguments evokes multiple priorities. Such problems are one reason that Cronbach (1989) stressed cross-argument criteria for assigning priority to a line of inquiry, such as the degree of prior uncertainty, information yield, cost, and leverage in achieving consensus.

The six aspects of construct validity afford a means of checking that the theoretical rationale or persuasive argument linking the evidence to the inferences drawn touches the important bases and, if not, of requiring that an argument be provided that such omissions are defensible. They are highlighted because most score-based interpretations and action inferences, as well as the elaborated rationales or arguments that attempt to legitimize them (Kane, 1992), either invoke these properties or assume them, explicitly or tacitly.

That is, most score interpretations refer to relevant content and operative processes, presumed to be reflected in scores that concatenate responses in domain-appropriate ways and are generalizable across a range of tasks, settings, and occasions. Furthermore, score-based interpretations and actions are typically extrapolated beyond the test context on the basis of presumed or documented relations with nontest behaviors and anticipated outcomes or consequences. The challenge in test validation is to link these inferences to convergent evidence supporting them as well as to discriminant evidence discounting plausible rival inferences. Evidence pertinent to all these aspects needs to be integrated into an overall validity judgment to sustain score inferences and their action implications or to provide compelling reasons why not, which is what is meant by validity as a unified concept, a concept that applies with equal force not only to traditional tests but also to alternative modes of assessment.

ACKNOWLEDGMENTS

Acknowledgments are gratefully extended to Randy Bennett, Ann Jungeblut, Donald Powers, and William Ward for their reviews of the manuscript of this chapter.

REFERENCES

American Psychological Association, American Educational Research Association, & National Council on Measurement in Education. (1985). *Standards for educational and psychological testing.* Washington, DC: American Psychological Association.

Baker, E. L., O'Neil, H. F., Jr., & Linn, R. L. (1993). Policy and validity prospects for performance-based assessment. *American Psychologist, 48,* 1210–1218.

Bejar, I. I. (1991). A methodology for scoring open-ended architectural design problems. *Journal of Applied Psychology, 76,* 522–532.

Bennett, R. E. (1993). On the meanings of constructed response. In R. E. Bennett & W. C. Ward (Eds.), *Construction versus choice in cognitive measurement: Issues in constructed response, performance testing, and portfolio assessment* (pp. 1–27). Hillsdale, NJ: Lawrence Erlbaum Associates.

Campbell, D. T., & Fiske, D. W. (1959). Convergent and discriminant validation by the multitrait-multimethod matrix. *Psychological Bulletin, 56,* 81–105.

Cook, T. D., & Campbell, D. T. (1979). *Quasi-experimentation: Design and analysis issues for field settings.* Chicago: Rand McNally.

Cronbach, L. J. (1971). Test validation. In R. L. Thorndike (Ed.), *Educational measurement* (2nd ed., pp. 443–507). Washington, DC: American Council on Education.

Cronbach, L. J. (1988). Five perspectives on validation argument. In H. Wainer & H. Braun (Eds.), *Test validity.* Hillsdale, NJ: Lawrence Erlbaum Associates.

Cronbach, L. J. (1989). Construct validation after thirty years. In R. L. Linn (Ed.), *Intelligence: Measurement, theory, and public policy: Proceedings of a symposium in honor of Lloyd G. Humphreys* (pp. 147–171). Chicago: University of Illinois Press.

Cronbach, L. J., & Gleser, G. C. (1965). *Psychological tests and personnel decisions* (2nd ed.). Urbana: University of Illinois Press.

Ebel, R. L. (1984). Achievement test items: Current issues. In B. S. Plake (Ed.), *Social and technical issues in testing: Implications for test construction and usage.* (pp. 141–154). Hillsdale, NJ: Lawrence Erlbaum Associates.

Embretson (Whitely), S. (1983). Construct validity: Construct representation versus nomothetic span. *Psychological Bulletin, 93,* 179–197.

Ferguson, G. A. (1956). On transfer and the abilities of man. *Canadian Journal of Psychology, 10,* 121–131.

Fitzpatrick, R., & Morrison, E. J. (1971). Performance and product evaluation. In R. L. Thorndike (Ed.), *Educational measurement* (2nd ed., pp. 237–270). Washington, DC: American Council on Education.

Frederiksen, J. R., & Collins, A. (1989). A systems approach to educational testing. *Educational Researcher, 18*(9), 27–32.

Frederiksen, N. (1984). The real test bias: Influences of testing on teaching and learning. *American Psychologist, 39,* 193–202.

Guilford, J. P. (1936). *Psychometric methods.* New York: McGraw-Hill.

Guion, R. M. (1976). Recruiting, selection, and job placement. In M. D. Dunnette (Ed.), *Handbook of industrial and organizational Psychology* (pp. 777–828). Chicago: Rand McNally.

Haladyna, T. M. (1992). Context-dependent item sets. *Educational Measurement: Issues and Practice, 11*(1), 21–25.

Heath, R. W. (1964). Curriculum, cognition, and educational development. *Educational and Psychological Measurement, 24,* 239–253.

Hunter, J. E., Schmidt, F. L., & Jackson, C. B. (1982). *Advanced meta-analysis: Quantitative methods of cumulating research findings across studies.* San Francisco: Sage.

Kane, M. T. (1992). An argument-based approach to validity. *Psychological Bulletin, 112,* 527–535.

Lennon, R. T. (1956). Assumptions underlying the use of content validity. *Educational and Psychological Measurement, 16,* 294–304.

Linn, R. L., Baker, E. L., & Dunbar, S. B. (1991). Complex, performance-based assessment: Expectations and validation criteria. *Educational Researcher, 20*(8), 15–21.

Loevinger, J. (1957). Objective tests as instruments of psychological theory. *Psychological Reports, 3,* 635–694 (Monograph supplement 9).

Messick, S. (1979). Potential uses of noncognitive measurement in education. *Journal of Educational Psychology, 71,* 281–292.

Messick, S. (1980). Test validity and the ethics of assessment. *American Psychologist, 35,* 1012–1027.

Messick, S. (1989). Validity. In R. L. Linn (Ed.), *Educational measurement* (3rd ed., pp. 13–103). New York: Macmillan.

Messick, S. (1993). Trait equivalence as construct validity across multiple methods of measurement. In R. E. Bennett & W. C. Ward, Jr. (Eds.), *Construction versus choice in cognitive measurement: Issues in constructed response, performance testing, and portfolio assessment* (pp. 61–73). Hillsdale, NJ: Lawrence Erlbaum Associates.

Messick, S. (1994). The interplay of evidence and consequences in the validation of performance assessments. *Educational Researcher, 23*(2), 13–23.

Moss, P. A. (1992). Shifting conceptions of validity in educational measurement: Implications for performance assessment. *Review of Educational Research, 62,* 229–258.

Peak, H. (1953). Problems of observation. In L. Festinger & D. Katz *(Eds.), Research methods in the behavioral sciences* (pp. 243–299). Hinsdale, IL: Dryden Press.

Scriven, M. (1994, April). *Death of paradigm: Replacing multiple choice with multiple ratings.* Paper presented to the annual meeting of the American Educational Research Association, New Orleans.

Sebrechts, M. M., Bennett, R. E., & Rock D. A. (1991). Agreement between expert system and human raters' scores on complex constructed-response quantitative items. *Journal of Applied Psychology, 76,* 856–862.

Shepard, L. A. (1993). Evaluating test validity. *Review of research in education, 19*, 405–450.

Shulman, L. S. (1970). Reconstruction of educational research. *Review of Educational Research, 40*, 371–396.

Snow, R. E. (1993). Construct validity and constructed response tests. In R. E. Bennett & W. C. Ward, Jr. (Eds.), *Construction versus choice in cognitive measurement: Issues in constructed response, performance testing, and portfolio assessment* (pp. 45–60). Hillsdale, NJ: Lawrence Erlbaum Associates.

Stiggins, R. J. (1991). Facing the challenges of a new era of educational assessment. *Applied Measurement in Education, 4*, 263–273.

Traub, R. E. (1993). On the equivalence of the traits assessed by multiple-choice and constructed-response tests. In R. E. Bennett & W. C. Ward, Jr. (Eds.), *Construction versus choice in cognitive measurement: Issues in constructed response, performance testing, and portfolio assessment* (pp. 45–60). Hillsdale, NJ: Lawrence Erlbaum Associates.

Wesman, A. G. (1971). Writing the test item. In R. L. Thorndike (Ed.), *Educational Measurement* (2nd ed., pp. 81–129). Washington, DC: American Council on Education.

Wiggins, G. (1993). Assessment: Authenticity, context, and validity. *Phi Delta Kappan, 75*, 200–214.

Wiley, D. E. (1991). Test validity and invalidity reconsidered. In R. E. Snow & D. E. Wiley.,(Eds.), *Improving inquiry in social science: A volume in honor of Lee J. Cronbach* (pp. 75–107). Hillsdale, NJ: Lawrence Erlbaum Associates.

7

A Construct Approach to Skill Assessment: Procedures for Assessing Complex Cognitive Skills

**Michael D. Mumford, Wayne A. Baughman,
Elizabeth P. Supinski, and Lance E. Anderson**
American Institutes for Research

A new wave of criticisms has been leveled at standardized tests over the past few years. These criticisms result in part from the failure of traditional testing procedures to provide a viable system for measuring complex performance skills. In this chapter, we propose a general model that might be used to develop measures of complex cognitive skills, and we describe some procedures that might be used to assess these skills. We then review the findings obtained in a series of studies intended to provide evidence for the validity of these skill-assessment measures. On the basis of the findings obtained in these studies, we argue that it is possible to assess complex skills cost effectively, but skill assessment may require the development of new measurement models and new assessment techniques.

Over the years the attacks on the need for, and merits of, educational and psychological testing have focused on several issues (Cole & Moss, 1989; Fallows, 1980). Some critics argue that tests are biased. Other critics stress the fact that educational and psychological tests are less than perfect predictors of future performance. Still others say that tests fail to capture the crucial capacities required to appraise people adequately.

Although the available evidence does not support these arguments (Cron-bach, 1990), there is no reason to hope that evidence per se can silence the critics. Educational and psychological tests are used to make a host of high-stakes decisions about people and programs. Test scores influence admission to some schools and professions, the kinds of job offers made available, continued funding for certain programs, and the decision to invest in these programs in the first place. Those who disagree with these decisions invariably criticize testing per se rather than address the issues.

This inherent antagonism is only a part, perhaps a very small part, of the new challenge to traditional testing. This new challenge comes from those who are concerned with performance, or competency, assessment (McClelland, 1994). Those interested in performance assessment do not eschew testing. Instead, they argue that what is required is a new approach to test development—one that focuses on observable, contextualized performance. In this chapter we contrast the traditional approach to test development with the performance-based approach and then argue that what is needed is an alternative approach drawing from both traditional test development and performance-assessment strategies. Finally, we consider the validation evidence obtained in a series of studies where we applied this integrative approach to develop a set for measures of creative problem-solving skills.

TRADITIONAL TESTING
AND PERFORMANCE ASSESSMENT

Traditional Testing

The traditional approach to test development had its origins in the problems confronting society at the turn of this century (Mislevy, 1993). Psychometri-cians were then concerned with the problem of identifying those people who would do well in school or on a job (Tyler, 1965). The approach used to solve this problem was based on the principles of trait theory (Guilford, 1954; Spearman, 1913), derived by early psychologists from Mendelian genetics (Snow, 1993). Essentially, the trait model of human behavior held that a few attributes, shared in varying degrees by all people, could account for perform-ance over time. The nature of these traits is illustrated by the now-familiar abilities such as intelligence, spatial ability, mathematical reasoning, and percep-tual speed (Carroll, 1993a; Fleishman & Reilly, 1992; Horn, 1976; Thurstone, 1938). It was assumed that a few traits would account for individual differences in performance across most domains and would provide an economical solution to the problem of efficient selection and classification.

The trait model of differential performance had profound implications for how researchers went about developing the items making up traditional tests: The objective of these tests was not to assess performance in a given domain directly or to identify a specific set of performance skills. Instead, the tests were intended to assess people with respect to relative levels of broader abilities underlying the development of performance skills. Thus, good test items, from a traditional test development perspective, were standardized: They were linked to abilities rather than to specific domains or performance skills. Second, good test items were necessarily those that could reliably differentiate people with respect to levels of a given ability. Finally, good test items represented general performance tasks. Items on traditional tests were general, or nonspecific, enough to provide everyone with much the same opportunity to display the trait of concern when responding. These three principles—standardization, differentiation, and use of general performance tasks—guided the development of nearly all traditional tests.

The procedures commonly used in traditional educational and psychological test development for multiple-choice tests flowed directly from these three general principles. Initially, a set of general performance tasks (items) was identified to tap the targeted ability. General reasoning ability, for example, might be assessed by having people solve analogy problems. Typically, these items were treated as having been drawn at random from a broader domain of related tasks, all of which called for expression of this ability (Ghiselli, Campbell, & Zedeck, 1981). Many items were written to sample this broad domain, where people were presented with a short description of a well-structured, unambiguous performance situation. After people had familiarized themselves with the performance requirements, they were asked to show how they would respond to this situation. To simplify scoring and ensure differentiation, some number of potential response options were typically presented, where one option reflected a correct response or a response reflecting effective application of the targeted ability. The remaining options represented incorrect responses varying in attractiveness (Nunnally, 1978). In developing tests based on these types of items, many "tryout items" were initially included in a test. Items were retained when they discriminated people from each other, and when they covaried with other items intended to measure the same ability. This selection of specific test items based on differentiation and covariation contributed to the accuracy of the differential statements that could be made about people on the basis of their test scores (Ghiselli, Campbell, & Zedeck, 1981; Stanley, 1971).

One advantage of these test development procedures is that they allow people to gather descriptive information and to score tests at low cost. More centrally, however, they appear to meet the criteria of generality, differentiation, and standardization set forth earlier. The bulk of the available evidence shows that well-developed ability tests typically yield reliability coefficients in the .80s (Anastasi, 1976; Cronbach, 1990). These tests, furthermore, are fair to people from different backgrounds (Cole & Moss, 1989; Jensen, 1980). Finally, the evidence accrued in various validity generalization studies shows that these tests predict performance across a variety of domains (Ree, Earles, & Teachout, 1994; Schmidt & Hunter, 1993).

Although traditional tests apparently serve their intended purpose, they are not designed to solve many problems confronting us today in psychological measurement (Mislevy, 1993; Sizer, 1986; Snow & Lohman, 1989). Information from traditional tests is most relevant when the interest is in assessing differences in the level of task performance between people (Carroll, 1993b; Glaser, 1963). Accordingly, the procedures used in test development, and the model underlying these procedures, effectively ignore qualitative differences among people (Gardner, 1983, 1993; Mumford, Stokes, & Owens, 1990). For these reasons, traditional tests cannot tell why individuals performed in a certain way or describe the strategies used to obtain correct or incorrect answers. These limitations impair the value of traditional tests as diagnostic tools (Gitomer & Rock, 1993; Snow & Lohman, 1989). In a search for simplicity and standardization, furthermore, traditional test design makes it difficult to detect how people develop and apply the particular skills needed in more specific, complex, "real-world" domains (Feltovich, Spiro, & Coulson, 1993; Lohman & Ippel, 1993; Resnick & Resnick, 1992).

Performance Assessment

The performance-assessment model most clearly departs from the classic measurement model in its focus on real-world performance. The intent of nearly all performance assessments is to evaluate, on an absolute scale, how well people perform particular domain-specific tasks (Baker, O'Neil, & Linn, 1993; Wilson & Wineburg, 1993). In assessment centers and work samples, people's performance is observed and evaluated as they work on performance exercises. Some exercises mimic job tasks; others involve the performance of actual job tasks (Bray, Campbell, & Grant, 1974; Klimoski, 1993; Schmitt & Landy, 1993). In portfolio assessments, performance is assessed by examining career achievement records or certain structured interview records and reports of previous task performance (Halpern, 1994; Hough, 1984; McDaniel, Whetzel, Schmidt, & Maurer, 1994).

Whatever the particular observational approach being applied, all performance-assessment techniques share four common characteristics (Baker, O'Neil, & Linn, 1993). First, observations or records of actual performance in a specific domain provide a basis for drawing inferences about people. Second, responses are constructed by the individual rather than chosen from a predefined list. Third, inferences about performance drawn from these responses are typically framed in terms of domain-specific performance skills rather than in terms of broad, underlying abilities. Fourth, at least in principle, these evaluations of requisite performance skills are made against an absolute standard that reflects the manifest quality of the observed performance.

Because performance assessment is referenced against a specific performance domain, the development of assessment exercises typically begins with an analysis of performance in this domain. This analysis is used to identify requisite performance skills and the tasks that might be used to elicit the application of these skills (Byham, 1980; Motowidlo, Dunnette, & Carter, 1990; Schmitt, 1977). On the basis of this information, a set of exercises, or tasks, intended to assess domain-specific performance skills, is developed . Although these exercises, or performance records, can vary in fidelity with respect to actual performance, they must elicit the skills underlying performance in the domain of interest (Russell & Kuhnert, 1992). Observations or documented records of task performance are then evaluated by a group of judges, typically experts in the field, who assess skill expression and overall performance against a set of absolute behavioral standards (Dreher & Sackett, 1981; Shore, Shore, & Thorton, 1992).

The performance-assessment model is attractive not only because it appears to capture complex, integrated performance skills, performance assessment does not necessarily constrain people to identify one right or wrong answer. Moreover, people are free to use different strategies to perform a task, and task performance can be evaluated against a fixed standard. Performance assessment, furthermore, does not require inferences about broad underlying abilities, but instead allows people to focus on observable skills. Performance-assessment exercises are often designed to elicit several skills and putatively provide a more comprehensive description of the individual's performance capabilities than do traditional methods. When these characteristics of performance assessment are considered in light of the demonstrated predictive validity of at least some performance-assessment systems, they appear to provide a compelling argument for use of this approach (Bray, Campbell, & Grant, 1974; Gaugler, Rosenthal, Thorton, & Benston, 1987; Thorton & Byham, 1982), particularly when the objectives of assessment are specific performance skills.

On the other hand, performance assessment suffers from several methodological and substantive problems. One set of problems arises from the use of judges in scoring exercise performance. Subjective evaluations are both costly and vulnerable to the effects of rater error. Although it is common practice to train judges and provide illustrations of both good and poor performance, judges do not always follow these rules (Reilly, Henry, & Smither, 1990; Sackett & Hakel, 1979). Their evaluations, moreover, may be influenced by a host of situational factors, such as candidate characteristics (Schmitt & Hill, 1977) and stereotypical assumptions about the nature of acceptable performance (Klimoski & Brickner, 1987). Further, although judges may agree (Shore, Shore, & Thorton, 1992), agreement may not reflect targeted skills, especially when exercises have not been carefully designed to call forth these skills (Russell, 1987; Russell & Kuhnert, 1992).

The problems associated with subjective scoring are exacerbated by the complex nature of most performance-assessment exercises. Not only does the complexity of these exercises make performance assessment expensive and scoring difficult (Sackett, 1982, 1987), their complexity makes it difficult to obtain an adequate sampling of skill expression. For example, a typical exercise may take anywhere from half an hour to 2 hours to complete. As a result, only four or five exercises can be included in an assessment, of which only one or two might measure a given skill. Under these conditions, the resulting performance scores may reflect exercise methods rather than the skill of concern, and thus may behave like a traditional test composed of one or two items (Schneider & Schmitt, 1992). To complicate matters further, many performance-assessment exercises are interactive in nature and occur in poorly controlled settings. It may be difficult to know how much of an individual's score reflects aspects of the assessment setting versus actual levels of the individual's skill. In an assessment center exercise, the individual's scores may reflect the actions of other group members; in portfolio assessment, scores may reflect the amount of help an individual received from others in preparing the portfolio responses.

These methodological problems are, however, not the only problems associated with the logic of performance assessment. The performance-assessment approach suffers from several broad substantive problems. One of these problems pertains to the generality of the resulting inferences. Performance assessment is necessarily tied to a specific performance domain. That is, the results of performance assessment cannot easily be generalized to new tasks and other domains. Thus, several different assessment systems may be required for related domains involving slightly different tasks. The need to create multiple systems results in a loss of efficiency and increased costs. Further, performance-assessment systems based on specific tasks may quickly become outdated as technology and job requirements change.

Another set of problems is associated with the focus in performance-assessment systems on manifest, observable performance. Not only is it difficult to see how these measures can be applied when people lack the requisite developmental background (e.g., educational and other resources); the measures may not be fair to individuals with atypical developmental histories. Moreover, because performance assessments focus on observed performance, they typically do not provide an understanding of the performance variables that underlie skilled performance. Performance assessments, as a result, may have limited value in helping people understand skilled performance and providing guidelines for skill development.

An Integrative Approach

Clearly, both performance assessment and the traditional approach to test development each have their own strengths and weaknesses. Table 7.1 contrasts these two measurement approaches. Perhaps the most clear-cut conclusion that can be drawn from the table is that, at least conceptually, performance assessment represents a more appropriate approach when the objective of measure-

TABLE 7.1

Differences Between Traditional and Performance Assessment Approaches to Test Development

	Traditonal Testing	Performance Assessment
Purpose	• Rank people with respect to levels of broad abilities underlying performance	• Assess level of developed skills on manifest performance
Measurement	• Narrow task performance • Tasks mark single underlying ability • Objective scoring	• Broad task performances • Tasks mark performance skills • Scoring via expert judgment
Inferences	• Discriminate between individuals in terms of overall level of broad abilities	• Discriminate between individuals in terms of domain-specific performance skills
Development	• Specification of performance-relevant constructs • Items are generally acceptable • Items maximally differentiate people • Items have high covariation	• Specification of performance-relevant knowledge and skills • Items domain specific • Items maximally realistic
Advantages	• Low cost • Objective scoring • Reliable • Unbiased • Predictive • Generality of inferences • Construct valid	• Absolute standard (criterion referenced) • Captures complex performance skills • Captures qualitative differences • Good diagnostic information • Highly face valid
Disadvantages	• Relative standard (norm referenced) • Does not capture complex skills • Insensitive to qualitative differences • Limited diagnostic information • No direct link to real world knowledge and skill application and development	• High cost • Subjective scoring • Inadequate domain sampling • Score contamination • Poor generality of inferences • Unfair to those of low socioeconomic levels

81

ment is that of specific requisite performance skills as expressed in context (Baker, O'Neil, & Linn, 1993). The methodological and substantive problems that plague performance assessment, however, leads researchers to question whether current assessment procedures really provide a sound basis for measuring requisite complex performance skills. The weaknesses of performance assessment are the strengths of the traditional approach to test development. Thus, finding a way to integrate these two approaches may represent a viable, alternative approach to the measurement of complex performance skills.

At first glance, it may not seem possible to integrate two such markedly different approaches to measurement. We argue, however, that integration of performance-assessment and traditional psychometric approaches might be possible based on the application of four principles. First, developing viable measures of complex performance skills requires defining the nature of a specific skill and the way this skill is applied in performance. Second, measuring these skills might be accomplished using simplified performance tasks expressly intended to elicit expression of the targeted skill. Third, performance on these simplified, low-fidelity simulations should be structured to elicit the crucial component characteristics of skilled performance. Fourth, scoring systems should be designed to capture these component characteristics of skilled performance.

Skill Definition.   Most performance-assessment efforts use a content-validation model in exercise development (Byham, 1980; Royer, Cisero, & Carlo, 1993). The basis for formulating skill measures is performance in a specific, targeted domain. An alternative to this content-based approach to measurement is a construct-based approach, where the major concern in exercise development is the skill or skills under consideration (Messick, 1989; Snow & Lohman, 1989, 1993). In a construct-based framework, measure development would begin with a definition of the skills contributing to performance and an analysis of how these skills are applied in performance. A variety of techniques, including expert–novice comparisons, think-out-loud protocols, critical incidents analysis, or a review of the relevant literature, might be used to identify specific skills and characteristics of skilled performance. What is essential is that such procedural analysis allows an a priori, substantive specification of performance-relevant skills and the manner in which they are applied in real-world contexts (Frederiksen, 1982; Snow & Lohman, 1993).

Performance Tasks.   After identifying the skill constructs of concern, the next necessary step is identification of the performance tasks to be used in assessing these skill constructs. In performance assessment, this is typically accomplished by using realistic task performance exercises that, at least in the appraisal of judges, call for the application of requisite skills (Assmann, Hixon, & Kacmarek, 1979). An alternative approach, however, is suggested by traditional test theory. Instead of using complex, highly realistic (high-fidelity) exercises, researchers might develop a series of low-fidelity exercises that are expressly intended to elicit the skill of concern. Mislevy (1993) called such exercises "controlled simulation" tasks, and Motowidlo, Dunnette, and Carter (1990) have evidence showing that use of more focused yet low-fidelity exercises yields results comparable to those obtained from more complex simulation exercises.

The development of low-fidelity exercises that elicit performance-relevant skills offers four distinct advantages. First, simple, exercises that consume little time reduce the total cost of assessment and enhance the accuracy of assessments by allowing more exercises to be administered. Second, simple, limited exercises should reduce the need for trained raters, streamline the development of scoring rules, and increase the reliability of assessments. Third, these simplified, structured exercises might make objective scoring of exercise performance possible. Fourth, by organizing assessments around underlying constructs, more general principles might be formulated. This process would allow the progressive construct-validation efforts needed for refinement of measures and the development of general theories (Landy, 1986; Messick, 1989).

Performance Task Characteristics. In measurement, researchers must identify a set of tasks that elicit requisite performance skills; then people must generate performances that reflect application of the targeted skills (Baker, O'Neil, & Linn, 1993; Royer, Cisero, & Carlo, 1993). In most performance assessments, application of requisite skills is inferred from overall task performance and this approach has its merits. An alternative approach, however, is suggested by the work of Frederiksen (Frederiksen, 1982; Frederiksen, Warren, & Rosenberg, 1985) and Hayes and Flower (1986). Rather than structuring response requirements in relation to overall performance, response requirements might be structured to call for application of crucial components of skilled performance. Thus, for writing, one component of writing skill—revision—might be assessed by asking people how they would revise an essay. Another component of writing skill—planning—might be assessed by asking people to outline an essay.

These illustrations are useful partly because they illustrate an important aspect of the task component, or construct-based, approach we are recommending with respect to response generation. A construct-based approach retains an element of the performance-assessment model in the sense that people's responses are obtained in ill-defined performance settings, settings in which they must structure their own activities. The activities called for, however, as with traditional tests, are designed to elicit or reflect use of the underlying attributes held to represent crucial components of skilled performance. Constructing task response requirements in relation to the component constructs underlying skilled performance may be accomplished in several ways. What is essential, however, is that people's responses to the task reflect these component constructs, or attributes, of skilled performance.

Scoring. As might be expected in a construct-based assessment framework, scoring would not be based on overall performance. Instead, scoring would be based on indices reflecting application or use of the attributes held to underlie skilled performance. This a priori scoring in relation to the use of relevant attributes requires a careful analysis of performance requirements; but such analysis also allows scoring based on an absolute rather than a differential scale and thus retains an important characteristic of the performance-assessment model. Further, because a scoring strategy based on relevant attributes would allow concrete, specific feedback, it should enhance the value of such measures as developmental tools.

When considering these observations, we are clearly recommending a construct-, rather than a content-based approach to performance assessment. Unfortunately, a construct-based approach to skill assessment has not traditionally been considered in the design of performance assessment systems. As a result, evidence is not available about the validity of this approach. Therefore, in the following discussion we review the results obtained in a series of studies in which this approach was used to develop a set of procedures for assessing complex, creative thinking skills.

ASSESSMENT OF CREATIVE PROBLEM-SOLVING SKILL

Background

Several theoretical systems have been proposed to account for the ways people go about solving novel, creative problems. Some investigations have stressed the importance of divergent thinking (Guilford, 1950; Runco, 1991). Others have stressed the need for systematic search-and-hypothesis testing (Kulkarni & Simon, 1988; Perkins, 1992). Still others have argued that creative problem solving is based on associational linkages (Mednick & Mednick, 1967; Poincaré, 1952).

In recent years, however, a growing body of evidence has led to the conclusion that, ultimately, creative problem solutions are based on the combination and reorganization of extant knowledge structures. Studies of eminent achievement in the arts and sciences by Koestler (1964), Kuhn (1970), and Rothenberg (1986) have suggested that new solutions are often associated with the fusion or linkage of two or more schemata. Along similar lines, Simonton (1988) showed that the rate of creative contributions can be accounted for on the basis of the number of concepts available for combination. Other work by Carlsson and Gorman (1992) and Mumford and Connelly (1993) suggested that many innovations in applied fields are based on the reorganization of available knowledge structures.

Evidence pointing to the importance of combination and reorganization processes is not limited to historic studies. In one set of experimental studies, Rothenberg and his colleagues (Rothenberg & Sobel, 1980; Sobel & Rothenberg, 1980) showed that experimental conditions intended to help combination and reorganization through superimposing different images led to the production of creative literary and artistic products. In another set of studies, Mumford and his colleagues (Baughman & Mumford, 1995; Mobley, Doares, & Mumford, 1992) presented people with a series of three lists of words representing three different taxonomic categories, such as *birds, sporting equipment,* and *planets.* People were asked to combine these three stimulus categories to generate a new category that would account for the category exemplars, that is, the contents of the three word lists. It was found that more original new categories, or concepts, were obtained when people were asked to combine diverse, as opposed to similar, stimulus categories.

In still another set of studies, Finke, Ward, and Smith (1992) presented people with various mechanical parts and asked them to combine these parts to create a useful, new tool. They found that exploration of these new combinations led to the production of creative, original, new products. Similarly, Owens (1969) asked engineers to combine and reorganize various parts and mechanical principles to create a new machine. Skill in combining and reorganizing these parts and principles was found to yield correlations of about .45, with indices of patent awards and supervisory assessments of creativity obtained more than 5 years later.

Combination and reorganization efforts, however, do not occur in isolation. In the real world, effective execution of the combination and reorganization process is likely to depend on other processes occurring before combination and reorganization (Merrifield, Guilford, Christensen, & Frick, 1962; Mumford, Mobley, Uhlman, Reiter-Palmon, & Doares, 1991). Initially, most creative problem-solving efforts are held to begin with defining or structuring the problem situation. Studies by Getzels and Csikszentmihalyi (1976); Hoover and Feldhusen (1990); Mumford, Reiter-Palmon, and Redmond (1994); and Okuda, Runco, and Berger (1991) have shown that this problem-definition process may represent another important component of creative problem solving.

Definition of the problem, however important, does not in itself provide an adequate basis for successful combination and reorganization efforts. Instead, people must use this information to encode or acquire information about the nature of the problem situation and must identify a set of categories or concepts that might be used to organize this information (Davidson & Sternberg, 1984; Kulkarni & Simon, 1988; Sternberg, 1986). The evidence compiled by Davidson and Sternberg (1984), Khandwalla (1993), and Perkins (1992), points to the importance of information-acquisition or information-encoding skills and the need for category selection or information organization in creative problem solving.

As a whole, these observations show that problem construction, information encoding, category selection, and category combination and reorganization may represent the crucial operations involved in creative thought. What is important to recognize, however, is that these four creative problem-solving skills might be applied in several different ways—one way people might differ in applying skills in terms of context, the type of information people work with, or generate, as they apply a given skill. For example, in problem construction, people might define problems in terms that emphasize the goals of the prob-lem-solving effort or they might define problems in terms of specific proce-dures that yield a solution (Mumford, Reiter-Palmon, & Redmond, 1994). In information encoding, people might focus on information pertaining to rele-vant principles or on information that is inconsistent with other observations (Kuhn, 1970; Perkins, 1992).

Differences in how people apply problem-solving skills provided the basis for the present set of studies. Specifically, we hoped to develop measures for assessing four creative problem-solving skills: problem construction, informa-tion encoding, category selection, and category combination and reorganiza-tion. In developing each of these measures, we attempted to identify a set of tasks that would elicit each of these four skills and permit assessment of the different contents or strategies people used as they applied the skills.

Study Design

The sample used to validate these measures was 124 undergraduates. The 47 men and 77 women who agreed to participate in this study were recruited from undergraduate psychology courses providing extra credit. Most students were in their junior year. Their academic ability, as indexed by self-reported scores on the Scholastic Aptitude Test, lay near the national average for entering first-year students.

The students were asked to participate in what was purported to be a study of problem solving. During the first hour of this study, the students completed a battery of reference measures. During the second hour, they completed a battery of computer-administered measures of problem construction, informa-tion encoding, category selection, and category combination and reorganiza-tion skill. Finally, they completed a complex, creative problem-solving task that served as our principal criterion measure.

Measures.   The battery of reference measures included a background infor-mation form. On this form, the students reported their current grade-point average and their total scores on the Scholastic Aptitude Test. Besides these traditional measures of academic achievement, they were asked to complete three measures of basic abilities and skills that might influence task perform-ance. One of these measures was the verbal reasoning test of the Employee Aptitude Survey. This measure was administered because it has been shown to provide a reliable measure of general intelligence (Ivancevich, 1976; Ruch & Ruch, 1980; Tenopyr, 1969). Because this study focused on creative problem solving, the students were asked to complete a divergent-thinking test, Guilford's Alternative Headlines Test (Guilford & Hoepfner, 1966), in which people are asked to rewrite a series of newspaper headlines. This test yielded inter-rater agreement coefficients in the .70s when scored for the manifest creativity apparent in the rewritten headlines. The final measure was a computer-administered measure of typing skill. This control measure seemed called for because the measures of creative problem-solving skills were administered using personal computers.

After the students completed these reference measures, they worked through the four measures intended to assess creative problem-solving skills. Finally, they completed the complex performance exercise intended to provide an assessment of creative problem-solving skills of a type that would typically be used in assessing creative problem solving.

Criterion Task.   The task used to assess creative problem solving was drawn from Redmond, Mumford, and Teach (1993). In this task, people were asked to develop an advertising campaign for a new product: the 3-D Holographic Television. This creative problem-solving task seemed especially appropriate for use with a general population, because most undergraduates have had substantial exposure to advertising during their lives.

To provide a basis for developing these advertising campaigns, the study participants were presented with a written product description illustrated in Fig. 7.1. After the students had read this product description, they were asked to write a three- or four-paragraph response to each of three tasks: describe the kinds of questions to include in a market survey to obtain information about market characteristics and optimal selling points; describe a 30-second television commercial that would be used to sell this product; and describe a full-page magazine advertisement that would be used to sell this product.

The solutions to each problem posed on this task were evaluated with the benchmark rating scales developed for this task by Redmond, Mumford, and Teach (1993), who asked 20 advertising executives to evaluate the quality and originality of the responses obtained for each of the three problems in a sample of responses. Figure 7.2 presents the resulting benchmark scales developed to assess the quality and originality of responses to the television advertisement problems.

In the present study, three judges were asked to evaluate the quality and originality of each response to the advertising task (i.e., task products) using the appropriate benchmark scale. The inter-rater agreement coefficients obtained for these evaluations of product quality and originality were in the .70s. Because previous research by Redmond, Mumford, and Teach (1993) showed that these indices of quality and originality are correlated, a total quality and originality score was computed for each person by summing the judges' average

---

Henderson & Co.
Consumer Electronics Division - New Products Department

NEW PRODUCT INTRODUCTION

New Product: 3-D Holographic TV

Firm: Zenith

Product Description:

One of our clients, Zenith, has developed and patented a three-dimensional holographic television. Using the latest in computer and laser technology, this brand new home entertainment system takes a standard two-dimensional television or videotape signal, and recreates it into a three-dimensional image, a hologram.

The computer technology was developed from research with high-density televisions. Unlike high-density televisions, however, the computer in the 3-D holographic TV generates the normally untelevised third dimension using known objects in its extensive memory. All three dimensions are then combined and projected using lasers and mirrors.

As illustrated by the enclosed sketch of the product, the 3-D holographic image is projected to an area *on top of the set*. This 3-D projection allows the created image to be viewed *from all angles* (front, back, and sides). For example, the enclosed illustration of the car scene is viewed from the front of the set. From this angle, the car appears to be traveling towards you. It will appear to be traveling away from you, however, if you were viewing the car scene from the rear of the set.

Other Features:

- Uses standard household current
- High-quality computer chips (Intel 586 chip)
- Extended memory of known objects
- State-of-the-art software
- Computer interface for custom hologram design
- Reasonable image quality
- Large image size (24" high, 24" wide, 18" deep)
- Easy to operate controls
- High-fidelity sound (four speakers)
- Wireless remote

Production Schedule:

Zenith currently has a working prototype of the 3-D holographic television built, and will be introducing it into the marketplace in *90 days*.

Retail Price:

The manufacturer's suggested retail price per unit is estimated to be $3,000-$4,000 for the first 10,000 units produced. As more units are produced, however, the average manufacturing cost per unit is projected to curve downward (production experience curve). This projected decline in manufacturing costs will enable Zenith to lower their suggested retail price per unit, as follows:

Retail Pricing Curve

Number of Units Produced	Manufacturer's Suggested Retail Price (per Unit)
1 - 10,000	$3,000 - $4,000
10,000 - 100,000	$2,500 - $3,000
100,000 - 1,000,000	$2,000 - $2,500
1,000,000 - 10,000,000	$1,500 - $2,000
10,000,000 - and up	$1,000 - $1,500

Competition:

RCA and Sony are also planning to produce 3-D holographic televisions. RCA is projected to introduce their first units in *one year*. However, due to increased development time, it will take Sony *two years* to introduce their first units.

The manufacturer's suggested retail price is expected to be similar for each of the three companies.

FIG. 7.1. Description of product to be marketed on the criterion-advertising task (from M. R. Redmond, M. D. Mumford, & R. Teach (1993)."Putting creativity to work: Effects of leader behavior on subordinate creativity," *Organizational Behavior and Human Decision Processes*, 55, 120. © 1993 by Lawrence Erlbaum Associates. Adapted by permission).

ratings across all three problems. It is of note that Mumford, Baughman, Supinski, Costanza, and Threlfall (1994) provided some evidence for the construct validity of this task. They showed that scores on this advertising task yield the expected correlations with divergent thinking and verbal reasoning: The correlations with divergent thinking were stronger than the correlations with verbal reasoning.

The question that now arises pertains to the central issue in the present effort: Do measures of creative problem-solving skills developed according to the four principles described earlier show the expected relation with performance on a relevant assessment exercise? We begin our attempt to answer this question by considering the results obtained for our measure of problem-construction skills.

Subject's Instructions:

Based upon the target market and the expected findings of your market research survey:

> Create and describe in detail a 30-second television advertisement that would be used to sell this product. When and where would you place this advertisement?

Originality Considerations:

The subject's answers to be above instructions should be rated on a five-point scale using the following dimensions:

UNEXPECTEDNESS: Did they approach the problem in a novel, imaginative, unpredictable, or innovative manner?

DESCRIPTION: Did they expand upon an idea, tell a story, or use fine detail to help the reader visualize the plan?

Five television advertisement plans are attached. Use these plans as examples of originality scale points (1 to 5). Please briefly review these plans at the beginning of each rating session. For reference purposes, the plans are summarized below.

Originality Scale Points:

(1) Vague description of ad: "Upbeat, youthful theme". Nondescriptive placement.

(2) Predictable placement (e.g., news, sports) to reach males primarily. Describes unoriginal ad: "Well dressed, upper class family watching new TV in living room." Unspecified 3D special effects. Good ideas, but no elaboration (e.g. airplanes dog fight, mushroom cloud).

(3) Specifies placement during current sporting event (e.g. Master's) to reach mostly male/upper class TM. Detailed ad: Specific golf star as spokesperson introduces himself on hole where he won tournament; shows flashback; introduces TV and stresses advantages; hits ball to show 3D effect of ball image. Unimaginative close: "It could make you the most popular guy in the house," with his family in living room.

(4) Detailed ad elicit consumer "curiosity." Ad uniquely demonstrates 3D effect by circling camera around 2D and 3D TVs. Camera first circles 2D TV showing back of cabinet, then circles scene on 3D TV to give 360 degree view. No audio words! Close: "Available now, from Zenith" on screen. Specific placement for "action/adventure person."

(5) Ad tells the 3D TV story using "flat/Columbus" theme with modern twist. Extremely detailed and imaginative description offsetting, images and dialogue (e.g. Columbus in lounge, with a Walkman, reading the Titanic, Crew enters and yells, "It's true, the earth the flat."). Product features described in story line. Placement discussed.

Subject's Instructions:

Based upon the target market and the expected findings of your market research survey:

> Create and describe in detail a 30-second television advertisement that would be used to sell this product. When and where would you place this advertisement?

Quality Considerations:

The subject's answers to be above instructions should be rated on a five-point scale using the following dimensions:

COMPLETENESS: Did they understand the instructions, use the information, and follow the instructions fully and completely?

EFFECTIVENESS: Is the plan usable, practical, and/or appropriate (reach and frequency)?

Five television advertisement plans are attached. Use these plans as examples of originality scale points (1 to 5). Please briefly review these plans at the beginning of each rating session. For reference purposes, the places are summarized below.

Quality Scale Points:

(1) Placement incomplete. Slogan: "You'll Love It On Holographic TV." Weak description of car ad. Unspecified as to how 3D effect shown.

(2) Placement: News/sports to reach professional man. Ignore females. Ad: family watching new TV. Mentions special effects to show advantages, but unspecified as to how 3D effects shown.

(3) Placement limited to current sporting event, e.g., Masters, to reach male/upper class. Ad: Golf star as spokesperson. Describes 3D effect of ball. Ineffective slogan, "It could make you the most popular guy in the house," with his family in living room watching him win on 3D TV.

(4) Appeals to "grown-up kids"/sports watchers. Ad starts with men watching Superbowl on 3D TV. Shows 3D effect: Fantastic football catch, bikinied women, stunt pilot, and shuttle lift off, all from different angles. Effective slogan: "Don't be left in the 2nd dimension." Mentions Zenith. No placement.

(5) Detailed ad description. Ad effectively demonstrate 3D effect by circling camera around 2D and 3D TVs. No audio words. Close with screen: "Available now, from Zenith". Specific placement: (a) Sports event for broad market, (b) segment watched by "high income action/adventure" people. Frequency considered.

FIG. 7.2. Benchmark rating scales for criterion-advertising task.

Problem Construction

Development of our measure of problem-construction skills was based on a model of the problem-construction process proposed by Mumford, Reiter-Palmon, and Redmond (1994). This model holds that individuals faced with problems define them by constructing a representation of the problem situation from experience and then draw inferences from their construction. People are held to search through and filter the mental representations activated by the situation to identify the specific elements included in these representations, which might serve to define the nature of the problem. On the basis of prior work by Gick and Holyoak (1983), Holyoak (1984), Novick (1990), and Reeves and Weisburg (1994), we hypothesized that these representations would include information about goals, key diagnostic information, requisite procedures, and restrictions involved in earlier problem-solving efforts. Accordingly, we developed this problem-construction measure to assess content elements reflecting the quality and originality of the goals, diagnostic information, requisite procedures, and restrictions people use in defining the nature of problems.

Development of a measure suitable for assessing use of these content elements was accomplished with a task proposed by Baer (1988) and Redmond, Mumford, and Teach (1993). On this task, people are presented with six complex, ill-defined situations that might be looked at, or structured, in several different ways. In responding to these problem situations, people are asked to find different ways of restating the problem. Thus, this task appears to satisfy the requirement that the task elicit the requisite problem-construction skills.

To assess the content that people preferred to apply in problem construction, we presented the students with 16 potential restatements or redefinitions of the problem situation. They were then asked to select the four restatements they thought would be most useful in addressing the problem. The restatements presented for each situation were varied to reflect the tendency to define problems in terms of goals, diagnostic information, procedures, and restrictions. Besides these four content dimensions, the response options were also varied to reflect two different levels of quality and originality.

The particular restatements presented on a given problem were derived from a pool of 64 potential restatements. These initial 64 problem restatements were generated by four graduate students in industrial and organizational psychology, who were instructed to generate independently a complete set of 16 responses for each problem. Specifically, they were instructed to generate responses in which each explicitly represented one of the four content dimensions and one of two levels of quality and originality. The final set of 16 restatements accompanying a given problem situation was selected from this initial pool, on the basis of the average ratings of 30 judges on the content dimension tapped by the restatement and its quality and originality. Accordingly, each problem situation was presented with two original and two high-quality restatements for each of the four content dimensions. Scores were derived by counting the number of times across all problems people selected high-quality or original statements derived for a particular content dimension. Figure 7.3 provides an example of one of these problems and illustrates how the various problem restatements reflect each content dimension.

Table 7.2 presents the correlations between scores on each of these content-dimension scales and the quality and originality scores obtained on the criterion-advertising task. This table also presents the multiple correlations and regression weights obtained when quality and originality scores on the criterion-advertising task were regressed onto the content dimensions incorporated in the problem construction skill measure. Here it was found that the tendency to select or use problem representations reflecting high-quality approaches was positively related to the production of high-quality ($r = .22, p .05$) and more original ($r = .17, p .05$) solutions on the criterion task. The tendency to select problem representations that reflected high-quality restrictions was also related to the quality ($r = .17, p .05$) and originality ($r = .18, p .05$) of solutions to the criterion-advertising task.

In the regressions analyses, these measures yielded multiple correlations of .34 and .33 when used to predict the quality and originality of solutions on the criterion-advertising task. We found that the tendency to select problem representations reflecting high-quality restrictions yielded the largest regression

SITUATION:		
YOU ARE SELECTED TO REPRESENT YOUR COUNTRY IN THE OLYMPIC TRACK AND FIELD. YOU ARE ONE OF THE TOP "HOPEFULS," BUT YOUR DOCTOR HAS ADVISED YOU TO HAVE SURGERY IMMEDIATELY OR RISK A DEBILITATING INJURY. HOWEVER, TO HAVE THE SURGERY WOULD MEAN MISSING THE GAMES.		
	QUALITY	ORIGINALITY
GOALS:		
How can I use my fame so as to help others avoid this condition?	HIGH	HIGH
How can I prevent myself from becoming discouraged?	HIGH	LOW
How can I intimidate opponents by convincing the press that I'm not really injured?	LOW	HIGH
How can I attend the games even if I don't participate?	LOW	LOW
PROCEDURES:		
How can I get a bionic replacement part so I can both participate and win?	HIGH	HIGH
How can I find a better solution?	HIGH	LOW
How can I get the games postponed?	LOW	HIGH
How can I convince the coach I should go?	LOW	LOW
KEY INFORMATION:		
How can I find out if other athletes dealt with this same condition successfully?	HIGH	HIGH
How can I find out if I can train to prevent injury?	HIGH	LOW
How can I find out if injured athletes can still make a lot of money?	LOW	HIGH
How can I find out if I can still win the games?	LOW	LOW
RESTRICTIONS:		
How can I make this decision on the basis of what is best for the team?	HIGH	HIGH
How can I participate, but not get hurt?	HIGH	LOW
How can I convince myself that the injury justifies not going to the games?	LOW	HIGH
How can I not let my country down?	LOW	LOW

FIG. 7.3. Description of problem-construction task and response options.

TABLE 7.2

Correlations and Regression With Performance for Problem Construction

	Advertising Task Quality		Advertising Task Originality	
	r	ß	r	ß
QUALITY				
Information	−.00	.09	.00	.09
Goals	−.00	.15	.00	.17
Approaches	.22**	.20*	.17**	.15
Restrictions	.17**	.20*	.18**	.21**
ORIGINALITY				
Information	−.13	−.11	−.10	−.08
Goals	−.16	−.15	−.17*	−.18
Approaches	.05	.03	.04	.05
Restrictions	.05	−.03	.05	−.04
MULTIPLE CORRELATION		.34*		.33*

Note:* = $p < .10$; ** = $p < .05$.

weights for solution quality (ß = .20, p .10) and solution originality (ß = .21, p .05). The use of problem restatements reflecting high-quality approaches (ß = .20), however, also yielded a marginally significant regression weight (p .10) for solution quality on the criterion task.

These findings are of interest not only because they suggest that problem-construction skills influence performance on creative problem-solving tasks. They also suggest that the type of representational content used in problem construction influences the nature and success of people's creative problem-solving efforts. Apparently, people who attempt to define or structure novel, ill-defined situations using high-quality material do better than those who do not, perhaps because the ambiguity of the situation calls for high-quality material, as opposed to original material that may be more difficult to use in creating a coherent problem definition. On the other hand, perhaps the use of high-quality material—reflecting content dimensions of alternative approaches and restrictions—allowed a flexible, procedure-based approach to problem solving (Mumford, Reiter-Palmon, & Redmond, 1994).

Our problem-construction measure represents one approach to the assessment of complex skills, in which people were given a range of choices about how they might approach a problem, and differences in preferences for using certain types of material were assessed. In information encoding, however, we used a different approach: The type of material people chose to work with as they went about solving certain problems provided the basis for assessment.

Information Encoding

On the problem-solving tasks making up the information-encoding measure, each problem was presented on a computer screen as a series of six "index cards." Two problems concerned public policy; the other two problems concerned business issues. In working through each problem, study participants were asked to read at their own pace all six cards describing the problem. After reading these cards once, they were asked to type a one-paragraph solution to the problem. As they read these cards, the amount of time they spent reading each card was recorded. These time-spent measures were then used to obtain relative time-spent measures, based on the total time spent reading all six cards. Figure 7.4 describes of the nature of this task.

On this task, we wished to assess what information people tended to focus on in problem solving. Research by Alissa (1972), Davidson and Sternberg (1984), Hogarth (1986), Kuhn (1970), and Snow and Lohman (1984) has shown that people's ability to solve problems may be related to the kind of information they look for during information encoding. Kuhn (1970), for example, has argued that the tendency to focus on inconsistent information may be related to performance on creative problem-solving tasks. Davidson and Sternberg's (1984) findings, furthermore, suggested that performance may be related to the time spent encoding important facts.

Accordingly, on this task the content of the information presented on the cards was varied. On three of the six cards, the information presented represented crucial information needed to solve the problem. Other kinds of information were presented on the remaining three cards. On one business and one public policy problem, a card presented information about principles that might be used to understand the situation (principles), a second card presented relevant facts that were inconsistent with the other facts (consistency), and a third card presented information about how the different facts were related to each other (relatedness). On the second business and public policy problem, these three additional cards presented information about the goals that needed to be addressed in problem solving (goals), organizational constraints on potential solutions (constraints), and additional information about the problem situation that was not specifically tied to the content of the problem at hand (range).

Table 7.3 presents the correlations between the average time spent encoding these different types of information and performance on the criterion-advertising task. As shown in Table 7.3, the relative time spent encoding crucial factual information ($\bar{r} = .23, p$ .05) and relative time spent encoding inconsistent facts ($\bar{r} = .24, p$ .05) were positively related to performance. These findings are consistent with the earlier observations of Davidson and Sternberg (1984) and Kuhn (1970), which showed that a focus on relevant facts and inconsistent observations contributes to problem solving. In keeping with this pattern of findings, the relative time spent on irrelevant information ($\bar{r} = -.22, p$ .05) was

SCENARIO

The amounts charged to the expense account were exorbitant. This was not the occasional three martini lunch or theater tickets--the sales rep was spending over one hundred and fifty thousand dollars a year--which was more than the whole regional office travel and entertainment budget. The receipts were all there, but the legitimacy of the expenses was questionable. However, the sales rep had been an assistant to the Undersecretary of the Navy during a previous administration and he really knew his way around Washington.

As the regional manager looked over his sales rep's expenses, he wondered why he initialed an expense account that listed three hundred dollar dinners night after night. After all, this division sold machinery to manufacturers and parts suppliers and no other sales rep spent a tenth of that amount.

When the rep had moved to the Washington office, he made it clear that the rules for expenses didn't apply to him because he reported directly to the vice-chairman of the company. When the issue of meeting sales goals came up, he said it might not be possible to meet them. He told the regional manager if he had a problem with this, he would have to take it up with the vice-chair.

Somewhat naively, the regional manager asked the rep why he wasn't working for the vice-chair. The man had responded that the vice chair wanted to keep his lobbying costs down. When the manager asked for a written statement regarding this, the rep merely laughed. the regional manager realized just then that he was going to have to take the blame for the expenses himself, or expose the would situation.

RESPONSE OPTIONS:

General Principles:
• Innocents easily become the victims of political schemes.
• What is ethical and what is practical are not always the same.

Specific Action Plans:
• The regional manager has to decide whether to take the fall of expose the situation.
• The regional manager should consider going to the chairman to try and save his job.

Long-Term Goals:
• Fiscal irresponsibility can set a bad precedent for other reps.
• Politicizing expenses and relationships could be bad for the company.

Evaluation of Others:
• The regional manager should take into account ethics, customary Washington lobbying practices, and personal and career considerations in deciding what to do.
• The regional manager could have gone to the vice-chair and requested an additional sales rep for his division in order to offset the lack of productivity on the part of the sales rep who only conducted public relations.

FIG. 7.4. Description of information-encoding task.

negatively related to performance, and the relative time spent encoding information about goals ($\bar{r} = -.18, p$ .05) was negatively related to the production of high-quality solutions.

TABLE 7.3

Correlations and Regression With Performance for Information Encoding

	Advertising Task Quality		Advertising Task Originality	
	r	ß	r	ß
Irrelevant	−.23**	−.05	−.21**	−.03
Inconsistent	.26**	.23*	.22**	.21
Principles	−.11	.08	−.09	.10
Restrictions	.06	.12	.02	.14
Goals	−.18**	−.11**	−.16**	−.08
Range	−.03	.01	.05	.10
Factual information	.23**	.25**	.24**	.28**
MULTIPLE CORRELATION		.39**		.36**

Note: * = $p < .10$; ** = $p < .05$.

When the performance indices obtained on the criterion task were regressed on the information-encoding measures, multiple correlations of .39 and .36 were obtained for solution quality and solution originality. Again, the tendency to focus on key facts ($\overline{\beta} = .26$, p .05) yielded sizable, significant regression weights. The tendency to attend to inconsistent information ($\overline{\beta} = .22$, p .10) also produced a marginally significant regression weight. Thus, the tendency to focus on relevant information, even when this information is inconsistent with other observations, contributes to creative problem solving. Moreover, these kinds of preferences can apparently be assessed by measuring the relative time people spend encoding certain types of information as they work on various problem-solving tasks.

Category Selection

The technique used to assess category selection was similar to the technique that we used in our attempt to measure problem-construction skills. We designed a measure intended to assess preferences for working with different types of concepts. On this measure, study participants were presented with four three- or four-paragraph descriptions of an organizational problem. These problem scenarios, drawn from Shorris (1981), presented complex, ill-defined situations, in which a variety of concepts or schemata might be used to understand the problem situation at hand.

To develop a measure of category or concept preferences using this material, we presented four doctoral candidates with the problem scenario and other relevant case study information bearing on potential response goals, principles, actions, and evaluation of others. Panel members were then asked to generate three or four concept statements describing relevant principles, long-term goals, evaluations of others, and specific action plans. Once these initial concept statements had been generated, they were reviewed by other panel members. Any concept statement that which was ambiguous, poorly worded, not clearly linked to the targeted type of concept, or not useful in understanding the problem situation was eliminated. This review was conducted to help ensure that all statements reflected viable, potentially useful concepts.

The 188 concept statements that survived this initial screening were presented to a second panel of judges. These 30 judges, all doctoral candidates in industrial and organizational psychology, were asked to rate the extent to which each concept statement reflected general principles, long-term goals, evaluations of others, or specific action plans. For each of the four content categories, the two concept statements that received the highest mean ratings and also had the lowest standard deviations were included as response options for each problem scenario. Thus, eight concept statements were presented to accompany each problem scenario. Study participants were asked to select the four concept statements they thought would be most useful in helping to understand the problem scenario. Figure 7.5 describes the nature of this task.

Responses to these problems were scored simply by determining the number of times concept statements reflecting a given content category were selected. Table 7.4 presents the correlations and regression weights obtained for each of these scales when they were used to account for the quality and originality of solutions to the criterion-advertising task. In the correlational analysis, only one significant relation was obtained. The selection of concept statements reflecting general principles was negatively related ($r = -.18, p .05$) to the quality of solutions to the criterion task. On the other hand, in the regression analysis, use of concept statements reflecting broad, general principles was negatively related to both criterion task-problem solution quality ($ß = -.24, p .05$) and solution originality ($ß = -.21, p .05$). Further, the tendency to select concepts based on specific action plans ($ß = -.21, p .05$) was negatively related to solution

TABLE 7.4

Correlations and Regression with Performance for Category Selection

	Advertising Task Quality		Advertising Task Originality	
	r	ß	r	ß
INFORMATION TYPE				
General principles	−.18**	−.24**	−.15*	−.21**
Evaluation of others	−.00	−.10	.00	−.09
Long-term goals	.08	−.03	.13	.01
Specific action plans	−.08	−.14	−.16*	−.21**
MULTIPLE CORRELATION		.23		.26**

Note: * = $p < .10$; ** = $p < .05$.

Your task is to look at these three categories and combine them into one category, imagining that the 12 words are a single list of words, and you had to invent a name for the list.

• seat	• glove	• bicycling
• tire	• baseball	• running
• brakes	• baseball bat	• swimming
• wheel	• football	• lifting weights

Type the NAME of your new category for these words

athletic necessities

Type a CHARACTERISTIC that describes your new category

entertaining
important
physical
enduring

Type a NEW ITEM, or word, that belongs in your new category

aerobics
softball
hockey
ski pole

FIG. 7.5. Description of category-selection task and response options.

originality. Perhaps the most plausible interpretation for this pattern of findings is that concepts must be tailored to the problem situation. Thus, both abstract and overly narrow, rigid concepts (i. e., specific action plans) inhibit performance. In considering this interpretation, however, it should be recognized that these effects were not strong. This point is illustrated by the multiple correlations of .23 and .26 obtained when these scales were used to predict the criterion task solution quality and originality.

Category Combination

A different pattern of results was obtained for our measure of combination and reorganization skills. This measure, unlike the category-selection and problem-construction measures, required study participants to generate three products. Here, people were presented with six category–exemplar-generation problems drawn from Mobley, Doares, and Mumford (1992). For these problems, expressly intended to elicit combination and reorganization skills, study participants were presented with three word lists. Each word list represented distinct categories or concepts, defined on the basis of relevant exemplars, as represented by the words in the lists. Thus, the category of *sporting equipment*, might be defined using the exemplars, *gloves, skates, bat*, and *ball*. In working through these problems, study participants were asked to review the exemplars defining each stimulus category and then to generate a new category to account for all presented exemplars. They were next asked to use this new, combined category to produce three products held to represent crucial elements of creative thought (Baughman & Mumford, 1995; Finke, Ward, & Smith, 1992). Specifically, they were asked to provide a label for their new category, to list additional exemplars or members of their new category, and to list the defining features emerging from their new category (e. g., *birds fly and have feathers*). Figure 7.6 illustrates the nature of this task and the requested products for category labels, defining features, and new exemplars.

To score the products generated in response to these questions, the category labels, exemplars, and features generated on each problem were presented to a panel of five judges. These judges were asked to rate the quality and originality of the set of products by using a variation on Hennessey and Amabile's (1988) consensual rating technique. These ratings of the quality and originality of the products obtained from this combination and reorganization task produced inter-rater agreement coefficients in the .80s. Total quality and originality scores for each product were obtained simply by summing the judges' average quality and originality ratings.

Table 7.5 presents the results obtained when our indices of performance on the criterion task were correlated with, and regressed on, the three product ratings reflecting performance on the combination and reorganization task. Perhaps the most clear-cut conclusion to emerge from this analysis was that all three types of products—new content category labels ($\bar{r} = .20$), new category

TABLE 7.5

Correlations and Regression With Performance for Category Combination

	Advertising Task Quality		Advertising Task Originality	
	r	ß	r	ß
PRODUCT QUALITY				
New category label	.25**	.11	.21*	.06
New category features	.40**	.87**	.39**	.83**
New category exemplars	.25**	−.20	.24**	−.28
PRODUCT ORIGINALITY				
New category label	.17*	−.11	.15	−.14
New category features	.31**	−.33	31**	−.27
New category exemplars	.22**	−.01	.24*	,.10
MULTIPLE CORRELATION		.47**		.44**

*Note: * = p < .10; ** = p < .05.*

CARD 1: RESTRICTIONS
Your company, CozyNight Inns, has recently expanded into the national arena by purchasing local hotels and converting them into upscale CozyNight Inns. In order to expedite the change, CozyNight has set up centralized Reservations, Marketing, Finance, Interior Decoration, Methods Standardization and Culinary departments at headquarters, but kept the preexisting general managers of each new CozyNight.

CARD 4: DATA
There are some problems at the local level, too. Hotel managers are often uncooperative with headquarters policies and are "too busy" to meet with visiting headquarters staff. Chefs at a number of hotels have complained that nationally prescribed menus violate local tastes, and a Texas head bartender insists that Texas customers want more than one ounce of gin in their gin fizzes!!

CARD 2: RANGE
You report directly to the CEO, who has told you, "I know you can handle it, so I'm putting you in charge of the expansion transition. I want my attention free to work on future planning with the board of directors--I don't want to do this day-to-day stuff. You have my authority to do whatever you think is needed to smooth over any transition problems. Just keep me posted once in a while, OK?"

CARD 5: DATA
Although there are problems at the top, you know that CozyNight's problems are restricted to management. The non-managerial employees are happy with better wages and benefits, the customers say they are very pleased with the new CozyNight Inns, and the stockholders have seen their shares triple in value. If only the managerial problems could be cleaned up, everyone would be happy with CozyNight.

CARD 3: DATA
Unfortunately, you know that friction is starting among staff departments. Finance is complaining that Interior Decoration is spending too much on original art work for the new Inns, but Decoration insists that the art is essential to the upscale image of CozyNight. Reservations is upset by Marketing's many introductory deals which they say are confusing computers, staff and customers.

CARD 6: GOALS
So, maybe your task won't be so bad after all. If only you can get the managerial staff to work together, you'll be able to give the CEO a great report. All you need to do is get the managers to agree on corporate priorities, and encourage them to work together to make everyone's life a little smoother. Now, the question is, just what should you do first?

FIG. 7.6. Description of category-combination measure with sample responses.

exemplars ($\bar{r} = .35, p$ .05), and new category-defining features ($\bar{r} = .24, p$ .05)—were positively related to the quality and originality of the solutions obtained from the criterion task. As might be expected, based on the size of these bivariate relationships, these three scales also yielded sizable multiple correlations when used to predict the quality and originality of criterion task solutions. A multiple correlation of .47 was obtained for criterion task solution quality, and the multiple correlation for solution originality was .44. More important, however, was the finding that the quality of new category-defining features produced the largest significant regression weight for both the quality of performance ($\beta = .87, p$ .05) and the originality of performance ($\beta = .83, p$ .05) on the criterion task. This finding is consistent with Finke, Ward, and Smith's (1992) observation that the quality of the new features emerging from people's combination and reorganization efforts represents an important determinant of creative performance.

Summary Findings

The results presented here show that, at least with complex problem-solving skills, it is possible to design alternative measures that can assess these skills. The low-fidelity, controlled simulation tasks we used to elicit these skills yield scores predicting overall performance on a complex, creative problem-solving task. Furthermore, the specific dimensional scores made unique contributions to performance that were consistent with other findings explaining how these skills contribute to performance. Thus, the tendency to attend to crucial facts and inconsistent observations during information encoding was related to the quality and originality of performance on the creative problem-solving task. Similarly, and according to Finke, Ward, and Smith's (1992) observations, we found that the quality of the new-category defining features emerging from people's combination and reorganization efforts were also effective predictors of performance on the creative problem-solving task.

These relationships, provide some important evidence for the construct validity of these measures. At this point, however, a new question that bears on the validity of these measures arises. Specifically, do these measures add anything to traditional measures of ability in predicting performance on the type of complex problem-solving tasks represented by the criterion problem-solving task?

To address this issue, we formed a summary scale for each of our four measures of problem-solving skills. To construct these aggregate scales, each content dimension included in a measure was assigned a weight based on the average regression weights obtained when these scales were used to predict solution quality and originality on the criterion-advertising task. These weighted dimensional scores were then used to formulate total scale scores for problem construction, information encoding, category selection, and category combination. The total scores obtained for each of these measures were then correlated with our reference measures of relevant abilities. In addition, scores for the quality and originality of solutions to the criterion task were correlated with, and regressed on, these total scores for the four skill measures, both before and after entering scores on the reference measures.

Table 7.6 presents the correlations among the four skill measures and their correlations with both the reference measures and our indices of performance on the criterion advertising task. As shown in the table, the four measures of problem-solving skills had weak, positive correlations among themselves ($\bar{r}$ = .19), with category combination producing most of the significant relationships ($\bar{r}$ = .21, p .05) with the other skill measures. More centrally, these measures were not apparently strongly related to our measures of relevant abilities. For example, verbal reasoning yielded positive correlations with only two scales: category combination (r = .20, p .05) and category selection (r = .22, p .05). Although divergent thinking produced a stronger pattern of relationships, with problem construction (r = .21, p .05), information encoding (r = .16, p .10), and category combination (r = .29, p .05) yielding significant relationships, these correlations were not of overwhelming power and yielded an average coefficient of .21. Similarly, for SAT scores, moderate but significant correlations were obtained for our measures of problem construction (r = .20, p .05) and category combination (r = .24, p .05). Course grades and keyboard skills, however, failed to yield significant relationships with these four measures of creative problem-solving skills.

The results obtained when performance on the criterion-advertising task was regressed on our measures of problem-solving skills and the reference measures are presented in Table 7.7. As shown in the table, the reference measures yielded multiple correlations of .46 and .47 when used to account for the quality and

TABLE 7.6
Correlation Among Skill and Ability Measures

	Problem Construct	Info. Encoding	Category Selection	Category Combin.	College GPA	Verbal Reasoning	Total SAT	Divergent Thinking
SKILLS								
Information encoding	.27**							
Category selection	.10	.12						
Category combination	.23**	.20**	.21**					
ABILITIES								
College GPA	−.00	.07	−.09	.00				
Verbal reasoning	.01	.12	.22**	.20**	.15*			
Total SAT	.20**	.17**	.13	.24**	.22**	.18**		
Divergent thinking	.21**	.16*	.16*	.29**	.14*	.28**	.30**	
Keyboard skills	−.04	−.09	.01	−.08	.01	−.02	−.07	.09

Note: * = p < .10: ** = p < .05.

TABLE 7.7

Overall Separate Regressions for Ability and Skill Measures

	Advertising Task Quality		Advertising Task Originality	
Measure	r	ß	r	ß
Ability Measures				
College GPA	.25**	.12	.21*	.05
Verbal reasoning	.40**	.13*	.39**	.17**
Total SAT	.25**	.11	.24**	.16*
Divergent thinking	.17*	.30**	.15	.29**
Keyboard skills	−.04	−.05	−.03	−.04
MULTIPLE CORRELATION		.46**		.47**
Skill Measures				
Problem construction	.30**	.18**	.29**	.15
Information encoding	.28**	.18**	.29**	.18**
Category selection	.21**	.14*	.25**	.17**
Category combination	.28**	.16*	.32**	.19**
MULTIPLE CORRELATION		.42**		.45**

Note: * = p < .10; ** = p < .05.

originality of solutions to the criterion task, with divergent thinking ($\overline{\beta}$ = .30, $\overline{p}$ .05) and verbal reasoning ($\overline{\beta}$ = .15, $\overline{p}$ .10) yielding the largest regression weights. The multiple correlations obtained when the four measures of problem-solving skills were used to predict criterion task–solution quality and originality were .42 and .45. This finding suggests that this set of four measures produced results comparable to those obtained from more traditional ability measures. Here, the information encoding ($\overline{\beta}$ = .18, $\overline{p}$ .05) and category combination ($\overline{\beta}$ = .18, $\overline{p}$ .05) measures produced the largest significant regression weights, although marginally significant regression weights were also obtained for problem construction ($\overline{\beta}$ = .17, $\overline{p}$ .10) and category selection ($\overline{\beta}$ = .16, $\overline{p}$ .10).

Taken as a whole, these findings show that, separately, both the ability measures and our measures of problem-solving skills were effective predictors of performance on the criterion task. Thus, the question that arises at this juncture is whether our measures of problem-solving skills added something to more traditional measures of task-relevant abilities. The results obtained in this analysis are presented in Table 7.8. When our measures of problem-solving skills were added to the ability measures, the multiple correlation for solution quality increased from .46 to .54. This change was significant at the .05 level, with problem construction yielding the largest significant regression weight (ß =

.16, p .05) among the measures of creative problem-solving skills. For solution originality, a significant increase (p .05) in the multiple correlation was again obtained with addition of the problem-solving skills measures. Here, the multiple correlation increased 8 points, with category selection (ß = .14, p .10) yielding the largest regression weight.

The findings obtained in these regression analyses are noteworthy for two reasons: First, it appears that our measures of creative problem-solving skills are effective predictors of performance on complex problem-solving tasks. Second, these measures appear to capture performance-relevant attributes beyond basic abilities. Thus, it seems plausible to conclude that the type of integrative approach to skill assessment on which we based the development of these measures does not simply represent an alternative framework for measuring traditional basic abilities.

TABLE 7.8

Overall Hierarchical Regressions for Ability and Skill Measures

Measures	Advertising Task Quality		Advertising Task Originality	
	r	ß	r	ß
Block 1				
College GPA	.25**	.12	.21*	.05
Verbal reasoning	.40**	.13*	.39**	.17**
Total SAT	.25**	.11	.24**	.16*
Divergent thinking	.17*	.30**	.15	.29**
Keyboard skills	−.04	−.05	−.03	−.04
MULTIPLE CORRELATION		.46**		.47**
Block 2				
College GPA	.25**	.16**	.21*	.09
Verbal reasoning	.40**	.09	.39**	.12
Total SAT	.25**	.05	.24**	.09
Divergent thinking	.17*	.22**	.15	.21**
Keyboard skills	−.04	−.04	−.03	−.03
Problem construction	.25**	.16**	.21*	.12
Information encoding	.40**	.11	.39**	.12
Category selection	.25**	−.12	.24**	.14*
Category combination	.17*	.08	.15	.10
MULTIPLE CORRELATION		.54**		.55**

Note: * = $p < .10$; ** = $p < .05$.

CONCLUSIONS

Before turning to the broader implications of our findings, certain limitations inherent in the present study should be noted. First, the results obtained in this effort were based on an undergraduate sample. Thus, some caution must be exercised in extrapolating our findings to occupational samples. Next, it should be recognized that the present study examined the predictive validity of these measures only with respect to a single criterion measure. As a result, it is quite possible that different results would be obtained if other criteria had been employed. Finally, it should be recognized that although we used a criterion measure expressly intended to call for complex, realistic performance, it cannot be assumed that this criterion fully reflects the complexity of many real-world performances.

Even bearing these cautionary notes in mind, we believe that the present study has several significant implications for the design of a new generation of measures. For some time, many psychologists have thought that traditional standardized tests do not provide an adequate basis for assessing complex performance skills (Baker, O'Neil, & Linn, 1993; Halpern, 1994; Perkins, Jay, & Tishman, 1994; Resnick & Resnick, 1992). Without an alternative to traditional measures, which may not be appropriate for use in the assessment of complex skills, the tendency has been to try to obtain direct samples of behavior or performance in the targeted domain. This task has typically been accomplished by using open-ended tasks drawn from the performance domain under consideration (Baker, O'Neil, & Linn, 1993).

Although this direct sampling approach to assessment suffers from several problems, including the cost of scoring, the complexity of exercises, and ambiguities about the meaning of judges' ratings (Dreher & Sackett, 1981; Klimoski, 1993), the central problem inherent in direct sampling is more subtle. Ultimately, all measurement is concerned with establishing the meaningfulness of the inferences drawn from a set of observations (Messick, 1989). Evidence bearing on the meaningfulness of a measure is generally provided by specifying the constructs to be measured by a test. Thus it must be established that the inferences implied by these constructs are justifiable (Cronbach, 1990; Landy, 1986). In most performance-assessment systems, the concern is with the measurement of some set of complex skills. The complex, integrated real-world performance tasks that comprise these assessment systems, however, may allow people to apply a variety of skills or aptitudes (Feltovich, Spiro, & Coulson, 1993; Sternberg, 1986). Thus, it cannot be assumed that scores on given performance-assessment exercises reflect the application of particular skills, any more than it can be assumed in measurement that random draws from an overly broad, poorly defined domain adequately represent specific relevant constructs.

The present effort represents an initial attempt to develop a construct-based framework for assessing complex skills. This framework is based on three propositions: First, a series of low-fidelity tasks can be used in skill assessment, if these tasks elicit the requisite skills. Second, response options that allow for simple, accurate, and objective scoring of performance focusing explicitly on expression of the skill of interest can be devised for these tasks. Third, responses can be scored on an absolute scale if they have been structured to elicit key components of a given skill.

The results obtained in the present study appear to provide some support for these three propositions. We designed tasks expressly intended to elicit certain problem-solving skills thought to influence creative thought, including problem construction, information encoding, category selection, and category combination and reorganization (Mumford, Mobley, Uhlman, Reiter-Palmon, & Doares, 1991). Subsequently, responses to these tasks were developed and scored with the expressed intent of assessing various components of skilled performance, but on an absolute, rather than a relative, scale. The resulting measures combine aspects of several types of constructed response test formats identified by Snow (1993).

We found that these measures examining components of the four skills that we targeted yielded an interpretable pattern of relation with performance on a complex, creative, problem-solving task. Thus, according to the observations of Davidson and Sternberg (1984) and Kuhn (1970), time spent encoding crucial factual information and the time spent encoding inconsistent information were related to the production of high-quality, original solutions on the creative problem-solving task. Similarly, we obtained results consistent with Finke, Ward, and Smith's (1992) observations of the importance of emergent features in generating creative products in combination and reorganization efforts. Specifically, we found that the index representing the quality of new category-defining features from the combination and reorganization task yielded strong positive relations with the production of high-quality, original solutions on the creative problem-solving task.

These findings provide some important evidence for the construct validity, or substantive meaningfulness, of the scale scores formulated using this construct-based approach. More compelling and perhaps less ambiguous evidence for the meaningfulness of the assessment measures constructed with this construct-based approach may be found in the relation between these scales and our measures of performance on the creative problem-solving task. The scales derived from the four skill measures not only yielded sizable multiple correlations with task performance, but they also added to the prediction obtained from traditional ability tests and displayed a pattern of correlations with traditional ability tests, which would be expected of measures intended to capture creative thinking skills.

Other validation evidence could be, and should be, provided for these measures of creative problem-solving skills. Nonetheless, the evidence now available does suggest that a construct-based approach to skill assessment can yield valid measures. This validation evidence, however, is not the only argument for applying a construct-oriented approach in the development of performance assessment measures.

One potential advantage of a construct-based approach was illustrated by the problem-construction, information-encoding, and category-selection measures. These measures, although apparently assessing relevant problem-solving skills, were not scored by using open-ended responses. Instead, by identifying component attributes involved in the application of a given skill, it proved possible to develop objective scoring systems for these measures. In encoding, for example, we assessed the relative time spent working with different types of information, and in problem construction we assessed preferences for using certain types of representational content. The development of objective, construct-based scoring systems for skill assessment is very important for two reasons. First, the availability of objective scoring procedures reduces the cost of assessment. Second, such objective scoring procedures are not subject to the rater–error problems that plague so many assessment efforts (Dreher & Sackett, 1981; Klimoski & Brickner, 1987).

It may not always be possible to formulate objective scoring systems for targeted skills assessment. In the present study, a case in point may be in the category–combination measure, where the nature of the skill dictated use of an open-ended response format. Even here, however, structuring the task and the requisite responses allowed many responses to be gathered. Further, the structured nature of these responses, with the availability of multiple responses, apparently contributed to more accurate and valid scoring.

Our observations about the combination and reorganization measure point to another important characteristic of this construct-based approach to skill assessment. By focusing on the assessment of skills per se, rather than on broad, overt manifestations of these skills in real-world performance, we could develop low-fidelity tasks capable of assessing these skills (Motowidlo, Dunnette, & Carter, 1990). The use of simplified skill-assessment tasks allows a great deal of descriptive information to be collected in a given time and contributes to the accuracy of skill measurement. It might be argued that these low-fidelity tasks do not capture some crucial aspects of performance, but the results we obtained for the prediction of performance on the criterion task show that low-fidelity measures may be highly effective predictors of performance on complex tasks, at least when similar skills are called for.

Another potential advantage of a construct-based approach pertains to its role in theory development. Most performance-assessment efforts are focused on a particular content domain. Accordingly, content overlap is often the only validation evidence of the meaningfulness of an assessment system. By using underlying skills as a basis for the design of assessment measures, however, it becomes possible to accrue compelling evidence for the validity of these measures that use the theory-based hypothesis-testing framework that has provided the basis for so many advantages in traditional measurement (Landy, 1986; Messick, 1989). Moreover, developing measures like these may make a contribution to theory development: A noteworthy pattern of findings in this study shows that the use of high-quality material, particularly in problem construction and information encoding, may be more important to creative thought than the use of highly original material. Although this finding contradicts some traditional wisdom (Lindzey, Hall, & Thompson, 1978), it is consistent with the difficult, demanding nature of the combination and reorganization process and the need for viable, high-quality material in people's combination and reorganization efforts (Carlsson & Gorman, 1992; Mobley, Doares, & Mumford, 1992).

Not only might a construct-based approach to skill assessment contribute to progressive refinement of theories and measures, it might also provide a general framework for the development of assessment systems. By virtue of their domain specificity and the complexity of the exercises they employ, it is difficult to apply assessment systems developed in one setting to other settings. Assessment systems, however, that focus on general skills and that assess these skills by using general tasks intended to elicit the skills, may evidence transportability across settings where these same skills are called for and may reduce the substantial development costs entailed in most performance assessment efforts.

Many argue for the need for assessment might object to this construct-oriented approach precisely because it does not stress the need for domain specificity. Often, particularly with certain domain-specific skills, it may not be possible to transport skill measures; but in cases where similar skills are involved in performance, it may prove possible to translate general skill-assessment formats into the language of the specific, targeted domain. This point is nicely illustrated in the Owens (1969) study cited earlier. There, a version of the general combination and reorganization tasks suited to engineers was developed by using mechanical parts and principles rather than standard taxonomic categories, such as birds and sporting equipment.

These observations bring us to our parting comment. Not so long ago, Landy (1986) performed an important service by reminding us that educational and psychological testing can progress as a science only by attending to constructs and general theories. While few would hold that skill constructs should be measured in the same way as ability constructs, skills nonetheless represent constructs. Until the field starts to apply construct-based approaches in skill assessment, it is difficult to see how performance assessment will move past stamp collecting and emerge as a true science. We hope that the present effort furthers the cause of performance assessment as a true branch of psychometrics by showing how it might be possible to develop construct-based skill-assessment systems.

ACKNOWLEDGMENTS

We would like to thank Stephen Zaccaro, T. Owen Jacobs, Steven Stewart, K. Victoria Threlfall, and David P. Costanza for their contributions to the present effort. Parts of this research were sponsored by a series of Small Business Innovation Research (SBIR) contracts (MDA903-92-C-0094 and MDA903-93-C-0081) from the United States Army Research Institute for Behavioral and Social Sciences to Management Research Institute, Bethesda, Maryland, Michael D. Mumford and Edwin A. Fleishman, Principal Investigators. Correspondence about this chapter should be addressed to Dr. Michael D. Mumford, American Institutes for Research, 3333 K Street, N.W., Washington, DC 20007.

REFERENCES

Alissa, I. (1972). Stimulus generalization and over-inclusion in normal and schizophrenic subjects. *Journal of Clinical Psychology, 34*, 182–186.

Anastasi, A. (1976). *Psychological testing.* New York: Macmillan.

Assmann, D. C., Hixon, S. H., & Kacmarek, R. M. (1979). *Clinical simulations for respiratory care workers.* Chicago: Year Book Medical Publishers.

Baer, J. M. (1988). Long-term effects of creativity training with middle-school students. *Journal of Early Adolescence, 8*, 183–193.

Baker, E. L., O'Neil, H. F., & Linn, R. L. (1993). Policy and validity prospects for performance-based assessment. *American Psychologist, 48*, 1210–1218.

Baughman, W. A., & Mumford, M. D. (1995). Process analytic models of creative capacities: Operations influencing the combination and reorganization process. *Creativity Research Journal, 8*, 73–98.

Bray, D. G., Campbell, R. N., & Grant, D. L. (1974). *The formative years in business: An AT&T study of managerial lives.* New York: Wiley.

Byham, W. C. (1980). Starting an assessment center the right way. *Personnel Administrator, 3*, 27–32.

Carlsson, W. B., & Gorman, M. E. (1992). A cognitive framework to understand technological creativity: Bell, Edison, and the telephone. In R. J. Weber & D. N. Perkins (Eds.), *Inventive minds: Creativity in technology* (pp. 48–79). New York: Oxford University Press.

Carroll, J. B. (1993a). *Human cognitive abilities.* New York: Cambridge University Press.

Carroll, J. B. (1993b). Test theory and the behavioral scaling of test performance. In N. Frederiksen, R. J. Mislevy, & I. I. Bejar (Eds.), *Test theory for a new generation of tests* (pp. 297–322). Hillsdale, NJ: Lawrence Erlbaum Associates.

Cole, N. S., & Moss, P. A. (1989). Bias in test use. In R. L. Linn (Ed.), *Educational measurement* (pp. 201–220). New York: Macmillan.

Cronbach, L. J. (1990). *The essentials of psychological testing.* New York: HarperCollins.

Davidson, J. E., & Sternberg, R. J. (1984). The role of insight in intellectual giftedness. *Gifted Child Quarterly, 28*, 58–64.

Dreher, G. F., & Sackett, P. R. (1981). Some problems in applying content validity evidence to assessment center procedures. *Academy of Management Review, 6*, 551–560.

Fallows, D. N. (1980). Tests: The best and the brightest. *Atlantic Monthly, 153*, 21–22.

Feltovich, P. J., Spiro, R. J., & Coulson, R. L. (1993). Learning, teaching, and testing for complex understanding. In N. Frederiksen, R. J. Mislevy, & I. I. Bejar (Eds.), *Test theory for a new generation of tests.* Hillsdale, NJ: Lawrence Erlbaum Associates.

Finke, R. A., Ward, T. B., & Smith, S. M. (1992). *Creative cognition: Theory, research, applications.* Cambridge, MA: MIT Press.

Fleishman, E. A., & Reilly, M. E. (1992). *Handbook of human abilities: Definitions, measurements, and job task requirements.* Palo Alto, CA: Consulting Psychologists Press.

Frederiksen, J. R. (1982). A componential theory of reading skills and their interactions. In R. J. Sternberg (Ed.), *Advances in the psychology of human intelligence* (pp. 125–180). Hillsdale, NJ: Lawrence Erlbaum Associates.

Frederiksen, J. R., Warren, B. M., & Rosenberg, R. S. (1985). A componential approach to training reading skills: Part I. Perceptual units. *Cognition and Instruction, 2,* 91–130.

Gardner, H. (1983). *Frames of mind: The theory of multiple intelligences.* New York: Basic Books.

Gardner, H. (1993). *Multiple intelligences: The theory in practice.* New York: Basic Books.

Gaugler, B. B., Rosenthal, D. B., Thorton, G. C., & Benston, C. (1987). Meta-analysis of assessment center validity. *Journal of Applied Psychology, 72,* 493–571.

Getzels, J. W., & Csikszentmihalyi, M. (1976). *The creative vision: A longitudinal study of problem finding in art.* New York: Wiley.

Ghiselli, E. E., Campbell, J. P., & Zedeck, S. (1981). *Measurement theory for the behavioral sciences.* New York: Freeman.

Gick, M. L., & Holyoak, K. J. (1983). Schema induction and analogical transfer. *Cognitive Psychology, 15,* 1–38.

Gitomer, D. H., & Rock, D. (1993). Addressing process variables in test analysis. In N. Frederiksen, R. J. Mislevy, & I. I. Bejar (Eds.), *Test theory for a new generation of tests* (pp. 243–268). Hillsdale, NJ: Lawrence Erlbaum Associates.

Glaser, R. (1963). Instructional technology and the measurement of learning outcomes. *American Psychologist, 18,* 519–521.

Guilford, J. P. (1950). Creativity. *American Psychologist, 14,* 469–479.

Guilford, J. P. (1954). *Psychometric methods* (2nd ed.). New York: McGraw-Hill.

Guilford, J. P., & Hoepfner, R. (1966). *Structure of intellect factors and their tests.* Los Angeles: Psychological Laboratory, University of Southern California.

Halpern, D. F. (1994). *A national assessment of critical thinking skills in adults: Taking steps towards the goal.* Washington, DC: National Center for Educational Statistics.

Hayes, J. R., & Flower, L. S. (1986). Writing research and the writer. *American Psychologist, 41,* 1106–1113.

Hennessey, B. A., & Amabile, T. M. (1988). The conditions of creativity. In R. J. Sternberg (Ed.), *The nature of creativity* (pp. 11–42). New York: Cambridge University Press.

Hogarth, R. M. (1986). *Decision making.* New York: Wiley.

Holyoak, K. J. (1984). Mental models in problem solving. In J. R. Anderson & S. M. Kosslyn (Eds.), *Tutorials in learning and memory* (pp. 193–218). New York: Freeman.

Hoover, S. M., & Feldhusen, J. F. (1990). The scientific hypothesis formulation ability of gifted ninth-grade students. *Journal of Educational Psychology, 82,* 838–848.

Horn, J. L. (1976). Human abilities: A review of research and theory in the early 1970s. *Annual Review of Psychology, 27,* 312–341.

Hough, L. M. (1984). Development and evaluation of the "accomplishment record" method of selecting and promoting professionals. *Journal of Applied Psychology, 69,* 135–146.

Ivancevich, T. M. (1976). Predicting job performance by the use of ability tests and studying job satisfaction as a moderator variable. *Journal of Vocational Behavior, 9,* 87–97.

Jensen, A. R. (1980). *Bias in mental testing.* New York: Free Press.

Khandwalla, P. N. (1993). An exploratory investigation of divergent thinking through protocol analysis. *Creativity Research Journal, 6,* 241–260.

Klimoski, R. J. (1993). Predictor constructs and theory measurement. In N. Schmitt & W. C. Borman (Eds.), *Personnel selection in organizations* (pp. 99–134). San Francisco: Jossey-Bass.

Klimoski, R. J., & Brickner, M. (1987). Why do assessment centers work? Puzzle of assessment center validity. *Personnel Psychology, 40*, 243–260.

Koestler, A. (1964). *The act of creation.* New York: Macmillan.

Kuhn, T. S. (1970). *The structure of scientific revolutions.* Chicago: University of Chicago Press.

Kulkarni, D., & Simon, H. A. (1988). The process of scientific discovery: The strategy of experimentation. *Cognitive Science, 12*, 139–175.

Landy, F. J. (1986). Stamp collecting versus science: Validation as hypothesis testing. *American Psychologist, 41*, 1183–1192.

Lindzey, G., Hall, C. S., & Thompson, R. F. (1978). *Creative thinking and critical thinking.* New York: Worth.

Lohman, D. F., & Ippel, M. J., (1993). Cognitive diagnosis: From statistically-based assessment toward theory-based assessment. In N. Frederiksen, R. J. Mislevy, & I. I. Bejar (Eds.), *Test theory for a new generation of tests* (pp. 41–71). Hillsdale, NJ: Lawrence Erlbaum Associates.

McClelland, D. C. (1994). The knowledge-testing–educational complex strikes back. *American Psychologist, 49*, 66–69.

McDaniel, M. A., Whetzel, D. L., Schmidt, F. L., & Maurer, S. D. (1994). The validity of employment interviews: A comprehensive review and meta-analysis. *Journal of Applied Psychology, 79*, 599–616.

Mednick, S. A., & Mednick, M. T. (1967). *Examiners' manual: Remote Associations Test.* Boston: Houghton-Mifflin.

Merrifield, P. R., Guilford, J. P., Christensen, P. R., & Frick, J. W. (1962). The role of intellectual factors in problem solving. *Psychological Monographs, 76*, 1–21.

Messick, S. (1989). Validity. In R. L. Linn (Ed.), *Educational measurement* (pp. 13–104). New York: Macmillan.

Mislevy, R. J. (1993). Foundations of a new test theory. In N. Frederiksen, R. J. Mislevy, & I. I. Bejar (Eds.), *Test theory for a new generation of tests.* Hillsdale, NJ: Lawrence Erlbaum Associates.

Mobley, M. I., Doares, L., & Mumford, M. D. (1992). Process analytic models of creative capacities: Evidence for the combination and reorganization process. *Creativity Research Journal, 5*, 125–156.

Motowidlo, S. J., Dunnette, M. D., & Carter, G. W. (1990). An alternative selection procedure: The low-fidelity simulation. *Journal of Applied Psychology, 75*, 640–647.

Mumford, M. D., Baughman, W. A., Supinski, E. P., Costanza, D. P., & Threlfall, K. V. (1994). *Cognitive and metacognitive skill development: Alternative measures for predicting leadership potential* (Tech. Rep. MRI 93-2). Bethesda, MD: Management Research Institute.

Mumford, M. D., & Connelly, M. S. (1993). Cases of invention: A review of Weber and Perkins' *Inventive minds: Creativity in technology. Contemporary Psychology, 38*, 1210–1217.

Mumford, M. D., Mobley, M. I., Uhlman, C. E., Reiter-Palmon, R., & Doares, L. (1991). Process analytic models of creative capacities. *Creativity Research Journal, 4*, 91–122.

Mumford, M. D., Reiter-Palmon, R., & Redmond, M. R. (1994). Problem construction and cognition: Applying problem representations in ill-defined domains. In M. A. Runco (Ed.), *Problem finding, problem solving, and creativity* (pp. 3–39). Norwood, NJ: Ablex.

Mumford, M. D., Stokes, G. S., & Owens, W. A. (1990). *Patterns of life history: The ecology of human individuality.* Hillsdale, NJ: Lawrence Erlbaum Associates.

Novick, L. R. (1990). Representational transfer in problem solving. *Psychological Science, 1*, 128–132.

Nunnally, J. C. (1978). *Psychometric theory.* New York: McGraw-Hill.

Okuda, S. M., Runco, M. A., & Berger, D. E. (1991). Creativity and the finding and solving of real-world problems. *Journal of Psychoeducational Assessment, 9*, 45–53.

Owens, W. A. (1969). Cognitive, noncognitive, and environmental correlates of mechanical ingenuity. *Journal of Applied Psychology, 53*, 199–208.

Perkins, D. N. (1992). The topography of invention. In R. J. Weber & D. N. Perkins (Eds.), *Inventive minds: Creativity in technology* (pp. 238–250). New York: Oxford University Press.

Perkins, D. P., Jay, E., & Tishman, S. (1994). *Assessing thinking: A framework for measuring critical thinking and problem solving skills at the college level.* Washington, DC: National Center for Educational Statistics.

Poincaré, H. (1952). *Science and method.* New York: Dover.

Redmond, M. R., Mumford, M. D., & Teach, R. J. (1993). Putting creativity to work: Leader influences on subordinate creativity. *Organizational Behavior and Human Decision Processes, 55,* 120–151.

Ree, M. J., Earles, J. A., & Teachout, M. S. (1994). Predicting job performance: Not much more than G. *Journal of Applied Psychology, 79,* 518–524.

Reeves, L. M., & Weisburg, R. W. (1994). The role of content and construct information in analogical transfer. *Psychological Bulletin, 115,* 381–401.

Reilly, R. R. S., Henry, S., & Smither, J. W. (1990). An examination of the effects of using behavior checklists on the construct validity of assessment center dimensions. *Personnel Psychology, 43,* 71–84.

Resnick, L. B., & Resnick, D. P. (1992). Assessing the thinking curriculum: New tools for educational reform. In B. R. Gifford & M. C. O'Connor (Eds.), *Changing assessments: Alternative views of aptitude, achievement, and instruction* (pp. 37–75). Boston: Kluwer.

Rothenberg, A. (1986). Artistic creation as simulated by superimposed versus combined-composite visual images. *Journal of Personality and Social Psychology, 50,* 370–381.

Rothenberg, A., & Sobel, R. S. (1980). Creation of literary metaphors as simulated by superimposed versus separated visual images. *Journal of Mental Imagery, 4,* 77–91.

Royer, J. M., Cisero, C. A., & Carlo, M. S. (1993). Techniques and procedures for assessing cognitive skills. *Review of Educational Research, 63,* 201–243.

Ruch, F. L., & Ruch, W. W. (1980). *Employees Aptitude Survey.* Los Angeles: Psychological Services.

Runco, M. A. (1991). The evaluative, valuative, and divergent thinking of children. *Journal of Creative Behavior, 25,* 311–314.

Russell, C. J. (1987). Person characteristics versus role conservancy explanations for assessment center ratings. *Academy of Management Journal, 30,* 817–826.

Russell, C. J., & Kuhnert, K. M. (1992). New frontiers in management selection systems: Where measurement technologies and theory collide. *Leadership Quarterly, 3,* 109–136.

Sackett, P. R. (1982). A critical look at some common beliefs about assessment centers. *Public Personnel Management, 11,* 140–146.

Sackett, P. R. (1987). Assessment centers and content validity. *Personnel Psychology, 40,* 13–25.

Sackett, P. R., & Hakel, M. D. (1979). Temporal stability and individual differences in using assessment information to form overall ratings. *Organizational Behavior and Human Performance, 23,* 120–137.

Schmidt, F. L., & Hunter, J. E. (1993). Tacit knowledge, practical intelligence, general mental ability, and job knowledge. *Current Directions in Psychological Science, 2,* 8–9.

Schmitt, N. (1977). Interrater agreement in dimensionality and combination of assessment center judgments. *Organizational Behavior and Human Performance, 23,* 120–137.

Schmitt, N., & Hill, T. E. (1977). Sex and race composition of assessment center groups as a determinant of peer and assessor ratings. *Journal of Applied Psychology, 62,* 261–264.

Schmitt, N., & Landy, F. J. (1993). The concept of validity. In N. Schmitt & W. C. Borman (Eds.), *Personnel selection in organizations* (pp. 275–309). San Francisco: Jossey-Bass.

Schneider, J. R., & Schmitt, N. (1992). An exercise design approach to understanding assessment center dimension and exercise constructs. *Journal of Applied Psychology, 77,* 32–41.

Shore, T. H., Shore, L. A., & Thorton, G. C. (1992). Construct validity of self- and peer evaluations of performance dimensions in an assessment center. *Journal of Applied Psychology, 77,* 42–54.

Shorris, E. A. (1981). *The oppressed middle: The politics of middle management.* New York: Anchor Press.

Simonton, D. K. (1988). Age and outstanding achievement: What do we know after a century of research? *Psychological Bulletin, 104,* 251–267.

Sizer, T. R. (1986). Changing schools and testing: An uneasy proposal. *Proceedings of the 1985 ETS Invitational Conference* (pp. 1–7). Princeton, NJ: Educational Testing Service.

Snow, R. E. (1993). Construct validity and constructed-response tests. In R. E. Bennett & W. C. Ward (Eds.), *Construction versus choice in cognitive measurement: Issues in constructed response, performance testing, and portfolio assessment* (pp. 45–60). Hillsdale, NJ: Lawrence Erlbaum Associates.

Snow, R. E., & Lohman, D. R. (1984). Toward a theory of cognitive aptitude from learning from instruction. *Journal of Educational Psychology, 76,* 347–376.

Snow, R. E., & Lohman, D. F. (1989). Implications of cognitive psychology for educational measurement. In R. L. Linn (Ed.), *Educational measurement* (pp. 263–332). New York: Macmillan.

Snow, R. E., & Lohman, D. F. (1993). Cognitive psychology, new test design, and new test theory: An introduction. In N. Frederiksen, R. J. Mislevy, and I. I. Bejar (Eds.), *Test theory for a new generation of tests* (pp. 1–18). Hillsdale, NJ: Lawrence Erlbaum Associates.

Sobel, R. S., & Rothenberg, A. (1980). Artistic creation assimilated by superimposed versus separated visual images. *Journal of Personality and Social Psychology, 39,* 953–961.

Spearman, C. (1913). Correlations of sums and differences. *British Journal of Psychology, 5,* 417–426.

Stanley, J. C. (1971). Reliability. In R. L. Thorndike (Ed.), *Educational measurement* (pp. 356–442). Washington, DC: American Council on Education.

Sternberg, R. J. (1986). Toward a unified theory of human reasoning. *Intelligence, 10,* 381–414.

Tenopyr, M. (1969). The comparative validity of selected leadership scales relative to success in production management. *Personnel Psychology, 22,* 77–85.

Thorton, G. C., & Byham, W. C. (1982). *Assessment centers and managerial performance.* New York: Academic Press.

Thurstone, L. L. (1938). Primary mental abilities. *Psychology Monographs, 1,* 1–66.

Tyler, L. E. (1965). *The psychology of human differences.* Englewood Cliffs, NJ: Prentice-Hall.

Wilson, S. M., & Wineburg, S. S. (1993). Wrinkles in time and place: Using performance assessments to understand the knowledge of history teachers. *American Educational Research Journal, 30,* 729–769.

8

Performance Assessment in Education and Professional Certification: Lessons for Personnel Selection?

Paul R. Sackett
University of Minnesota

Educational testing and testing for professional certification are areas in which considerable attention is being paid to the question of alternatives to traditional testing (paper-and-pencil testing, primarily of the multiple-choice variety). There has been a ground swell of support in recent years for the use of *authentic assessments*, with traditional testing increasingly viewed as an impediment to both accurate assessment and to educational reform. I write this chapter as an industrial/organizational (I/O) psychologist who has had the opportunity to come in close contact with the areas of educational testing and professional certification as a result of several large scale projects over the last few years. The two most significant of these projects involve an evaluation of the examination process for admitting new attorneys to the bar (Millman, Mehrens, & Sackett, 1993) and an ongoing project under the auspices of the National Board for Professional Teaching Standards (NBPTS) to develop assessment systems for the identification of highly accomplished teachers. This chapter provides an overview of the performance assessment movement; discusses assertions that performance assessment requires a rethinking of traditional concepts of reliability and validity; explores the notion that performance assessment reduces, if not eliminates, subgroup differences; investigates practical impediments to the implementation of performance assessments, such as concerns about collaboration and about cost; and analyzes the implications of these issues for personnel selection.

AN OVERVIEW OF PERFORMANCE ASSESSMENT

A voluminous literature has developed on performance assessment, authentic assessment, portfolio assessment, and other such terms. Readers interested in these issues can consult sources such as Hambleton and Murphy (1992), Linn, Baker, and Dunbar (1991), Mehrens (1992), Meyer (1992), and Worthen (1993).

Several terms used in the field of educational measurement lack consensus about precise meanings. *Performance assessment, authentic assessment*, and *portfolio assessment* are sometimes used interchangeably; at other times distinctions are made. With the caveat that terms can be used differently, I attempt to make meaningful distinctions between these concepts. *Performance assessment* is a generic term, referring to an assessment characterized by a relatively unconstrained response mode and by placing respondents in a meaningful context. In essence, examinees engage in performances that could conceivably occur outside an assessment setting. The concept of performance assessment closely parallels an I/O psychologist's familiar notion of a work sample test: What is observed is a sample of the criterion behavior of interest or at least a relatively high-fidelity simulation of this behavior. Writing an essay, rather than responding to multiple-choice questions about rules of grammar, is a performance assessment, as is performing a piece of music, delivering a speech, and using mathematical tools to address a complex real-world problem. More precisely, such behaviors become performance assessments when attempts are made to evaluate the behavior for some purpose.

The distinction is not perfectly clean. At the extremes, it is easy to give examples of what is a performance assessment (unconstrained behavior in a realistic context, e. g., writing a short story on a self-chosen topic) and what is not (decontextualized constrained behavior, e. g., being told to spell words correctly as an instructor reads them orally). As more constraints are placed on behavior, the distinction blurs (e. g., being assigned to write a paragraph on each of five topics assigned by a teacher imposes some response constraints on examinees, but certainly far less than in the case of a multiple-choice test). This distinction parallels the debates in I/O psychology as to the settings in which content validity can serve as the basis for inferences of job relatedness.

The term *authentic assessment* is more ambiguous in its meaning and much more emotionally loaded. Various criteria may be specified for an assessment to qualify as authentic. For some, the criteria parallel those just outlined as the key characteristics of performance assessment, namely, unconstrained response format and the embedding of performance in a meaningful context. For others, authenticity imposes additional requirements. One is the removal of constraints not only from the response format, but also from the stimulus requirements. For example, to assess writing skills, it is not enough to move from a multiple-choice test of rules of grammar, spelling, and punctuation to a format in which students are asked to produce writing samples meeting various specifications. The imposition of specifications as to topic, length, style, and the like detracts from the authenticity of the assessment. It can be hypothesized that students who are not motivated by the required topic or format do not reveal their true skill level. Authentic assessments allow students to choose the mode in which their writing skills are manifested.

Closely related is another characteristic posited by some as required for authentic assessment, namely, allowing students rather than teachers or the instructional system to choose when to perform. The observation that a student performs poorly when told "In the next 45 minutes write three paragraphs about the person you admire most" confounds writing ability with motivation to perform on demand.

One final posited requirement for authentic assessment is that evaluation requires knowledge of examinees' life circumstances and performance histories. In the context of student performance assessment, teachers play an important role in evaluation. For example, a third party brought in to evaluate a written student performance may miss subtleties that are very evident to the teacher who has worked with the student over an extended time. Although the third party's evaluation may be overly dominated by some idiosyncratic errors on the part of the student, the teacher may be better able to see past these errors and to recognize other meritorious aspects of the student's performance.

Thus at the extreme the requirements for authentic assessment are quite demanding and would require a radical departure from not only traditional modes of educational assessment but also from many forms of performance assessment. Performance on demand, standardized stimulus material, and evaluation by neutral third parties are common characteristics of traditional approaches to measurement, which are challenged by concepts of authentic assessment.

It is important to note some philosophical undercurrents in these testing characteristics. The term *authentic assessment* is a label carefully chosen for its provocativeness. The label itself casts traditional forms of assessment as *nonauthentic*. Advocates of authentic assessment commonly view traditional testing as a major cause of the perceived problems with the U.S. educational system. Teaching to the test, emphasis on rote learning, and destroying motivation by decontextualizing learning are among the problems asserted to be caused by traditional testing. An additional undercurrent is that traditional testing may give a distorted picture of learning in the United States. The hypothesis is that U. S. students are not really learning less than desired; rather, the assessment methods used do not detect true learning. This idea is also extended to the commonly observed ethnic differences in test performance. The differences are posited to be a mirage caused by traditional testing methods that are incompatible with the needs of students not part of White middle-class culture. Thus not only is authentic assessment said to produce better evaluation of students, but it also is thought to reveal a very different picture of the degree of learning occurring in U. S. schools, of the U. S. students' level of achievement, and of the differences in achievement among subgroups.

The final term for discussion here is *portfolio assessment*. As the name implies, this process involves the collection by examinees of a set of performance products, which are then submitted for evaluation. Portfolio assessment is a subset of performance assessment and emphasizes some of the features of authentic assessment, namely, examinees' freedom to select work products produced over time. Portfolio assessment systems differ in the degree to which they constrain the content: A writing assessment system that asks students to include a poem, an essay, and a short story offers less flexibility than one that invites students to include whatever work products they wish.

These concepts of performance assessment, authentic assessment, and portfolio assessment contain some elements quite familiar to I/O psychologists as well as some that are startlingly different. The basic notion of performance assessment is well known; where conceptually and pragmatically feasible, I/O psychologists would probably prefer work sample tests to paper and pencil measures of the same constructs. More jarring is the idea that performance on demand renders an assessment *nonauthentic*: performance on demand is a characteristic of virtually all selection devices in the repertoire, except for forms of life history data such as application blanks or accomplishment records that candidates complete on their own time. I/O psychologists do not share authentic assessment advocates' concerns about performance on demand, perhaps because psychologists implicitly assume that job candidates are, in fact, motivated to perform well. I/O psychologists might not express much sympathy if told that an applicant did not do well on a selection procedure because the applicant "didn't feel like trying today." They might observe that on the job there is little opportunity to selectively decide when and when not to perform. It must be acknowledged, however, that when trying to describe an examinee's standing on a characteristic of interest, variations in the motivation to perform well constitute a source of bias in the measure of this characteristic.

NEW VIEWS OF RELIABILITY AND VALIDITY?

In the performance assessment movement, various efforts have been aimed to reconceptualize the concepts and roles of reliability and validity. Because these concepts are traditionally seen as central to sound assessment practice, challenges to traditional views can cause considerable controversy. In this section, two developments are discussed. First, a recent paper by Moss (1994) is entitled

"Can There Be Validity Without Reliability" a question that the psychometric community is likely to view as unnecessary to address in light of decades of well-developed psychometric theory. That Moss's answer to the question was "Yes" has raised many eyebrows. I review and respond to Moss's position. Second, a new concept under the rubric of consequential validity is receiving considerable attention in the educational community; I also review and comment on this concept.

Validity Without Reliability?

Moss's article contrasted two views of assessment, which she labeled psychometric versus hermeneutic. To the psychometric view she attributed several requirements. The first is the use of multiple independent measures (items or tasks), that permit an examination of the adequacy of item or task sampling from a specified domain and an examination of consistency of performance across items or tasks. The second is the use of interchangeable impartial evaluators, which permit the evaluation of inter-rater reliability and precludes the possibility of bias brought into the process by an evaluator with previous knowledge of an examinee or a stake in a particular examinee's outcome. The third is the standardization of items or tasks, so that all candidates respond to a common set of stimulus materials.

This approach was contrasted with a hermeneutic approach. Although Moss offered a brief outline of hermeneutic philosophical traditions, it is not clear that either the background or the label is needed for her argument. The key ideas were that assessment should be holistic and integrative, should evaluate performances in context, should respect the particular expertise that an evaluator or various evaluators bring to the process, and should use discussion and consensus as mechanisms for decision making.

Moss illustrated her ideas with several real-world settings in which important decisions are made about individuals in a holistic, integrative, contextually based manner. The academic tenure process is one example. Candidates are not given a set of items or tasks to which to respond, but rather assemble work products reflecting their scholarship, teaching, and service. Outside letters of evaluation are commonly solicited from scholars who know a candidate's work, and an internal reading committee, made up of appropriate faculty members, evaluates the candidate's work. Integrative discussion leading to a vote at the department level, the college level, or both occurs, and is often followed by one or more additional levels of administrative review. The process is integrative and holistic, and allows evaluation of the candidate's work in context. For example, a candidate's publication record is viewed in the context of the research questions addressed: a seminal piece in a growth area is viewed differently from a fine-tuning piece in a well-developed area. Disagreements about a candidate's work are discussed, often at great length, in an attempt to reach consensus.

Although this process violates traditional concerns of standardization of stimulus material, multiple independent items, and multiple interchangeable raters, Moss asserted that a strong case can be made for the validity and fairness of the tenure decision. The process looks at the whole in light of its parts, gives heavy weight to evaluators most knowledgeable about the area of study, requires that evaluators ground their interpretations in the evidence available, and uses rational debate among participants. Other similar examples include the granting of PhD degrees by a faculty examining committee and the decision process used for publication decisions by scientific journals. (Let me note parenthetically that Moss's examples confound two distinct problems: evaluating a person and evaluating a work product. Educational and psychological assessment involves the evaluation of a person's standing on a construct of interest, such as achievement in an area of study. It is because the construct of interest commonly goes beyond the performances used to draw conclusions about the person's standing on the construct that concerns about task sampling arise. Evaluating a product [e. g., a journal manuscript] does not involve inferences beyond the particular performance: The determination that a manuscript makes a sufficient scientific contribution to merit publication differs from a judgment about an author's general skill or contribution as a researcher.)

In this context Moss framed the question "Can there be validity without reliability?" And it is with very important qualifications that she answers the question "Yes." Specifically, the answer to the question is yes when "reliability is defined as consistency among independent measures intended as interchangeable." On the basis of these qualifications, I do not view her statement as particularly controversial, but it is important to make a distinction between *reliability* and *documented reliability*. Moss did not make a clear distinction between the fundamental notions of reliability, namely replicability and freedom from error of measurement and particular mechanisms for documenting reliability.

Consider four different variants of the question "Can there be validity without reliability?" The first is "Can there be validity without documented reliability?". The answer here is a clear "Yes." In a personnel selection setting, if a well-done criterion-related validity study produces, say, a validity coefficient of .40, would people discount the study because predictor reliability was not reported? I see no reason to do so, although knowledge of predictor reliability is certainly desirable.

The second variant is "Can there be validity without the hallmarks of the psychometric approach as characterized by Moss, namely, multiple standardized tasks with interchangeable raters?" Again, the answer is a clear "Yes." I/O psychology has embraced approaches that have many features of the holistic, integrative approach advocated by Moss, with assessment centers as perhaps the best example. Although context is simulated, attempts are made to create psychological, if not physical, fidelity to a job situation. Holistic judgments are made following integrative consensus discussion. Particular rater expertise is recognized; as different raters observed candidates in different exercises, those with firsthand knowledge of candidate performance in a particular exercise are relied on as key informants about particular aspects of performance. Thus there is a history of using techniques in Moss's hermeneutic tradition and a relatively extensive body of evidence about the techniques' criterion-related validity (Gaugler, Rosenthal, Thornton, & Bentson, 1987). The use of a holistic, integrative process is not inherently at odds with concerns about the reliability of the evaluations produced using this process, and it is certainly possible to examine the reliability of complex, integrative decision processes.

A third variant I view as crucial, namely, "Can there be validity with documented unreliability?" One of Moss's examples is the use of an individual teacher, rather than standardized assessments, as the source of high-stakes decisions about students (e.g., meeting minimum competency requirements in a particular area of study for graduation). Her argument was that the teacher has unmatched expertise about the student, and is uniquely qualified to evaluate the student's work in context. Although the teacher's evaluation of a portfolio of the student's work is not consistent with the psychometric requirements outlined earlier, Moss argued for the validity of the teacher's judgment.

I would like to pose a thought experiment. What if a second, equally qualified teacher had spent just as much time with the student, and the two teachers reached very different conclusions about the student's level of achievement? In other words, what if reliability were zero? I believe that this is the crucial question because it cleanly distinguishes between rejecting the concept of reliability (i.e., replicability), or accepting the concept in principle and merely calling for the consideration of assessment approaches that do not lend themselves to reliability analysis on a routine basis.

It is clear that Moss accepted the concept of reliability in principle, as she viewed reliability as one contributor to the overarching concern of construct validity, namely, that the evidence supports the intended inference drawn from a behavior sample over other interpretations. Lack of agreement in the thought experiment would certainly be evidence countering the construct validity of the first teacher's evaluation. To me, the answer to the question "Can there be validity with documented unreliability?" is a clear "No."

A fourth variant is "Can there be validity when the availability of but a single appropriate judge precludes assessing reliability?" This question is really at the heart of Moss's concern. She wished to make a case for the potential value of portfolio assessment by a student's teacher and argued that the teacher has unique expertise about the particular student. Yet in the interests of creating an evaluation system that is amenable to reliability analysis, various features of standardized assessment, including evaluation by parties other than a student's teacher, are commonly incorporated in the assessment process. The discussion to this point should make clear that the answer to this question is "Yes": Following the logic developed earlier that there can be validity without documented validity, it is certainly possible in principle for a system with but one uniquely qualified judge to be valid. The availability of but a single appropriate judge does not, however, lessen the degree of scrutiny to be applied to the evaluation of the assessment system. Although Moss emphasized the unique expertise of the individual teacher, others have feared that personal and political issues may inappropriately influence the high-stakes decisions that the teacher is makes (e.g., giving higher than warranted evaluations in the interests of student self-esteem or in the interests of success rate comparisons with other teachers or other schools). Binet's initial forays into testing were motivated by concerns about favoritism and bias on the part of teachers. Thus although traditional reliability analysis may be unavailable, all sorts of mechanisms for investigating validity and for indirectly assessing reliability can be devised. As one example, imagine an experiment in which two groups of teachers conduct portfolio assessments, one with high-stakes consequences and the other without. A higher mean in the high-stakes condition would be evidence against the validity of the proposed assessment system.

I do not believe that Moss's paper presents the degree of challenge to ways of thinking about reliability and validity that it might. Moss did not distinguish between *reliability* and *reliability analysis*, and the conclusion that there can be validity without reliability would more accurately be stated as that there can be validity without one particular form of reliability analysis.

Consequential Validity

The term *consequential validity* is likely to be new to many I/O psychologists. It has emerged from the work of Messick (1989), though many have used it in ways that I believe are quite different from Messick. In a highly influential chapter, Messick differentiated between what he termed evidentiary and consequential bases for validity. Evidentiary bases generally correspond to the forms of criterion-related, content, and construct validity evidence long familiar to psychologists. Consequential bases refer to a consideration of intended and unintended consequences resulting from testing. Adverse impact resulting from a personnel selection system and the narrowing of a curriculum to focus on material perceived to be the focus of an educational assessment system would be examples of unintended and undesirable consequences resulting from test use.

Messick (1989) wrote that adverse consequences affect judgments about validity only when the consequences are empirically traceable to sources of test invalidity. I do not believe that this view is controversial: To advocate a review of potential consequences and to investigate whether the consequences are the result of test invalidity are well within a framework that views validity as the pattern of evidence supporting a proposed inference to be drawn from a test. It is when consequences per se, even if not linked to test flaws, are incorporated into the notion of validity that the matter becomes controversial. The term *consequential validity* has come to refer inappropriately to any situation in which unintended negative consequences are observed, in which case the test or assessment is branded as lacking consequential validity.

Assume that the inference I wish to draw is that a particular test predicts a carefully chosen and well-designed measure of job performance. I conduct a high-quality predictive validity study, including an examination of differential validity by ethnicity. I find three things: large majority–minority test differences, no evidence of differential prediction, and a highly significant predictive validity coefficient. I conclude that I have evidence to support my intended inference. Yet the use of the test would have adverse social consequences: Limited minority hiring could result. The finding of no differential prediction argues against test invalidity as the source of the adverse consequences.

Now assume that the best alternative measure I can find reduces adverse impact but is also a markedly inferior predictor. There are adverse social consequences with this alternative as well: More potentially good performers are denied jobs; more individuals prove to be poor performers after hire and are humiliated by failure on the job; and company performance could suffer and could lead indirectly to other consequences (e. g., a company lays off employees, is able to provide jobs for fewer new employees, or is less able to offer good wages to employees).

If validity is an overall judgment about the appropriateness of my proposed test use and you and I differ in terms of which of these above adverse consequences we consider more serious, is it the case that the proposed test inferences are valid for me and not valid for you? Or if Democrats and Republicans differ in terms of which of these adverse consequences they consider more serious, is it the case that the proposed test inferences are valid and sanctioned when Democrats are in office and invalid and prohibited when Republicans are in office? If it becomes the case that "validity is in the eyes of the beholder," then I fear that the concept of validity loses its stature as the most important consideration in test development and use.

Thus I agree with the call for an investigation of intended and unintended consequences of test use and with the proposition that such an investigation may lead to the identification of flaws in test design or implementation, which reduce or destroy construct validity; but I do not agree with the notion of a new type of validity called *consequential validity*. I endorse the elimination of the term from the vocabulary.

EXAMPLES OF PERFORMANCE ASSESSMENTS

I offer two examples that offer insights into the search for performance-based alternatives to paper and pencil testing. The first example involves a program of research to investigate alternatives to the traditional bar examination as a mechanism for certification to practice law. Each state has its own examination procedures, but they tend to follow a common pattern. Most states make use of the Multistate Bar Examination (MBE), a 200-item multiple choice test created by the National Conference of Bar Examiners. A state-specific multiple choice exam is commonly used, as is a state-specific essay examination.

Criticism of the examination process come from several quarters. One set of criticisms is based on the observation that passing rates typically vary quite dramatically by ethnicity. A recent study of the bar examination process in New York (Millman et al., 1993) reported passing rates of 81.6% for Whites, 37.4% for Blacks, 48.6% for Hispanics, and 53% for Asian Americans. Critics of the testing process have made two-pronged attacks: First, the existing test is a flawed measure of legal knowledge and reasoning, and second, even if the test were a sound measure of legal knowledge and reasoning, it measures only a subset of the knowledge, skills, and abilities needed for the practice of law. Oral communication, trial advocacy, law office management, and legal research are examples of skills that job analysis indicates are aspects of the practice of law, but are not covered in the bar examinations. People concerned about the disparity in passing rates have posited that smaller subgroup differences would be observed on measures of these excluded skills. As noted earlier, one aspect of the performance assessment movement is a belief that some portion of the subgroup differences observed on achievement tests are an artifact of traditional testing technology. As assessments become more "authentic," it is asserted that examinee achievement will be more appropriately revealed and that differences by subgroup will be reduced, if not eliminated.

Concerns about excluded skills also come from the legal community. Employers of newly minted attorneys have expressed surprise to find examples of individuals who passed the bar with flying colors but who cannot do legal research, write a brief, interview a witness, or conduct a cross-examination. Those responsible for the bar examination process have responded that the bar examination makes no pretense of measuring all lawyering skills. Those that are measured are the foundation skills of legal knowledge and legal reasoning; their absence essentially precludes effectively performing other lawyering skills. Millman et al. (1993) presented data showing that effective performance of other lawyering skills indeed rests on this foundation.

In light of concerns about the current bar examination process from both the employer community and the minority advocacy community, there has been considerable interest in alternative examination methods. A number of efforts to develop performance assessments have been undertaken, with the most extensive set of studies conducted in California by Klein and his colleagues. I have attempted to extract and synthesize information from these studies to give a picture of the effects of these performance assessment approaches on subgroup differences. I focus on Black–White differences, as samples are large enough for meaningful interpretation. In the Millman et al. (1993) study of the MBE, the standardized White–Black difference was .89 standard deviations, with a sample of over 7,000. As the MBE has an internal consistency reliability of .91, the White–Black difference is .93 after correcting for error of measurement. With this as a reference point, I contrast three different approaches to performance assessment with results obtained using the MBE. Table 8.1 contains reliability estimates for each measurement approach, correlations of each approach with the MBE (both observed and corrected for error of measurement), and standardized White–Black differences (also both observed and corrected).

Approach 1: The Research Test

This approach simulated the process of doing legal research. Candidates were given background material about a case and a legal position that their firm wished to advocate in the case. Candidates were then given what was referred to as a mini-library, containing a set of five judicial opinions. Their task was to review each case and evaluate whether the case supported, was neutral toward, or contradicted the proposition in question. Candidates also prepared memoranda in response to questions from a senior partner about interpretations of the cases in question. Candidates had 3 hours to respond. Over 7,000 individuals

TABLE 8.1

White-Black d and r with MBE for Bar Examination Performance Assessments

		d	r with MBE
MBE		.89	
($r_{xx} = .91$)		(.93)	
Research test		.89	.57
($r_{xx} = .78$)		(1.01)	(.67)
Trial practice		.89	.68
($r_{xx} = .64$)		(1.11)	(.89)
Assessment center			
	Total	.76	.50
	($r_{xx} = .67$)	(.93)	(.65)
	6 oral exercises	.46	.39
	($r_{xx} = .53$)	(.63)	(.57)
	5 written exercises	.84	.44
	($r_{xx} = .60$)	(1.08)	(.61)
	1 oral exercise	.22	
	($r_{xx} = .12$)		
	1 written exercise	.61	
	($r_{xx} = .32$)		

took this test in conjunction with the state bar examination.

Klein (1981) did not report standardized mean differences by ethnicity, but did state that the gap between groups did not narrow compared with the MBE. On the basis of this statement, I use a value of .89—the same as was obtained for the MBE—as the best estimate of the White–Black difference. Klein reported a reliability estimate of .78, and a correlation with the MBE of .57.

Approach 2: The Trial Practice Test

After reading background materials on a case, candidates viewed a videotape of a hearing related to the case. At different points the video was stopped, and candidates were asked factual ("Was the objection raised valid?") and strategic ("Was it appropriate to raise the objection at this point?") questions about the hearing. Candidates had 90 minutes to respond; 860 candidates took the test on trial tractice in conjunction with the bar examination.

Klein (1983) again did not report standardized mean differences by ethnicity, but again stated that the gap between groups did not narrow compared with the MBE. On the basis of this statement, I use a value of .89 as the best estimate of White–Black difference. Klein reported a reliability estimate of .64, and a correlation with the MBE of .68.

Approach 3: The Assessment Center

A 2-day assessment center was designed. Each day simulated a separate trial, with a candidate representing the plaintiff on one day and the defendant on the second. Each case took 6 hours. The center consisted of 11 different tasks, 6 oral and 5 written. These included conducting a client interview, delivering opening and closing statements, conducting a cross-examination, writing a discovery plan, and preparing a case summary memo. Actors played the other roles in the trial. Exercises were videotaped for later scoring by trained attorneys. Candidates received a score on each of the 11 tasks; 485 individuals participated in conjunction with the bar examination.

From means and standard deviations reported by Klein and Bolus (1982), a Black–White d of .76 was computed for the overall assessment center score. d values of .46 and .84 were computed for the oral and written exercises, respectively. I applied the Spearman–Brown formula to determine the White–Black difference on a single exercise, and obtained values of .22 for a single oral exercise and .61 for a single written exercise. Klein and Bolus reported a reliability estimate of .67 and a correlation with the MBE of .50.

Several observations about these findings are in order. First, these three attempts at performance assessments did not reduce subgroup differences, much less eliminate them. The research test and the trial practice test had the same observed White–Black difference as the MBE; after correcting for unreliability, these two performance assessments have a Black–White difference larger than the MBE. At the observed score level, the assessment center had a somewhat smaller White–Black difference (.76 versus .89); but after correcting for unreliability the assessment center and the MBE produced identical White–Black differences of .93 standard deviation units. Thus in this setting the multiple-choice format of the MBE was not the cause of the subgroup differences. Performance assessments focusing on trial practice and legal research produced comparable, if not larger, subgroup differences.

Second, if the assessment center is decomposed into separate oral and written components, a different pattern emerges. The written exercises parallel the results already described: Like the research test and the trial practice test, the White–Black difference on a composite of the written assessment center exercises after correcting for unreliability was larger than the difference found on the MBE. But the difference on a composite of the five oral exercises produced a difference of .46 standard deviation units; even after correcting for unreliability the difference of .63 was smaller than the corrected value of .93 for the MBE. Thus it appears that some performance assessment components may produce smaller subgroup differences. Oral exercises appeared to rely more on skills outside the cognitive realm than did the other forms of performance assessments. Oral presentation skills per se, separate from the content of the presentation, may have contributed to individuals' scores; as oral presentation skills were less cognitively loaded, smaller group differences would be expected.

Third, group differences can be reduced dramatically by using a smaller number of assessment center exercises. The subgroup difference on a single oral exercise was estimated to be .22. This is indeed a dramatic reduction in the degree of subgroup difference, and it is attributable to the low reliability of the single exercise. The single exercise functions like a single item in traditional tests: It is the aggregation across items that produces a reliable measure.

Because that the assessment center exercises required 12 hours to administer, it is not unreasonable to imagine attempts to make use of a much shorter subset of exercises. In the case of the bar examination, attempts to incorporate performance assessment components have taken place in the context of limited testing time (Klein, 1991). By shortening other components, several states have been able to find time to include a 2-hour performance assessment within the constraints of a 2-day bar exam process. The performance assessments now used are similar to the research test previously described. Their addition has not reduced subgroup differences, a finding consistent with the research summarized here. Performance assessments have served as a catalyst for change in law school curriculum in states where these performance assessments are used: Applied research skills are now emphasized more heavily in the curriculum. Thus the bar examination experience with performance assessments effectively highlights the issue of broader consequences of test use: Changing the bar exam content led quickly to a change in the law school curriculum.

Although the bar examination performance assessments are responsive to some criticisms made of multiple-choice examinations, they stop short of some criteria for authentic assessments. For instance, they do involve performance on demand.

I now turn to a second example of a performance assessment system, one that illustrates the portfolio assessment notion outlined earlier. The NBPTS is in the process of developing assessment systems for the certification of highly accomplished teachers. The board has a clear vision of what highly accomplished teaching means, and it thinks that the identification and recognition of highly accomplished teachers can contribute to improvements in the quality of education in the United States. Such certification would be sought voluntarily by teachers; the NBPTS hopes that school systems will recognize and reward this certification. The state of North Carolina has passed legislation calling for a pay increase for teachers receiving certification from the NBPTS.

Separate assessment systems are planned for over 30 different specialty areas. One initial pilot project focused on early adolescent generalists; I focus on this system here. The assessment system has several components, including two portfolio exercises and an assessment center.

Teaching and Learning Exercise

In this exercise, teachers were asked to focus on one unit of instruction in one class over one 3- to 6-week period. During this period they were to prepare three products. The first was a "videoclips tape"—a videotape of 3 to 5 segments, totaling 1 hour, in a variety of settings, including not only presentations by the teacher, but also interaction with classes. The second was an "unedited lesson tape"—a 30- to 60-minute tape representing a single lesson that a teacher views as his or her best work. The third is "student work samples," in which a teacher selects three students and collects examples of each student's work and the teacher's written feedback to each student, and then prepares a "reflections journal" describing the work with each student.

Professional Outreach Exercise

In this exercise teachers were asked to select and document activities about working with students to foster social development (5–7 items), working with families (3–5 items), and working with colleagues (3–5 items). Teachers wrote an explanation of each item, and this material was the subject of a follow-up interview at the assessment center.

Assessment Center

The assessment center had several exercises. In "applying and analyzing content" a teacher responded to 10 vignettes describing various occurrences. In "instructional design" a teacher was asked to plan a unit on "communication." In "peer collaboration" a teacher viewed and evaluated a video of a colleague's lesson. In "student conflict" a teacher read a scenario and outlined the planned response. In "team collaboration," a group of teachers engaged in curriculum planning on the topic of fostering thinking skills.

A pilot study with 287 teachers has been completed, and I quickly note several aspects of the findings. First, teacher reactions to the portfolio were very favorable. Candidates were more positive about the portfolio than about the assessment center as a way to measure accomplishment, an interesting finding in light of the favorable reaction that assessment centers commonly receive compared to other personnel selection methods. Second, reliability of portfolio evaluations proved low, and a change to the use of two evaluators had to be made to increase reliability. Third, candidates reported spending an average of 100 hours in completing the portfolio portion of the assessment; the assessment center required an additional 2 days. Thus the time investment on the part of candidates is substantial. Fourth, 50% of the candidates reported that they collaborated with others in preparing their portfolios.

This issue of collaboration merits some discussion. The issue of whose work went into the portfolio can become a serious concern. One radical solution is that collaboration should be mandated! Collaboration among teachers is seen as desirable in school settings; why should something encouraged at work be prohibited in assessment?

A response to this suggestion focuses on construct validity: The construct being assessed blurs with collaboration. Tom Sawyer succeeded in getting a fence whitewashed in record time by cajoling other children to do the work for him: Would people rate him high in "fence-painting skill" based on this outcome? Can psychologists project the same performance for other fences where the availability of persuadable children differs?

A second response deals with the issue of a level playing field. More than one third of teachers in the pilot study reported that if collaboration were mandated, it would be a burden: Some teachers have easier access to high-quality collaborators than do others. In my cub scout days, a big event each year was the Pinewood Derby, in which each scout built and raced a small wooden car. Collaboration, that is, assistance from parents, was encouraged. I vividly recall the contrast between the sleek designs, meticulous balancing, and graphite wheel lubrication produced by scouts with engineer fathers and the crude products offered by other scouts. Without access to equally able and willing collaborators, the issue of collaboration remains, in my opinion, a pressing concern for portfolio assessments.

DISCUSSION AND IMPLICATIONS
FOR I/O PSYCHOLOGY

Here I discuss several summary issues of performance assessment and its implications for I/O psychology. The first issue deals with performance assessment methods: Do they offer something new to I/O psychology? My sense is that we are already among the converted in several ways. Work sample or simulation measures are well regarded, and are used where conceptually and pragmatically feasible. Attempts at realism and fidelity to the job in designing selection systems are valued. The less familiar issues are some aspects of authentic or portfolio assessment, such as rejection of performance on demand, calls for examinee choice as to the materials submitted for evaluation, and desire to encourage collaboration. I foresee limited acceptance of these issues in employment settings, partly because of the differences between the overarching goals of assessment in education and in employment. In education the goal is description of achievement level; in employment the goal is the prediction of job performance. Performance in response to the demands of the situation is central to most, if not all, work roles, and thus seeing how individuals rise to the challenge put before them in an assessment setting parallels similar demands in work settings.

Another issue is the question of whether there is reason to change the concepts of reliability and validity as a result of developments in performance assessment. In this chapter I have reviewed proposals for rethinking these concepts, and have concluded that it is unnecessary to rethink our current views. I/O psychology has viewed reliability as equally applicable to complex performance assessments and to traditional tests: How reliability is operationalized may be different, but concerns about the overarching principle are the same. As to validity, the consideration of consequences is certainly important, but I rejected the notion of a separate form of validity under the label of consequential validity earlier in this chapter. Testing can have consequences that go beyond the immediate purpose; this important issue merits careful attention by I/O psychologists. The bar examination discussion offered a useful example of testing consequences: The addition of a performance assessment component on the bar examination led to curriculum modification to give increased emphasis to the legal research skills tapped by the performance assessment.

A third issue is the role of performance assessments in reducing subgroup differences. The bar examination experience with performance assessment is instructive. Performance assessment per se apparently does not reduce subgroup differences: The data clearly show comparable and sometimes larger differences for performance assessments versus the multiple-choice MBE. In several cases, an apparent reduction of subgroup differences is nothing more than the result of lowering the reliability of the assessment. In other cases, the reduction of subgroup differences appears attributable to a shift to the measurement of skill areas with a lower cognitive component, as in the case of oral presentation exercises in the bar examination assessment center. The message here is important: Care must be taken to decide whether apparent reductions in subgroup differences are due to format per se, to changes in the reliability of measurement, or to changes in the construct being addressed.

A fourth issue involves costs. Complex performance assessments often impose unfeasible resource demands. The bar examination example is telling:

Despite evidence that oral assessment center exercises tap relevant skills not measured elsewhere and that subgroup differences are smaller than on other components, the oral exercises have not been put into use. The testing time needed to administer enough exercises to achieve acceptable levels of reliability and the resources needed to score these exercises make their use prohibitive. The same is true for NBPTS assessment, in which candidates averaged over 100 hours to complete the portfolio package. In a professional certification setting, where people seek credentials that are valued by many employers, candidates may be willing to make such an investment. A similar investment on the part of applicants for a job with a particular employer seems unlikely.

Thus at present the developments reviewed in this chapter do not appear to call for major changes in selection practices. I believe that it is useful to monitor developments in educational testing and professional certification and to continue to carefully consider the implications for employment settings. Confronting different perspectives is a useful device to prompts reviewing and rethinking theory and practice.

REFERENCES

Gaugler, B., Rosenthal, D. B., Thornton, G. C. III, & Bentson, C. (1987). Meta-analysis of assessment center validity. *Journal of Applied Psychology, 72*, 493–511.

Hambleton, R. K., & Murphy, E. (1992). A psychometric perspective on authentic assessment. *Applied Measurement in Education, 5*, 1–16.

Klein, S. P. (1981). *Testing research skills on the California Bar Examination*. Unpublished manuscript.

Klein, S. P. (1983). *An analysis of the relationship between trial practice skills and bar examination results*. Unpublished manuscript.

Klein, S. P (1991). *Performance testing on the bar examination*. Unpublished manuscript.

Klein, S. P., & Bolus, R. E. (1982). *An analysis of the relationship between clinical legal skills and bar examination results*. Unpublished manuscript.

Linn, R. L., Baker, E. L., & Dunbar, S. B. (1991). Complex, performance-based assessment: Expectations and validation criteria. *Educational Researcher, 20*, 15–21.

Mehrens, W. A. (1992). Using performance assessment for accountability purposes. *Educational Measurement: Issues and Practice, 11*, 3–20.

Messick, S. (1989). Validity. In R. L. Linn (Ed.), *Educational measurement* (3rd ed., pp. 13–103). Washington, DC: American Council on Education and National Council on Measurement in Education.

Meyer, C. A. (1992). What's the difference between authentic and performance assessment? *Educational Leadership, 49*, 39–40.

Millman, J., Mehrens, W. A., & Sackett, P. R. (1993). *An evaluation of the New York State Bar Examination*. Unpublished manuscript.

Moss, P. A. (1994). Can there be validity without reliability? *Educational Researcher, 23*, 5–12.

Worthen, B. R. (1993). Critical issues that will determine the future of authentic assessment. *Phi Delta Kappan, 74*, 444–454.

9

Personality at Work: Issues and Evidence

Leaetta Hough
The Dunnette Group, Ltd.

Personality measurement has a long history in psychology, but industrial/organizational (I/O) psychologists consider personality variables alternative predictors of work performance. This chapter briefly examines the history of personality variables in I/O psychology in an effort to explain this perspective. The main focus, however, is on evidence that supports the use of personality variables to predict work performance and on issues that emerge as a result of using personality variables to predict work performance.

A construct-oriented framework is needed to investigate the usefulness of personality variables. Indeed, evidence for the criterion-related validity of personality variables emerges only when both predictor and criterion domains are conceptualized in terms of constructs. Different frameworks, or taxonomies, however, result in different conclusions. This chapter demonstrates the usefulness of personality constructs for predicting major work-related criteria and shows the results obtained when different taxonomic structures are used.

At least three implementation issues are important when considering personality variables for inclusion in a personnel selection or placement decision-making system. One issue is the impact of intentional distortion on the criterion-related validity of personality measures. A second issue is the impact of using personality measures on the selection ratio of protected groups compared to the selection ratio of White men. Does the use of personality measures have adverse impact on protected groups? A third issue is the impact of the Americans with Disabilities Act of 1990 (ADA) on the use of personality testing in industry. In addition to examining the history of personality measurement in I/O psychology and the criterion-related validity of personality variables (including differences in concurrent and predictive validities), this chapter provides information relevant to implementation issues.

HISTORICAL PERSPECTIVE

Jack and Ronda Hunter (1984) conducted a meta-analysis of the validity of 16 different types of predictors of job performance. The predictors they considered, as well as their validities, are shown in Table 9.1. Personality variables were

TABLE 9.1

Hunter & Hunter (1984)
Average Validity of Predictors

Predictors Considered	Validity
Work sample test	.54[1]
Ability composite	.53[2]
Peer ratings	.49[1]
Behavioral consistency experience ratings	.49[1]
Job knowledge test	.48[1]
Job tryout	.44[2]
Assessment center	.43[1]
Biographical inventory	.37[2]
Reference check	.26[2]
Experience	.18[2]
Interview	.14[2]
Training and experience ratings	.13[2]
Academic achievement	.11[2]
Education	.10[2]
Interest	.10[2]
Age	−.01[2]

Note: From "Validity and utility of alternative predictors of job performance" by J. E. Hunter and R. F. Hunter, 1984, *Psychological Bulletin, 96,* 72–98. Copyright 1984 by the American Psychological Association, Inc. Reprinted by permission.

[1] Validities for predictors to be used for promotion or certification where current performance on the job is the basis for selection.

[2] Validities for predictors for entry-level jobs for which training will occur after hiring.

then generally held in such low esteem that the Hunters did not even include them as predictors of job performance.

Yet, about 20 years earlier, Ghiselli (1966) had published a book, *The Validity of Occupational Aptitude Tests*, in which he presented evidence that personality measures had useful validities for predicting job performance. Ghiselli summarized criterion-related validities separately for types of predictor measures, jobs, and criteria. Table 9.2 summarizes his results, with an aggregation of data from several of Ghiselli's tables; Table 9.2 shows the validity of different predictors for different jobs for the criterion job proficiency. Across different jobs, the best predictor is personality; the median validity is .24. At about the same time, Guion and Gottier (1965), after a thorough review of personality variables, concluded that "personality measures have had predictive validity more often than can be accounted for simply by chance" (p. 141), but they could discern no guiding principles to account for the not quite random results. Ghiselli and Guion, two highly respected I/O psychologists, indeed giants in the field, reached very different conclusions about the merits of personality variables for

TABLE 9.2

Edwin Ghiselli, 1966
The Validity[1] of Occupational Aptitude Tests
Criterion: Job Proficiency

Type of Job	Type of Predictor				
	Intellectual Abilities	Spatial & Mechanical	Perceptual Accuracy	Personality[2]	Interest
Executives	.29	.18	.24	.27	.31
Foremen	.24	.23	.14	.15	.15
Clerks	.27	.20	.27	.24	.12
Sales clerks	−.10	—	−.05	.35	.34
Commission sales	.31	.07	.21	.24	.31
Protective services	.23	.16	.17	.24	−.01
Personal service	.03	—	−.10	.16	—
Vehicle operators	.14	.20	.36	—	.26
Trades and crafts	.19	.23	.22	.29	−.13
Industrial occupations	.16	.16	.18	.50	.14
Median Validity	.21	.19	.20	.24	.15

Note: Adapted from *The Validity of Occupational Aptitude Tests*, (tables 3.1 to 3.8, pp. 34–56) by E. E. Ghiselli, 1966, New York: Wiley. Copyright 1966 by John Wiley & Sons, Inc. Adapted with permission.

[1] Observed validities.

[2] "Only those results were included in this summary where the trait seemed pertinent to the job in question" (Ghiselli, 1966, p. 21).

I/O psychology. One important difference in Ghiselli's review was that he included only those results "where the trait seemed pertinent to the job in question" (Ghiselli, 1966, p. 21). Unfortunately, Ghiselli did not describe how he determined the appropriateness of the trait for the job in question.

CONSTRUCT APPROACH

In the early 1980s, the Army Research Institute funded a large research project, Project A, to investigate the predictors of job performance in military occupational specialties. An important goal of the project was to investigate the usefulness of "alternative" predictors, that is, alternatives to the Armed Services Vocational Aptitude Battery (ASVAB), a measure of cognitive abilities. I was assigned responsibility for all the *non*cognitive variables; personality variables constituted one set of noncognitive variables.

We were familiar with the prevailing wisdom about personality variables. Luminaries in the field—Robert Guion, John Hunter, Neal Schmitt, and Ken Pearlman—all regarded personality variables as having minimal value for predicting job performance (Guion, 1965; Guion & Gottier, 1965; J. E. Hunter & R. F. Hunter, 1984; Pearlman, 1985; Schmitt, Gooding, Noe, & Kirsch, 1984).

We were also familiar with and respected Ghiselli's work. We, therefore, speculated on guiding principles that might be brought to bear to explain Ghiselli's validity results for personality variables. The zeitgeist of Project A was construct oriented; both predictors and criteria were conceptualized as constructs. Our hope was that different personality constructs might correlate with performance constructs differently, that previous researchers had aggregated and summarized validities across constructs, and that this approach had attenuated the validity of personality constructs. Thus, a search for an adequate taxonomy of personality constructs began.

Predictor Constructs: Structure of Personality

At the time, personality psychologists were rediscovering Tupes and Christal's (1961/1992) five factors—surgency, dependability, adjustment, agreeableness, and culture—which were beginning to be called the Big Five. We classified existing personality scales into these five constructs, obtained as many criterion-related validity studies as possible, and summarized the validities in constructs.

On the basis of the Big Five as the predictor taxonomy and overall job performance as the criterion, the results were not encouraging (Kamp & Hough, 1986; see also Hough, Eaton, Dunnette, Kamp, & McCloy, 1990). A few years later, Barrick and Mount (1991) conducted a similar literature review. Both reviews yielded similarly low validity levels. Table 9.3 shows the results. Both meta-analyses found similar levels of observed validities for four of the

TABLE 9.3

Validities[1] of the Big Five

	Job Proficiency	
Big Five Construct	*Barrick & Mount*[2]	*Kamp & Hough*[3]
Dependability (conscientiousness)	.13	.13
Surgency (extraversion)	.06	.04
Agreeableness (cooperativeness)	.04	−.01
Adjustment (emotional stability)	.04	.13
Culture (openness to experience, intellectance)	−.02	.01

[1]Observed correlations.

[2]Adapted from "The big five personality dimensions and job performance: A meta-analysis" by M. R. Barrick and M. K. Mount, 1991, *Personnel Psychology, 44*, 1–26. Copyright 1991 by Personnel Psychology, Inc. Adapted with permission.

[3]Adapted from "Criterion-related validities of personality constructs and the effect of response distortion on those validities" [Monograph] by L. M. Hough, N. K. Eaton, M. D. Dunnette, J. D. Kamp, & R. A. McCloy, 1990, *Journal of Applied Psychology, 75*, 581–595. Copyright 1990 by American Psychological Association. Adapted with permission. See also "Utility of personality assessment: A review and integration of the literature" by J. D. Kamp and L. M. Hough, 1986, in L. M. Hough (Ed.), *Utility of temperament, biodata, and interest assessment for predicting job performance: A review and integration of the literature* (ARI Research Note No. 88-02, pp. 1–90), Alexandria, VA: U.S. Army Research Institute for the Behavioral and Social Sciences.

Big Five variables. Both the Kamp and Hough, and Barrick and Mount studies found a mean observed validity for Dependability of .13. The only noteworthy difference in level of validity is for the personality variable Adjustment. Kamp and Hough obtained a mean observed validity of .13 for Adjustment; Barrick and Mount obtained a mean observed validity of .04. These validities were not at the level that Ghiselli had reported. Indeed, the magnitude of the validities was more in line with the results obtained by researchers who concluded that personality variables had little merit for predicting job performance criteria.

Undaunted by our apparent failure, we examined the taxonomy of personality constructs we had used, that is, the Five-Factor Model. Many existing personality scales did not fit well in the Five-Factor Model; a large miscellaneous category of scales did not correlate sufficiently highly with scales classified into the five factors. An examination of the miscellaneous personality category produced three more constructs: achievement, locus of control, and masculinity/femininity. Masculinity/femininity was relabeled rugged individualism. In addition, the affiliation scales were removed from the surgency construct based on Hogan's (1982) work. The taxonomy thus had nine variables.

Our most recent taxonomy consists of eight variables. Locus of control is no longer a separate taxon. (See Schneider & Hough [1995] for a thorough analysis of taxonomic issues about the structure of personality variables and Hough & Schneider [1996] for a discussion of the usefulness of different taxonomies for I/O psychologists.) The definitions for the eight constructs in our personality taxonomy are the following:[1]

Affiliation—The affiliation construct refers to the degree of sociability a person exhibits. A person high in affiliation likes to be with people, is outgoing, participative, and friendly. A person low in affiliation feels uneasy in social situations, is shy, reserved, and prefers to work alone.

Potency—Potency is defined as the degree of impact, influence, and energy that a person displays. A person high on this characteristic is appropriately forceful and persuasive, is optimistic and vital, and has the energy to get things done. A person low on this characteristic is timid about offering opinions or providing direction and is likely to be lethargic and pessimistic.

Achievement—The achievement construct is defined as the tendency to strive for competence in work. An achievement or work-oriented person works hard, sets high standards, tries to do a good job, endorses the work ethic, and concentrates on, and persists in, completion of the task at hand. This person is also confident, feels success from past undertakings, and expects to succeed in the future. A less achievement-oriented person has little ego involvement in his or her work, feels incapable and self-doubting, does not expend undue effort, and does not feel that hard work is desirable.

Dependability—The dependability construct refers to a person's characteristic degree of conscientiousness. A dependable person is disciplined, well-organized, planful, respectful of laws and regulations, honest, trustworthy, wholesome, and accepting of authority. Such a person prefers order and thinks before acting. A less dependable person is unreliable, acts on the spur of the moment, and is rebellious and contemptuous of laws and regulations.

Adjustment—Adjustment is defined as the amount of emotional stability and stress tolerance that a person possesses. A well-adjusted person is generally calm, displays an even mood, and is not overly distraught by stressful situations. He or she thinks clearly and maintains composure and rationality in situations of actual or perceived stress. A poorly adjusted person is nervous, moody, easily irritated, tends to worry a lot, and "goes to pieces" in times of stress.

Agreeableness—The agreeableness–likability construct is defined as the degree of pleasantness versus unpleasantness exhibited in interpersonal relations. An agreeable and likable person is pleasant, tolerant, tactful, helpful, not defensive, and generally easy to get along with. His or her participation in a group adds cohesiveness rather than friction. A relatively disagreeable and unlikable person is critical, fault finding, touchy, defensive, alienated, and generally contrary.

---

[1]From "The 'Big Five' personality variables—construct confusion: Description versus prediction," by L. M. Hough, 1992, *Human Performance, 5,* 139–155. Copyright 1992 by Lawrence Erlbaum Associates. Reprinted with permission.

Intellectance—The intellectance construct refers to the degree of culture that a person possesses and displays. A person high on intellectance is cultured, esthetically fastidious, imaginative, quick witted, curious, socially polished, intellectual, and independent minded. A person low on intellectance is artistically insensitive, unreflective, and narrow.

Rugged Individualism—This construct refers to what are often regarded as masculine rather than feminine characteristics and values. A person who is high on this construct is decisive, action oriented, independent, and rather unsentimental. A person low on this construct is sympathetic, helpful, sensitive to criticism, tends to interpret events from a personal point of view, and often feels vulnerable.

Figure 9.1 shows the eight constructs in comparison with other personality taxonomies. Most taxonomies are variants of the Big Five. Our taxonomy is shown at the top. The original Tupes and Christal (1961/1992) Big Five is in bold print. Figure 9.1 shows that Rugged Individualism has no counterpart in the Five-Factor Model. The figure also shows that in our model surgency (extraversion) is split into affiliation and potency, and achievement is a separate construct. The figure also shows that the five factors of the Five-Factor Model, especially dependability and extraversion, have been defined differently by different theorists and researchers. For example, in the original Tupes and Christal Five-Factor Model, ambition and ascendance (elements of our achievement construct) were incorporated into their surgency construct. In the Costa and McCrae (NEO-PI-R, 1992) version of the Five-Factor Model, striving for competence (an element in our achievement construct) was incorporated into their conscientiousness factor. Similarly, Five-Factor proponents Digman and Inouye (1986) incorporated our achievement construct into the conscientiousness (dependability) construct. They even labeled the conscientiousness factor "will to achieve." Our achievement construct is thus confounded with extraversion (surgency) in some models and conscientiousness (dependability) in others.

The dependability/conscientiousness factor in the Five-Factor Model is so broad that in some versions of the Five-Factor Model, dependability encompasses achievement striving and competence as well as dutifulness, order, self-discipline, and deliberation. Achievement striving and competence, which relate to White's (1959) concept of effectance, involve self-expansive striving and setting goals to master the environment. On the other hand, dutifulness, order, self-discipline, and deliberation involve self-restrictive caution, conventionality, and adapting to goals set by others. These variables are dissimilar and, as data in subsequent tables demonstrate, correlate differently with different criterion constructs. Achievement is thus a separate construct in our model.

An important feature of the Project A work was that job performance was considered multidimensional. This construct-oriented approach characterized all phases of Project A, including the literature review. The criterion space was

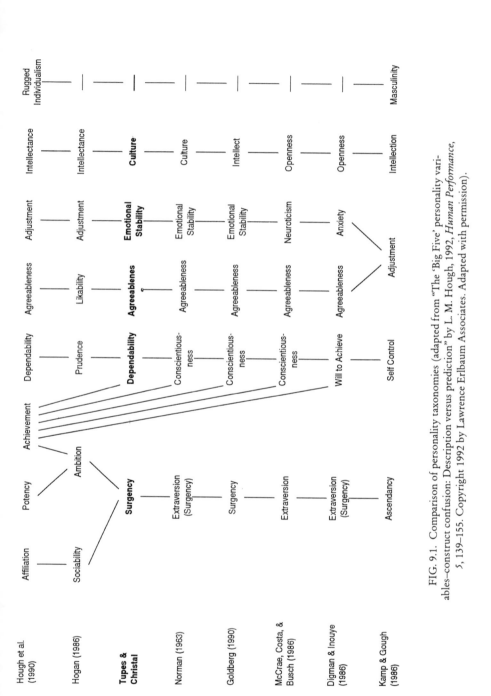

FIG. 9.1. Comparison of personality taxonomies (adapted from "The 'Big Five' personality variables–construct confusion: Description versus prediction" by L. M. Hough, 1992, *Human Performance*, 5, 139–155. Copyright 1992 by Lawrence Erlbaum Associates. Adapted with permission).

138

thus conceptualized as consisting of distinct criteria such as job proficiency, training success, educational success, and counterproductive behavior. Criterion-related validities from previous research were summarized according to both predictor construct (using our revised taxonomic structure) and various criterion constructs.

Validity of Personality Constructs

Table 9.4 shows the mean observed validities for each predictor–criterion combination, as well as the number of correlations and total sample size for each mean *observed* validity. (Correlations are not corrected for unreliability or restriction in range.) The best predictor of all the criteria is Achievement. It correlates .15, .21, .29, and −.38 with job proficiency, training success, educational success, and counterproductive behavior, respectively. Dependability correlates .08, .11, .12, and −.35 respectively with the same criteria. Potency (Extraversion without the Affiliation component) correlates .10, .07, .12, and −.17 respectively with the same criteria. Our results thus suggest that merging Achievement with either Dependability or Extraversion dilutes the criterion-related validity of Achievement scales. (Data in subsequent tables indicate that, depending on the performance construct being predicted, the criterion-related validities of Achievement and Dependability scales are in *opposite* directions for some types of criteria.)

The most predictable criterion is Counterproductive Behavior. Achievement, Dependability, and Adjustment scales predict it very well. Validities are −.38, −.35, −.34, respectively, for Achievement, Dependability, and Adjustment. Educational Success, however, is also predicted quite well with Achievement and Adjustment measures. Validities are .29 and .20, respectively.

Concurrent Versus Predictive Validity Coefficients

Table 9.5 shows the results for the subset of studies that were *concurrent* validity studies. Table 9.6 shows the results for the subset of studies that were *predictive* validity studies.

In general, the same conclusions apply. First, Achievement is again the best predictor of the criteria. Concurrent criterion-related validity coefficients (Table 9.5) for Achievement are .13, .35, and −.42, respectively, for Job Proficiency, Educational Success, and Counterproductive Behavior. Predictive criterion-related validity coefficients (Table 9.6) for Achievement are .19, .19, .23, and −.33, respectively, for Job Proficiency, Training Success, Educational Success, and Counterproductive Behavior. Merging Achievement with either Dependability or Extraversion/Surgency dilutes the validity coefficients of Achievement measures. The most predictable criterion is again Counterproductive Behavior: Achievement, Dependability, and Adjustment predict it very well in both concurrent and predictive validity studies. Achievement, Dependability, and

TABLE 9.4

Relationship Between Personality Constructs and Criterion Constructs: Summary of Observed Criterion-Related Validities

| | Criterion Construct | | | | | | | | | | |
| Personality Construct | Job Proficiency | | | Training Success | | | Educational Success | | | Counterproductive Behavior | | |
	No.Corr.	Sum of Samples	Mean r	No.Corr.	Sum of Samples	Mean r	No.Corr.	Sum of Samples	Mean r	No.Corr.	Sum of Samples	Mean r
Affiliation	23	3,390	.00	—	—	—	9	2,953	.01	—	—	—
Potency	274	65,876	.10	70	8,389	.07	128	63,057	.12	23	82,635	-.17
Achievement	28	2,811	.15	9	1,160	.21	31	12,639	.29	4	10,062	-.38
Dependability	141	46,116	.08	34	4,710	.11	42	18,661	.12	66	113,427	-.35
Adjustment	182	35,148	.09	69	8,685	.12	162	70,588	.20	21	56,765	-.34
Agreeableness	87	22,060	.05	7	988	.08	15	7,330	.01	4	24,259	-.08
Intellectance	46	11,297	.01	35	8,744	.02	8	3,628	.13	1	747	.24
Rugged individualism	28	3,007	.08	11	1,614	.03	27	12,358	-.02	4	14,075	.01

Note: Correlations are *not* corrected for unreliability or restriction in range.
Boxes indicate validities that are equal to or greater than .15 and are based on sample sizes equal to or greater than 500.
Adapted from "The 'Big Five' personality variable–construct confusion: Description versus prediction," by L. M. Hough, 1992, *Human Performance, 5,* 139–155. Copyright 1992 by Lawrence Erlbaum Associates. Adapted with permission.

TABLE 9.5

Summary of Observed Criterion-Related Validities: *Concurrent* Studies

	Criterion Construct											
	Job Proficiency			*Training Success*			*Educational Success*			*Counterproductive Behavior*		
Personality Construct	*No. Corr.*	*Sum of Samples*	*Mean r*	*No. Corr.*	*Sum of Samples*	*Mean r*	*No. Corr.*	*Sum of Samples*	*Mean r*	*No. Corr.*	*Sum of Samples*	*Mean r*
Affiliation	21	3,200	.00	—	—	—	2	150	-.15	—	—	—
Potency	195	51,592	.10	10	600	.19	13	7,885	.19	14	60,254	-.24
Achievement	19	2,129	.13	—	—	—	4	2,056	.35	2	5,918	-.42
Dependability	96	35,119	.09	10	693	.12	6	1,971	.28	41	55,302	-.39
Adjustment	123	23,443	.11	7	377	.03	15	9,247	.32	16	43,876	-.39
Agreeableness	69	14,648	.08	2	111	-.05	2	170	.02	1	7,666	-.21
Intellectance	35	4,522	.05	2	111	.20	2	170	.26	—	—	—
Rugged Individualism	18	2,232	.13	1	50	.18	1	1,371	-.18	3	6,152	.02

Note: Correlations are *not* corrected for unreliability or restriction in range.
Boxes indicate validities that are equal to or greater than .15 and are based on sample sizes equal to or greater than 500.

TABLE 9.6
Summary of Observed Criterion-Related Validities: *Predictive Studies*

	Criterion Construct											
	Job Proficiency			*Training Success*			*Educational Success*			*Counterproductive Behavior*		
Personality Construct	No. Corr.	Sum of Samples	Mean r	No. Corr.	Sum of Samples	Mean r	No. Corr.	Sum of Samples	Mean r	No. Corr.	Sum of Samples	Mean r
Affiliation	2	190	.12	—	—	—	7	2,803	.02	—	—	—
Potency	69	13,580	.07	50	7,199	.07	80	27,564	.15	9	22,381	-.04
Achievement	7	556	.19	7	1,042	.19	21	5,262	.23	2	4,144	-.33
Dependability	40	9,930	.04	22	3,899	.11	28	10,982	.13	24	56,603	-.23
Adjustment	59	11,705	.05	50	7,600	.11	108	28,799	.21	5	12,889	-.17
Agreeableness	18	7,412	.01	5	877	.10	11	6,702	.00	3	16,593	-.01
Intellectance	11	6,775	-.02	33	8,633	.02	5	3,229	.12	1	747	.24
Rugged individualism	10	775	-.05	8	1,446	.02	19	5,437	-.03	1	7,923	.00

Note: Correlations are *not* corrected for unreliability or restriction in range.
Boxes indicate validities that are equal to or greater than .15 and are based on sample sizes equal to or greater than 500.

Adjustment correlate −.42, −.39, and −.39, respectively, with Counterproductive Behavior in concurrent criterion-related validity studies (Table 9.5). They correlate −.33, −.23, and −.17, respectively, with Counterproductive Behavior in predictive criterion-related validity studies (Table 9.6). Third, Educational Success is again predicted quite well with Achievement and Adjustment measures. They correlate .35 and .32, respectively, with Educational Success in concurrent criterion-related validity studies. They correlate .23 and .21, respectively, with Educational Success in predictive criterion-related validity studies.

An apparent conclusion when the magnitude of the concurrent validity coefficients is compared to the magnitude of the predictive validity coefficients is that the predictive validity coefficients are lower than the concurrent validity coefficients. When each mean concurrent validity coefficient is compared to its mean predictive validity coefficient counterpart, the average difference is .07. Concurrent validity studies produce validity coefficients that are, on average, .07 points higher than predictive validity studies. If the comparison is done within criterion construct, the difference in means ranges from .04 to .15. That is, concurrent validity coefficients are from .04 to .15 higher than predictive validity coefficients depending on the criterion construct.

One criterion that Ones, Viswesvaran, and Schmidt (1993) included in their comprehensive meta-analysis of the validities of integrity tests was counterproductive behavior, a criterion that we had also included in our meta-analysis. Integrity tests are saturated with the dependability construct; thus, mean correlations between dependability measures and counterproductive behavior obtained in the two different meta-analyses can be compared. The *observed* correlation coefficients from both studies appear in Table 9.7[2]. Both meta-analyses also separately report mean observed validities for concurrent and predictive validity studies.

In the Ones et al. (1993) meta-analysis, the mean observed correlation between integrity tests (all studies) and counterproductive behavior was −.33. In our database, the mean observed correlation between dependability measures (all studies) and counterproductive behavior is −.35. When only concurrent validity studies are compared, Ones et al. obtained a mean observed validity of −.39; our analyses also yield −.39. When only predictive validity studies are compared, the results are again similar. The validities in both studies are in the mid 20s. Both meta-analyses show useful levels of criterion-related validity for dependability measures in both concurrent and predictive validity studies, and both show lower validity levels when only predictive validity studies are examined.

---

[2]Hough, in her meta-analytic work, codes the sign of a validity coefficient to indicate the direction of the relationship with the definition of the criterion construct. For example, achievement, dependability, and adjustment correlate negatively with counterproductive behavior. Thus, a −.20 in Hough's (1992) data is the same as a +.20 in Ones et al.'s (1993) data.

TABLE 9.7

Comparison Between Hough (1992) and Ones, Viswesvaran, & Schmidt (1993)
Observed Validities for Dependability Construct[1]

Integrity/Dependability Measures	Validities for Criterion Construct:Counterproductive Behavior	
	Ones, Viswesvaran, & Schmidt Database[2,3]	Hough Database
All studies	−.33	−.35[4]
Concurrent validity studies	−.39	−.39
Predictive validity studies	−.25	−.23

[1] Integrity tests are saturated with Dependability construct.
[2] Observed validities. Signs are reversed to be comparable to how Hough keys predictor and criterion.
[3] Adapted from "Comprehensive meta-analysis of integrity test validities: Findings and implications for personnel selection and theories of job performance" [Monograph] by D. S. Ones, C. Viswesvaran, and F. L. Schmidt, 1993, *Journal of Applied Psychology, 78*, 679–703. Copyright by American Psychological Association. Adapted with permission.
[4] Adapted from "The 'Big Five' personality variables–construct confusion: Description versus prediction," by L. M. Hough, 1992, *Human Performance, 5*, 139–155. Copyright 1992 by Lawrence Erlbaum Associates. Adapted with permission.

Importance of Criterion Dimensions

In the last few years considerable effort has been devoted to defining and conceptualizing the dimensions of job performance. Borman and Motowidlo (1993), for example, distinguished task performance from contextual performance. Smith, Organ, and Near (1983) coined the term *organizational citizenship*; whereas, Brief and Motowidlo (1986) use the term *prosocial organizational* behavior to describe similar criterion dimensions.

Many studies have reported validities for specific job performance constructs. Hough (1992) summarized many of these validity coefficients within personality construct. Table 9.8 shows the average validities for personality constructs and several specific job performance constructs—Irresponsible Behavior, Sales Effectiveness, Creativity, Teamwork, Effort, and Combat Effectiveness. A box indicates validities that appear useful.

In the table, every one of the nine personality constructs shows a useful relation with at least one criterion. Achievement is *not* necessarily the best predictor—it depends on the criterion. Moreover, the relations make sense.

That the relations do make sense is revealed by, for example, an examination of the predictors of Creativity. Agreeableness correlates −.29 with Creativity; Affiliation correlates −.25 with Creativity; and Potency, which is defined as degree of impact, influence, and energy, correlates +.21 with Creativity. Interestingly, Dependability correlates −.07 with Creativity. Although the total sample size for the −.07 value is only 268, conformity is an element of Dependability and probably accounts for this negative relation. Achievement, on the

TABLE 9.8
Relationship Between Personality Constructs and Job Performance Constructs

Personality Construct	Job Performance Construct																	
	Irresponsible Behavior			Sales Effectiveness			Creativity			Teamwork			Effort			Combat Effectiveness		
	No. Corr.	Sum of Samples	Mean r	No. Corr.	Sum of Samples	Mean r	No. Corr.	Sum of Samples	Mean r	No. Corr.	Sum of Samples	Mean r	No. Corr.	Sum of Samples	Mean r	No. Corr.	Sum of Samples	Mean r
Affiliation	1	667	.01	1	667	.19	2	116	-.25	—	—	—	1	667	.00	2	600	-.02
Potency	14	38,578	-.06	7	1,111	.25	11	550	.21	39	2,307	.08	16	17,156	.17	9	2,695	.08
Achievement	4	19,476	-.19	2	162	.27	2	116	.14	3	233	.14	4	15,530	.21	1	300	.13
Dependability	69	98,676	-.24	5	2,236	.06	5	268	-.07	25	1,340	.17	11	25,408	.14	5	1,490	.08
Adjustment	9	21,431	-.15	3	778	.18	8	442	-.05	31	2,067	.13	15	9,562	.16	13	3,880	.19
Agreeableness	4	24,259	-.08	—	—	—	3	174	-.29	7	329	.17	1	7,666	.15	1	300	-.04
Intellectance	2	1,414	-.15	1	667	.15	1	58	.07	1	667	.11	1	667	.11	1	300	-.07
Rugged individualism	1	7,923	.00	—	—	—	1	58	.01	4	306	.08	2	198	-.03	2	595	.25

Note: Correlations are *not* corrected for unreliability or restriction in range.

From "The 'Big Five' personality variables—construct confusion: Description versus prediction" by L. M. Hough, 1992, *Human Performance, 5,* 139–155. Copyright 1992 by Lawrence Erlbaum Associates. Reprinted by permission.

other hand, does not have conformity as a part of it, and it correlates +.14 with Creativity. Adjustment also has a small negative relation with Creativity –.05. These relations suggest that creativity is characterized by people's marching to their own drummer as opposed to being oriented to smooth, harmonious, and agreeable relationships.

Teamwork is an important criterion for many organizations, especially as more and more organizations incorporate teams as part of their work processes and structure. Personality characteristics that correlate the highest with Teamwork are Dependability and Agreeableness.

This pattern of correlations for the two criteria Creativity and Teamwork suggests some interesting hypotheses about the composition of effective teams. For example, if a team has a creative task to accomplish, scoring high on Agreeableness may not be an asset. Indeed, it may work against effective task accomplishment. Team members selected because they are likely to work harmoniously with each other may be highly effective at some tasks, but such a team may not be particularly effective at creative problem solving.

The data in Table 9.8 suggest other useful relations as well. For example, Sales Effectiveness is best predicted by Achievement and Potency measures. Achievement correlates .27 with sales effectiveness, and Potency correlates .25. Of less interest to civilian organizations but highly relevant for military organizations are the predictors of combat effectiveness. Rugged Individualism (masculinity/femininity) correlates .25 with Combat Effectiveness, and Adjustment correlates .19 with Combat Effectiveness.

Incremental Validity

Personality variables do predict some parts of the criterion space, but do they provide increased validity when they are used in combination with measures of cognitive ability?

An important part of Project A was a concurrent validity study. Several predictors were administered to soldiers, including cognitive ability tests and personality measures. Performance data were gathered on several criterion measures. The criteria were categorized into five broad criteria—core technical proficiency, general soldiering proficiency, effort and leadership, personal discipline, and physical fitness and military bearing. The multiple correlations of the cognitive ability tests and personality scales with each criterion are shown in Table 9.9. The correlations are corrected for restriction in range and adjusted for shrinkage.

Clearly, the cognitive ability tests are very good predictors of the two proficiency criteria, Core Technical Proficiency and General Soldiering Proficiency, and they do correlate with the other three criteria. The personality scales correlate primarily with Effort and Leadership, Personal Discipline, and Physical Fitness/Military Bearing. The multiple correlations of the combined cognitive and personality measures indicate that the personality measures do indeed

TABLE 9.9

Incremental Validity of Personality Variables: Project A Results

Predictor	Core Technical Proficiency	General Soldiering Proficiency	Effort & Leadership	Personal Discipline	Military Bearing
	Job Performance				
General cognitive ability	.63	.65	.31	.16	.20
Personality	.26	.25	.33	.32	.37
Combined	.63	.66	.42	.35	.41

Note: Validity coefficients were corrected for range restriction and adjusted for shrinkage. $N \sim 4,000$.
Adapted from "Project A validity results: The relationship between predictor and criterion domains," by J. J. McHenry, L. M. Hough, J. T. Toquam, M. A. Hanson, & S. Ashworth, 1990, *Personnel Psychology, 43*, 335–354. Copyright by Personnel Psychology, Inc. Adapted with permission.

increment the validity of the cognitive measures. For the Effort and Leadership criterion, they increment validity by .11. For the Personal Discipline criterion they increment validity by .19. For the Physical Fitness/Military Bearing criterion, the personality variables increment validity by .21. It is clear that when the criterion space is expanded to include organizational citizenship or contextual variables, such as counterproductive behavior and effort, personality measures are useful additions to the predictor battery.

IMPLEMENTATION ISSUES

Issues other than validity are also important when personality variables are considered as part of a predictor battery to make real-life employment decisions. One important issue is faking or intentional distortion. Applicants are motivated to present themselves in a favorable light. In such cases, what is the effect of intentional distortion on criterion-related validity? The U.S. Civil Rights Acts of 1964 and 1991 prohibited discrimination on the basis of ethnic background, gender, and religious preferences. Employment tests that show adverse impact against minorities and women come under severe scrutiny. Moreover, diversity in an organization's workforce is increasingly recognized as an asset. Thus, an important issue is how minorities and women score on personality scales. A final implementation issue relates to the ADA of 1990. How does the Equal Employment Opportunity Commission (EEOC) intend to enforce ADA with regard to personality measures? These three issues are addressed in this section.

Faking

The magnitude of validities of personality tests obtained in predictive validity studies indicates that personality tests are useful predictors of important criteria even when individuals are tested under conditions in which they are motivated to, and do, distort their responses. Although the magnitude of the validity coefficients is lower than that in concurrent validity studies, the magnitude of these validities is such that personality measures are still useful predictors of criteria. Of course, the decrease in the magnitude of validity may be due to factors other than distortion.

Project A researchers examined the effect of distortion on the level of validities of personality scales. They developed and administered a personality inventory in two contexts: a concurrent criterion-related validity study and a faking experiment. Sample sizes were 9,188 and 245, respectively. Results showed that the unlikely virtues scale, which was designed to detect intentional distortion, was responsive to motivational set; people can and do distort their responses when instructed to do so; and criterion-related validities remain stable regardless of possible distortion by respondents (Hough et al., 1990).

The data showing the effects of social desirability on criterion-related validity appear in Table 9.10, which shows the validities for an Accurate group and an Overly Desirable group for two criteria—Effort and Leadership and Personal Discipline. The numbers in bold show the differences in validities between the Accurate and Overly Desirable groups for the two criteria. The sample size for the Accurate group is about 5,900; the sample size for the Overly Desirable group is about 2,500. Four of the differences are statistically significant. Of these four, one is in the direction of increased validity for the group providing Overly Desirable self descriptions. The average difference in validity between the Accurate and Overly Desirable groups across all the personality measures for the Effort and Leadership criterion is a −.03. That is, validity is .03 points lower for the Overly Desirable group. The average difference in validity for the Personal Discipline criterion is +.01; validity increased. The difference in validity is not significant, but it is not lower.

Adverse Impact

Mean score differences between men and women and mean score differences between Whites and ethnic groups are also important when considering personality measures for a selection system because people in the lower scoring group are hired at a lower rate than those in the higher scoring group. How do women score relative to men on personality variables? How do Blacks, Hispanics, and Native Americans score relative to Whites on personality variables?

Means, standard deviations, and sample sizes were obtained from manuals of many different personality inventories. Mean score differences were com-

TABLE 9.10

Effects of Social Desirability on Criterion-Related Validity

	Effort & Leadership			Personal Discipline		
	Accurate	Overly Desirable	Difference	Accurate	Overly Desirable	Difference
Potency:						
Dominance	.15	.14	−.01	.00	.06	+.06*
Energy Level	.23	.20	−.03	.13	.15	+.02
Achievement:						
Self-esteem	.21	.18	−.03	.12	.12	.00
Work orientation	.25	.20	−.05*	.17	.16	−.01
Dependability:						
Traditional values	.14	.11	−.03	.26	.22	−.04
Nondelinquency	.13	.12	−.01	.28	.29	+.01
Conscientiousness	.19	.14	−.05*	.22	.22	.00
Adjustment:						
Emotional stability	.17	.16	−.01	.11	.12	+.01
Agreeableness:						
Cooperativeness	.16	.13	−.03	.20	.21	+.01
Average Difference			−.03			+.01

Note: Validities are *not* corrected.
Sample sizes for Accurate group range from 5,896 to 5,997. Sample sizes for Overly Desirable group range from 2,428 to 2,480.
Adapted from "Criterion-related validities of personality constructs and the effect of response distortion on those validities," [Monograph] by L. M. Hough, N. K. Eaton, M. D. Dunnette, J. D. Kamp, and R. A. McCloy, 1990, *Journal of Applied Psychology, 75,* 581–595. Copyright 1990 by the American Psychological Association, Inc. Adapted with permission.
* Denotes statistical significance at $p. < 05$.

puted between men and women and between Whites, Blacks, Hispanics, and Native Americans and converted to effect sizes so that mean score differences could be summarized and examined across inventories and scales.

Dozens of validity coefficients have appeared in previous tables. Interpretation of the data in the next tables, however, requires a change in set. Tables 9.11 to 9.14 show effect sizes, which are interpreted in terms of *standard deviations*. (Effect size is the standardized mean difference between two groups' scores, i.e., $\overline{X}_1 - \overline{X}_2 \div SD_{pooled}$.) Table 9.11 shows mean score differences between men and women. Tables 9.12, 9.13, and 9.14 show mean score differences between Whites and Blacks, Whites and Hispanics, and Whites and Native Americans, respectively. All effect sizes in Tables 9.11 to 9.14 are relative to the protected group. That is, a positive value (effect size) indicates higher scores for the protected group; a negative value indicates lower scores for the protected group.

Three columns in each of these tables are especially important. They are Average Effect Size for Scales, Average Effect Size for Construct—Inventory Based, and Weighted Effect Size for Construct—Inventory Based. The values in the Average Effect Size for Scales were calculated by computing the effect size of the difference between, for example, female and male scores on each scale and computing the average of the effect sizes for the scales in each personality construct. In most instances this column would be the most relevant, but personality inventories often contain at least two scales that measure different facets of a personality construct. In these instances, the Average Effect Size for Scales values may not be the best estimate of the difference between women and men on the construct because the sample may not be representative of women and men in the population. In the Average Effect Size for Scales column, the sample values are entered as many times as the inventory has scales included in the construct. Thus, if an inventory has three dependability scales, the sample contributes three estimates of the effect size of the difference between mean scores for women and men. Additional average effect sizes were calculated to address this concern. Those values are presented in the Average Effect Size for Construct—Inventory Based column. Values in this column were obtained by averaging the effect size of the differences between women and men on scales measuring the same construct in an inventory and using this average effect size as the value to represent the effect size for the construct for this inventory or sample. Thus, if an inventory had three dependability scales, the average effect size of the difference between mean scores for women and men for these three scales was calculated. This average effect size was then used to represent the value of the mean score differences between women and men for this inventory. The sample thus did not contribute three values to the calculation of the average effect size. Sample size is, however, an important characteristic. Thus, a third column of values was calculated: Weighted Effect Size for Construct—Inventory Based. The values in this last column were calculated by weighting the values in the Average Effect Size for Construct—Inventory Based column by the sample size to which the inventory was administered. The values in this column may be the best estimate of the difference (in terms of standard scores, i.e., effect sizes) between mean scores. If the sample size for one inventory is much larger than those for other inventories, the author's operationalization of the construct (with all its idiosyncrasies) is given greater weight.

The information about effect sizes of the differences in mean scores for women and men is shown in Table 9.11. A positive value in the Average Effect Size columns indicates that women score higher than men; a negative value means that women score lower than men. The largest effect size is for Rugged Individualism; women score about 1.50 to 1.75 standard deviations lower than men. This result is not surprising—Rugged Individualism is Masculinity/Femi-

TABLE 9.11
Mean Score Differences Men and Women (Effect Sizes)

Personality Construct	No. Inv.	No. Scales	Male Sample Size	Female Sample Size	Range of Effect Sizes for Scales	Average Effect Size for Scales	Range of Effect Sizes for Construct Inventory Based[1]	Average Effect Size for Construct Inventory Based[1]	Weighted[2] Average Effect Size for Construct Inventory Based[1]
Affiliation	3	7	10,215	5,590	-.15 to +.86	.21	-.14 to +.39	.10	-.06
Potency	8	19	27,903	24,179	-.55 to +.22	-.14	-.42 to +.03	-.17	-.18
Achievement	4	6	18,236	19,093	-.13 to +.23	-.02	-.09 to +.08	-.02	-.04
Dependability	11	21	66,853	62,570	-.22 to +.67	.17	-.22 to +.54	.18	.27
Adjustment	7	15	26,874	23,177	-.44 to +.31	-.11	-.39 to +.13	-.20	-.21
Agreeableness	7	12	26,903	23,179	-.87 to +.59	.10	-.09 to +.28	.08	.09
Intellectance	4	4	10,331	5,726	-.39 to +.10	-.12	-.39 to +.10	-.12	-.27
Rugged individualism	3	3	1,481	1,498	-1.95 to -1.25	-1.57	-1.95 to -1.25	-1.57	-1.74
Response validity: Unlikely Virtues	4	4	18,236	19,093	-.05 to +.01	-.01	-.05 to +.01	-.01	.00

Note. Effect size is the standardized mean difference between the two groups' scores. All effect sizes in this table are relative to the Female group. A positive value indicates higher scores for Females; a negative value indicates lower scores for the Females.
Inventories included in analyses are: ABLE; CABLE; California Psychological Inventory; Comrey Personality Scales; Guilford-Zimmerman Temperament Survey; Hogan Personality Inventory; Job Candidate Profile; PDI Employment Inventory; Personality Research Form; Personnel Reaction Blank; 16 PF.
[1] Several inventories have multiple scales that measure different facets of the same construct. The figures in this column were obtained by averaging the effect size of the differences between Female and Male on scales measuring the same construct in an inventory and using this average effect size as the value to represent the effect size for the construct for the inventory.
[2] Weighted by sample size.

151

ninity. Also not surprising, women score .18 standard deviations below men on Potency, which is defined as dominance and influence, and women score .27 standard deviations above men on Dependability measures. These values are very likely stable estimates of the differences between men and women—some of the sample sizes are very large. For example, the number of men in the Dependability comparison is over 66,800; the number of women in the Dependability comparison is over 62,500. Except for Rugged Individualism, the differences between men and women are small.

Information about effect sizes of the differences in mean scores for Blacks and Whites is shown in Table 9.12. Again a positive value means that the protected group, in this case Blacks, scores higher than Whites; a negative value means that Blacks score lower than Whites. Examination of the average effect size columns indicates that the difference between Black and White mean scores is very small, and except for the Affiliation and Intellectance scales, the sample sizes are very large. For the Dependability construct, the Black sample size is almost 31,000. For the Potency, Achievement, Adjustment, and Agreeableness constructs, the sample sizes are about 15,000. For these constructs the values are likely stable estimates of differences between Blacks and Whites, and again, the differences are very small.

Information about effect sizes of the differences in mean scores for Hispanics and Whites is shown in Table 9.13. The sample sizes for the Hispanic group range from 911 to 7,493; thus, the estimates are less stable. The only noteworthy difference between Hispanics and Whites is for the unlikely virtues scale. Hispanics score about .60 standard deviations higher on unlikely virtues scales than do Whites.

Information about effect sizes of the differences in mean scores for Native Americans and Whites is shown in Table 9.14. The sample sizes for the Native American group are very small. The sample size for the Dependability construct is 552; the sample size for the other constructs is 73. Although the sample sizes are small and these may not be stable estimates, some data are better than no data.

Implications of Americans with Disabilities Act (ADA) for Personality Measurement

The ADA prohibits disability-related inquiries of applicants, and it prohibits a medical examination before a conditional job offer. How does this affect the use of personality inventories for selection? The EEOC issued its enforcement guidelines for the ADA in 1995. (Excerpts of the EEOC ADA Enforcement Guidance notice, which are relevant to personality testing, are reproduced in Appendix A.)

Disability-related Inquiries.   The EEOC specifically allows asking about work attendance, including number of days absent from a previous job, but does not

TABLE 9.12
Mean Score Differences: Blacks & Whites (Effect Sizes)

Personality Construct	No.Inv.	No.Scales	White Sample Size	Black Sample Size	Range of Effect Sizes for Scales	Average Effect Size for Scales	Range of Effect Sizes for Construct Inventory Based[1]	Average Effect Size for Construct Inventory Based[1]	Weighted[2] Average Effect Size for Construct Inventory Based[1]
Affiliation	1	1	5,606	1,034	—	-.31	—	-.31	-.31
Potency	4	6	28,376	15,053	-.05 to +.26	.15	+.08 to +.21	.15	.15
Achievement	3	6	22,770	14,019	-.09 to +.27	.08	-.08 to +.25	.08	.01
Dependability	6	12	74,942	30,803	-.27 to +.29	.12	-.27 to +.26	.07	-.08
Adjustment	4	4	28,376	15,053	-.02 to +.21	.09	-.02 to +.21	.09	.04
Agreeableness	5	5	31,224	15,418	-.12 to +.27	.04	-.13 to +.27	.04	-.01
Intellectance	1	1	5,606	1,034	—	-.28	—	-.28	-.28
Locus of control	2	2	10,075	3,754	-.07 to -.06	-.07	-.07 to -.06	-.07	-.06
Response validity: unlikely virtues	3	3	22,770	14,019	-.13 to +.21	.09	-.13 to +.21	.09	.00

Note: Effect size is the standardized mean difference between the two groups' scores. All effect sizes in this table are relative to the Black group. A positive value indicates higher scores for Blacks; a negative value indicates lower scores for Blacks.
Inventories included in analyses are ABLE; CABLE; Hogan Personality Inventory; Job Candidate Profile; PDI Employment Inventory.
[1] Several inventories have multiple scales that measure different facets of the same construct. The figures in this column were obtained by averaging the effect size of the differences between Blacks and Whites on scales measuring the same construct in an inventory and using this average effect size as the value to represent the effect size for the construct for the inventory.
[2] Weighted by sample size.

153

TABLE 9.13

Mean Score Differences: Hispanics & Whites (Effect Sizes)

Personality Construct	No. Inv.	No. Scales	White Sample Size	Hispanic Sample Size	Range of Effect Sizes for Scales	Average Effect Size for Scales	Range of Effect Sizes for Construct Inventory Based[1]	Average Effect Size for Construct Inventory Based[1]	Weighted[2] Average Effect Size for Construct Inventory Based[1]
Potency	3	5	22,770	1,911	-.06 to +.21	.07	-.06 to +.16	.05	.01
Achievement	3	6	22,770	1,911	-.02 to +.11	.05	+.02 to +.10	.05	.04
Dependability	5	11	69,336	7,493	-.36 to +.32	.09	-.36 to +.23	.01	-.09
Adjustment	3	3	22,770	911	-.04 to +.07	.00	-.04 to +.07	.00	-.01
Agreeableness	4	4	25,618	2,160	-.15 to +.10	-.01	-.15 to +.10	-.01	-.05
Response Validity: Unlikely Virtues	3	3	22,770	1,911	+.48 to +.79	.67	+.48 to +.79	.67	.60

Note: Effect size is the standardized mean difference between the two groups' scores. All effect sizes in this table are relative to the Hispanic group. A positive value indicates higher scores for Hispanics; a negative value indicates lower scores for Hispanics.
Inventories included in analyses are ABLE; CABLE; Job Candidate Profile; PDI Employment Inventory.
[1] Several inventories have multiple scales that measure different facets of the same construct. The figures in this column were obtained by averaging the effect size of the differences between Hispanics and Whites on scales measuring the same construct in an inventory and using this average effect size as the value to represent the effect size for the construct for the inventory.
[2] Weighted by sample size.

TABLE 9.14

Mean Score Differences: Native Americans & Whites (Effect Sizes)

Personality Construct	No. Inv.	No. Scales	White Sample Size	Native American Sample Size	Range of Effect Sizes for Scales	Average Effect Size for Scales	Range of Effect Sizes for Construct Inventory Based[1]	Average Effect Size for Construct Inventory Based[1]	Weighted[2] Average Effect Size for Construct Inventory Based[1]
Potency	1	1	12,695	73	—	—	—	—	-.09
Achievement	1	2	12,695	73	.00 to +.03	—	—	—	.02
Dependability	2	2	56,413	552	-.20	—	—	—	-.20
Adjustment	1	1	12,695	73	—	—	—	—	-.05
Agreeableness	1	1	12,695	73	—	—	—	—	-.14
Response validity: Unlikely virtues	1	1	12,695	73	—	—	—	—	-.04

Note: Effect size is the standardized mean difference between the two groups' scores. All effect sizes in this table are relative to the Native American group. A positive value indicates higher scores for Native Americans; a negative value indicates lower scores for Native Americans. Inventories included in analyses are: CABLE; PDI Employment Inventory.

[1] Several inventories have multiple scales that measure different facets of the same construct. The figures in this column were obtained by averaging the effect size of the differences between Native Americans and Whites on scales measuring the same construct in an inventory and using this average effect size as the value to represent the effect size for the construct for the inventory.

[2] Weighted by sample size.

allow asking about the number of *sick* days. It is all right to ask if an applicant has used *illegal* drugs, but it is not all right to ask about the *amount* of illegal drug use or about prescription drugs. Similarly, asking whether a person consumes alcohol is permitted, but asking about the amount of alcohol consumed is not; alcoholism is considered a disease. The EEOC Enforcement notice specifically states that employers can ask about honesty, tastes, and habits. Clearly, it is important to examine each item in an inventory.

Defining Characteristics of a Medical Examination.   A second area of concern is whether a personality inventory is considered a medical examination. If it is, it can be administered only after a conditional job offer is made.

The EEOC Notice lists the following factors that they consider when determining whether a procedure or test is a medical examination:

- If a test is administered or interpreted by a health care professional or someone trained by a health care professional, the test is considered a medical examination.
- If a test is *designed* to reveal or is *administered* to determine an applicant's physical or mental health or impairments, the test is considered a medical examination. According to the EEOC notice, psychological examinations are medical if they provide evidence that would lead to identifying a mental disorder or impairment (for example, those listed in the American Psychiatric Association's most recent *Diagnostic and Statistical Manual of Mental Disorders* [DSM]). (For more detail, read Appendix A.)
- If a test is invasive, such as drawing blood, collection of urine, or analyzing breath, the test is considered a medical examination.
- If a test measures physiological or biological responses, the test is considered a medical examination.
- If a test is normally administered in a medical setting or requires use of medical equipment or devices, the test is considered a medical examination.

Personality measures are not necessarily considered medical examinations; the particular circumstances determine the classification. Because of the way the Minnesota Multiphasic Personality Inventory (MMPI) was developed and the way it is often used, it is likely to be considered a medical examination. In general, personality inventories developed by I/O psychologists and used to predict job performance are not likely to be considered medical examinations. It is, however, very important to examine individual items and scales for compliance with the EEOC's interpretation of what constitutes a disability-related question or item.

SUMMARY

Personality measures can contribute to I/O psychologists' tool kit used to predict job performance. The usefulness of these measures emerges, however, only when validity coefficients are summarized according to constructs in a personality taxonomy. Criterion-related validities of the Big Five constructs in the Five-Factor Model suggest that these constructs are too "fat." Greater specificity and greater diversity of constructs are needed to discover useful levels of validity. An alternative taxonomy developed during Project A research revealed more useful levels of validity.

Construct analysis of the performance domain is also important for identifying relevant personality constructs to use as predictors. When both predictor and criterion domains are considered, specific personality constructs predict *targeted* performance criteria such as effort and leadership, personal discipline, counterproductive behavior, creativity, sales effectiveness, educational success, training success, and combat effectiveness. Specific personality measures do less well predicting overall job performance and technical proficiency. Once specific personality constructs are identified as predicting a particular criterion construct, the specific personality measures can be combined to form a composite or compound (heterogeneous) personality measure that thereby increments the criterion-related validity of the personality predictor.

When personality measures are included in prediction batteries and the information is used to make important decisions, people are motivated to present themselves in an acceptable way, to distort their responses to personality items. As a result, decision makers are often skeptical of including personality measures in a battery of tests. Although predictive criterion-related validities appear to be lower than concurrent criterion-related validities, intentional distortion does not appear to be the reason. Project A research suggested that socially desirable responding does not appear to moderate the validity of personality variables.

Important legal issues must be considered before using personality variables as part of a decision system that affects employment in the U. S. For example, the U.S. Civil Rights Acts of 1964 and 1991 prohibit certain employer activities. A comparison of mean scores of men, women, Whites, Blacks, Hispanics, and Native Americans on personality constructs likely to be useful for predicting work performance indicates that protected groups score similarly to White men. Increasingly, organizations are recognizing the value of having a diverse workforce. Personality measures are useful for predicting criterion constructs that are not well predicted with cognitive measures, and they result in little or no adverse impact.

The ADA of 1990 also prohibits certain employer activities such as administering a medical examination before giving an applicant a conditional job offer. The ADA also prohibits disability-related inquiries. The EEOC Enforcement notice indicates that personality measures are not necessarily considered medical examinations—the particular circumstances determine the classification. A careful review of the circumstances is important. For example, each item must be reviewed to ensure that no disability-related questions are asked. A careful review of test development activities is also important. The purpose of the test and what it was designed to measure are important factors in determining whether or not the test is considered a medical examination.

In short, personality variables predict work-related criteria even when people are motivated to present themselves in a favorable manner. Moreover, when combined with cognitive measures, personality measures increment criterion-related validity and reduce adverse impact against protected groups. These outcomes are likely to result in personality measures being considered as additions to many performance prediction batteries.

REFERENCES

Barrick, M. R., & Mount, M. K. (1991). The big five personality dimensions and job performance: A meta-analysis. *Personnel Psychology, 44*, 1–26.

Borman, W. C., & Motowidlo, S. J. (1993). Expanding the criterion space to include elements of contextual performance. In N. Schmitt, W. C. Borman, & Associates, *Personnel selection in organizations* (pp. 71–98). San Francisco, CA: Jossey-Bass.

Brief, A. P., & Motowidlo, S. J. (1986). Prosocial organizational behaviors. *Academy of Management Review, 11*, 710–725.

Costa, P. T., Jr., & McCrae, R. R. (1992). *Revised NEO Personality Inventory (NEO-PI-R) and NEO Five-Factor Inventory (NEO-FFI) professional manual.* Odessa, FL: Psychological Assessment Resources, Inc.

Digman, J. M., & Inouye, J. (1986). Further specification of the five robust factors of personality. *Journal of Personality and Social Psychology, 50*, 116–123.

Ghiselli, E. E. (1966). *The validity of occupational aptitude tests.* New York: Wiley.

Goldberg, L. R. (1990). An alternative "description of personality": The Big-Five factor structure. *Journal of Personality and Social Psychology, 59*, 1216–1229.

Guion, R. M. (1965). *Personnel testing.* New York: McGraw-Hill.

Guion, R. M., & Gottier, R. F. (1965). Validity of personality measures in personnel selection. *Personnel Psychology, 18*, 135–164.

Hogan, R. J. (1982). A socioanalytic theory of personality. In M. M. Page (Ed.), *1982 Nebraska Symposium on Motivation: Personality—current theory and research* (pp. 55–89). Lincoln: University of Nebraska Press.

Hogan, R. J. (1986). *Hogan Personality Inventory manual.* Minneapolis, MN: National Computer Systems.

Hough, L. M. (1992). The "Big Five" personality variables—construct confusion: Description versus prediction. *Human Performance, 5*, 139–155.

Hough, L. M., Eaton, N. L., Dunnette, M. D., Kamp, J. D., & McCloy, R. A. (1990). Criterion-related validities of personality constructs and the effect of response distortion on those validities [Monograph]. *Journal of Applied Psychology, 75*, 581–595.

Hough, L. M., & Schneider, R. J. (1996). Personality traits, taxonomies, and applications in organizations. In K. R. Murphy (Ed.), *Individual differences and behavior in organizations* (pp 31–88). San Francisco: Jossey-Bass.

Hunter, J. E., & Hunter, R. F. (1984). Validity and utility of alternative predictors of job performance. *Psychological Bulletin, 96*, 72–98.

Kamp, J. D., & Gough, H. G. (1986, August). *The Big Five personality factors from an assessment context.* Paper presented at the 94th annual convention of the American Psychological Association, Washington, DC.

Kamp, J. D., & Hough, L. M. (1986). Utility of personality assessment: A review and integration of the literature. In L. M. Hough (Ed.), *Utility of temperament, biodata, and interest assessment for predicting job performance: A review and integration of the literature* (ARI Research Note No. 88-02, pp. 1–90). Alexandria, VA: U. S. Army Research Institute for the Behavioral and Social Sciences.

McCrae, R. R., Costa, P. T., Jr., & Busch, C. M. (1986). Evaluating comprehensiveness in personality systems: The California Q-set and the five-factor model. *Journal of Personality, 54*, 430–446.

Norman, W. T. (1963). Toward an adequate taxonomy of personality attributes: Replicated factor structure in peer nomination personality ratings. *Journal of Abnormal and Social Psychology, 66*, 574–583.

Ones, D. S., Viswesvaran, C., Schmidt, F. L. (1993). Comprehensive meta-analysis of integrity test validities: Findings and implications for personnel selection and theories of job performance [Monograph]. *Journal of Applied Psychology, 78*, 679–703.

Pearlman, K. (1985, November). *Validity generalization: From theory to application.* Paper presented at the Center for Human Resources Programs, Institute of Industrial Relations, University of California at Berkeley, Berkeley, CA.

Schmitt, N., Gooding, R. Z., Noe, R. A., & Kirsch, M. (1984). Meta-analysis of validity studies published between 1964 and 1982 and the investigation of study characteristics. *Personnel Psychology, 37*, 407–422.

Schneider, R. J., & Hough, L. M. (1995). Personality and industrial/organizational psychology. In C. L. Cooper & I. T. Robertson (Eds.), *International review of industrial and organizational psychology* (pp. 75–129). Chichester, England: Wiley.

Smith, C. A., Organ, D. W., & Near, J. P. (1983). Organizational citizenship behavior: Its nature and antecedents. *Journal of Applied Psychology, 68*, 653–663.

Tupes, E. C., & Christal, R. E. (1992). Recurrent personality factors based on trait ratings. *Journal of Personality, 60*, 225–251. (Originally released 1961.)

White, R. W. (1959). Motivation reconsidered: The concept of competence. *Psychological Review, 66*, 297–333.

APPENDIX A
EEOC Notice About Enforcement of ADA
ADA Enforcement Guidance: Preemployment
Disability-Related Questions and Medical Examinations

Issued by U.S. Equal Employment Opportunity Commission

1995 (Excerpts)

INTRODUCTION

Under the Americans with Disabilities Act of 1990 (the "ADA"), an employer may ask disability-related questions and require medical examinations of an applicant only *after* the applicant has been given a conditional job offer.

STATUTORY AND REGULATORY FRAMEWORK

Although employers may not ask disability-related questions or require medical examinations at the pre-offer stage, they *may* do a wide variety of things to evaluate whether an applicant is qualified for the job, including the following:

Employers *may* ask about an applicant's ability to perform specific job functions. For example, an employer may state the physical requirements of a job (such as the ability to lift a certain amount of weight, or the ability to climb ladders), and ask if an applicant can satisfy these requirements.

Employers *may* ask about an applicant's non-medical qualifications and skills, such as the applicant's education, work history, and required certifications and licenses.

Employers *may* ask applicants to describe or demonstrate how they would perform job tasks.

Once a conditional job offer is made, the employer may ask disability-related questions and require medical examinations as long as this is done for all entering employees in that job category. If the employer rejects the applicant after a disability-related question or medical examination, investigators will closely scrutinize whether the rejection was based on the results of that question or examination.

If the question or examination screens out an individual because of a disability, the employer must demonstrate that the reason for the rejection is "job-related and consistent with business necessity."

In addition, if the individual is screened out for safety reasons, the employer must demonstrate that the individual poses a "direct threat." This means that the individual poses a significant risk of substantial harm to him/herself or others, and that the risk cannot be reduced below the direct threat level through reasonable accommodation.

Medical information must be kept confidential. The ADA contains narrow exceptions for disclosing specific, limited information to supervisors and managers, first aid and safety personnel, and government officials investigating compliance with ADA. Employers may also disclose medical information to state workers' compensation offices, state second injury funds, or workers' compensation insurance carriers in accordance with state workers' compensation laws and may use the medical information for insurance purposes.

PRE-OFFER STAGE

What is a Disability-Related Question?

Definition: "Disability-Related Question" means a question that is *likely to elicit* information about a disability.

At the pre-offer stage, an employer cannot ask questions that are *likely to elicit* information about a disability. This includes directly asking whether an applicant has a particular disability. It also means that an employer cannot ask questions that are *closely related* to disability. (Of course, an employer can always ask about an applicant's ability to perform the job.)

On the other hand, if there are many possible answers to a question and only some of those answers would contain disability-related information, that question is not "disability-related." (Sometimes, applicants disclose disability-related information in responding to an otherwise lawful pre-offer question. Although the employer has not asked an unlawful question, it still cannot refuse to hire an applicant based on disability unless the reason is "job-related and consistent with business necessity.")

Below are some commonly asked questions:

May an employer **ask whether an applicant can meet the employer's attendance requirements**?

Yes. An employer may state its attendance requirements and ask whether an applicant can meet them. An employer also may ask about an applicant's prior attendance record (for example, how many days the applicant was absent from his/her last job). These questions are not likely to elicit information about a disability because there may be many reasons unrelated to disability why someone cannot meet attendance requirements or was frequently absent from a previous job (for example, an applicant may have had day-care problems).

An employer also may ask questions designed to detect whether an applicant abused his/her leave because these questions are not likely to elicit information about a disability.

Example: An employer may ask an applicant, "How many Mondays or Fridays were you absent last year on leave other than approved vacation leave?"

However, at the pre-offer stage, an employer may not ask how many days an applicant was *sick*, because these questions relate directly to the *severity of an individual's impairments*. Therefore, these questions are likely to elicit information about a disability.

May an employer ask applicants about their **arrest or conviction records**?
Yes. Questions about an applicant's arrest or conviction records are not likely to elicit information about disability because there are many reasons unrelated to disability why someone may have an arrest/conviction record.[1]

May an employer ask questions about an **applicant's impairments**?
Yes, if the particular question is not likely to elicit information about whether the applicant has a disability. It is important to remember that not all impairments will be disabilities; an impairment is a disability *only* if it substantially limits a major life activity. So, an employer may ask an applicant with a broken leg how she broke her leg. Since a broken leg normally is a temporary condition which does not rise to the level of a disability, this question is not likely to disclose whether the applicant has a disability. But, such questions as "Do you expect the leg to heal normally?" or "Do you break bones easily?" would be disability-related. Certainly, an employer may not ask a broad question about impairments that is likely to elicit information about disability, such as "What impairments do you have?"

May an employer ask **whether applicants can perform major life activities**, such as standing, lifting, walking, etc.?
Questions about whether an applicant can perform major life activities are almost always disability-related because they are likely to elicit information about a disability. For example, if an applicant cannot stand or walk, it is likely to be a result of a disability. So, these questions are prohibited at the pre-offer stage *unless* they are specifically about the ability to perform job functions.

---

[1] However, investigators should he aware that Title VII of the Civil Rights Act of 1964, as amended, applies to such questions and that nothing in this Enforcement Guidance relieves an employer of its obligations to comply with Title VII. The Commission has previously provided guidance for investigators to follow concerning an employer's use of arrest/conviction records. *See* Policy Guidance No. N-915-061 (9/7/90) ("Policy Guidance on the Consideration of Arrest Records In Employment Decisions under Title VII of the Civil Rights Act of 1964, as amended, 42 U.S. C. § 2000e *et seq.* [1982]"; EEOC Compliance Manual, Vol. II, Appendices 604-A ("Conviction Records") and 604-B (" Conviction Records—Statistics").

May an employer ask applicants about their **workers' compensation history?**

No. An employer may not ask applicants about job-related injuries or workers' compensation history. These questions relate directly to the severity of an applicant's impairments. Therefore, these questions are likely to elicit information about disability.

May an employer ask applicants about their **current illegal use of drugs?**

Yes. An employer may ask applicants about current illegal use of drugs[2] because an individual who currently illegally uses drugs is not protected under the ADA (when the employer acts on the basis of the drug use).

May an employer ask applicants about their **lawful drug use?**

No, if the question is likely to elicit information about disability. Employers should know that many questions about current or prior lawful drug use are likely to elicit information about a disability, and are therefore impermissible at the pre-offer stage. For example, questions like, "What medications are you currently taking?" or "Have you ever taken AZT?" certainly elicit information about whether an applicant has a disability.

However, some innocuous questions about lawful drug use are not likely to elicit information about disability.

> Example: During her interview, an applicant volunteers to the interviewer that she is coughing and wheezing because her allergies are acting up as a result of pollen in the air. The interviewer, who also has allergies, tells the applicant that he finds "Lemebreathe" (an over-the-counter antihistamine) to be effective, and asks the applicant if she has tried it. There are many reasons why someone might have tried "Lemebreathe" which have nothing to do with disability. Therefore, this question is not likely to elicit information about a disability.

May an employer ask applicants about their **lawful drug use** if the employer is administering a test for illegal use of drugs?

Yes, *if* an applicant tests positive for illegal drug use. In that case, the employer may validate the test results by asking about lawful drug use or possible explanations for the positive result other than the illegal use of drugs.

> Example: If an applicant tests positive for use of a controlled substance, the employer may lawfully ask questions such as, "What medications have you taken that might have resulted in this positive test result? Are you taking this medication under a lawful prescription?"

May an employer ask applicants about their **prior illegal drug use?**

Yes, provided that the particular question is not likely to elicit information about a disability. It is important to remember that past *addiction* to illegal drugs

---

[2]"Drug" means a controlled substance, as defined in schedules 1 through V of Section 202 of the Controlled Substances Act (21 U.S.C. § 812). 29 C.F.R. § 1630.3(a)(1).

or controlled substances is a covered disability under the ADA (as long as the person is not a current illegal drug user), but past *casual* use is not a covered disability. Therefore, the question is fine as long as it does not go to past drug *addiction*.

> Example: An employer may ask, "Have you ever used illegal drugs?" "When is the last time you used illegal drugs?" or "Have you used illegal drugs in the last six months?" These questions are not likely to tell the employer anything about whether the applicant was addicted to drugs.

However, questions that ask how much the applicant used drugs in the past *are* likely to elicit information about whether the applicant was a past drug addict. These questions are therefore impermissible at the pre-offer stage.

> Example: At the pre-offer stage, an employer may not ask an applicant questions such as, "How often did you use illegal drugs in the past?" "Have you ever been addicted to drugs?" "Have you ever been treated for drug addiction?" or "Have you ever been treated for drug abuse?"

May an employer ask applicants about their **drinking habits**?

Yes, unless the particular question is likely to elicit information about alcoholism, which is a disability. An employer may ask an applicant whether s/he drinks alcohol, or whether s/he has been arrested for driving under the influence because these questions do not reveal whether someone has alcoholism. However, questions asking *how much* alcohol an applicant drinks or whether s/he has participated in an alcohol rehabilitation program *are* likely to elicit information about whether the applicant has alcoholism.

What is a Medical Examination?

> Definition: A "Medical Examination" is a procedure or test that seeks information about an individual's physical or mental impairments or health.

At the pre-offer stage, an employer cannot require examinations that seek information about physical or mental impairments or health. It is not always easy to determine whether something is a *medical* examination. The following factors are helpful in determining whether a procedure or test is *medical*:

Is it administered by a health care professional or someone trained by a health care professional?

Are the results interpreted by a health care professional or someone trained by a health care professional?

Is it designed to reveal an impairment or physical or mental health?

Is the employer trying to determine the applicant's physical or mental health or impairments?

Is it invasive (for example, does it require the drawing of blood, urine or breath)?

Does it measure an applicant's performance of a task, *or* does it measure the applicant's physiological responses to performing the task?

Is it normally given in a medical setting (for example, a health care professional's office)?

Is medical equipment used?

In many cases, a combination of factors will be relevant in figuring out whether a procedure or test is a *medical* examination. In some cases, one factor may be enough to determine that a procedure or test is medical.

Example: A psychological test is designed to reveal mental illness, but a particular employer says it does not give the test to disclose mental illness (for example, the employer says it uses the test to disclose just tastes and habits). But, the test also is interpreted by a psychologist, and is routinely used in a clinical setting to provide evidence that would lead to a diagnosis of a mental disorder or impairment (for example, whether an applicant has paranoid tendencies, or is depressed). Under these facts, this test is a medical examination.

May an employer give **psychological examinations** to applicants?

Yes, unless the particular examination is *medical*. This determination would be based on some of the factors listed above, such as the purpose of the test and the intent of the employer in giving the test. Psychological examinations are medical if they provide evidence that would lead to identifying a mental disorder or impairment (for example, those listed in the American Psychiatric Association's most recent (*Diagnostic and Statistical Manual of Mental Disorders* [DSM]).

Example: An employer gives applicants the RUOK Test (hypothetical), an examination which reflects whether applicants have characteristics that lead to identifying whether the individual has excessive anxiety, depression, and certain compulsive disorders (DSM-listed conditions). This test is medical.

On the other hand, if a test is designed and used to measure only things such as honesty, tastes, and habits, it is not *medical*.

Example: An employer gives the IFIB Personality Test (hypothetical), an examination designed and used to reflect only whether an applicant is likely to lie. This test, as used by the employer, is not a medical examination.

THE POST-OFFER STAGE

After giving a job offer to an applicant, an employer may ask disability-related questions and perform medical examinations. The job offer may be conditioned on the results of post-offer disability-related questions or medical examinations.

At the "post-offer" stage, an employer may ask about an individual's workers' compensation history, prior sick leave usage, illnesses/diseases/impairments, and general physical and mental health. Disability-related questions and medical examinations at the post-offer stage do not have to be related to the job.[3]

If an employer asks post-offer disability-related questions, or requires post-offer medical examinations, it must make sure that it follow certain procedures:

- all entering employees in the same job category must be subjected to the examination/inquiry, regardless of disability, and
- medical information obtained must be kept confidential.

---

[3]But, if an individual is screened out because of disability, the employer must show that the exclusionary criterion is job-related and consistent with business necessity. 42 U.S.C. § 12112(h]; 29 C.F.R. §§ 1630.10, 1630.14(b)(3).

10

Biodata and Differential Prediction: Some Reservations

Neal Schmitt
Michigan State University

Elaine D. Pulakos
Personnel Decisions Research Institute

Because of the relatively great adverse impact produced by many cognitive ability tests and multiaptitude test batteries, most researchers and practitioners would welcome an alternative with equal validity that produces less or no adverse impact. Even with less validity, the alternative, if uncorrelated with cognitive ability, might dampen the adverse impact to some extent when used in combination with cognitive ability (Sackett & Wilks, 1994). It has also been argued that individuals' standing on alternative job-relevant constructs, perhaps measured via biodata, that evidence little, if any, adverse impact, should be considered before (or at least simultaneously with) cognitive ability. This process would allow members of lower-scoring groups the best opportunity to exhibit their skill and ability on the full range of relevant selection attributes. Because of evidence that biodata exhibit little or no subgroup differences (at least along racial divisions), they appear to be a popular alternative or adjunct to cognitive ability measures (Stokes, Mumford, & Owens, 1994).

This study arose from disappointing and confusing results of an attempt to develop and validate a biodata instrument to measure several constructs judged important for the success of incumbents working as professionals in a large federal agency. First, we present the procedure we employed to develop rational biodata scales and the results of a criterion-related validation of these scales. We then present the results of log-linear analyses of differences in the rate of option choice by members of three different racial and ethnic subgroups and our attempt to interpret the differences we observed. At the outset, it is emphasized that this research is exploratory and post hoc, but we think the results provide some evidence of interpretable differences between subgroups in the way that they respond to biodata; further research of this type ought to examine the meaning and implications of the use of biodata measures.

PREVIOUS RESEARCH ON DIFFERENTIAL PREDICTION USING BIODATA

Recent reviews of biodata research (Hogan, 1994; Mumford & Stokes; 1992) have cited only a handful of studies that have examined differential prediction of members of racial subgroups; all the studies date to 1981 or earlier and were reported in Reilly and Chao's (1982) review of alternative selection procedures. Reilly and Chao reported 10 studies (half of which were published) in which the performance of racial and ethnic subgroups on biodata measures was examined. In most of these studies, researchers reported similar validities and no mean differences in minority and majority scores on biodata indices. Three studies did report some differences. Lefkowitz (1972) developed separate scoring keys for Black and White subgroups as well as for his total sample of female production employees. The key based on the total sample was not valid for either of the racial subgroups, and the keys developed for separate racial subgroups did not hold up on cross-validation. Toole, Gavin, Murdy, and Sells (1972) analyzed the validity of biodata scales for different race–age combinations and found no valid biodata items across more than one age–race subgroup. They also reported mean differences in biodata composite scores across race subgroups. Finally, Sharf (undated) reported no significant differences in standard errors of estimate, slopes, or intercepts across Black, Hispanic, and White subgroups, but he did report significant differences in biodata means.

A more recent meta-analytic review of biodata research (Rothstein, Schmidt, Erwin, Owens, & Sparks, 1990) provided data that indicated that validity of a 128-item biodata instrument developed so as to be generalizable across a wide variety of jobs and organizations was equally valid for different racial subgroups. This biodata key was empirically based, but items were retained only if a "rationale or psychological explanation" for the keyed relationship was possible and the relationship held in a Black subsample.

Although the preponderance of the data suggests that biodata provide unbiased and valid predictions of the performance of members of various race and ethnic subgroups, both Hogan (1994) and Mumford and Stokes (1992) cautioned that the "blind empirical" approach to biodata key development can lead to the selection of items that are correlated with race, ethnicity, or sex. One commonly cited example of this occurrence was provided by Pace and Schoenfeldt (1977) who found that having a Detroit address was related to a criterion. Obviously this item would produce a majority–minority difference if the sample included people living in the suburbs. Owens (1976) suggested that rational screening of items should be undertaken as a method of decreasing the likelihood that such items be included in a scale. The problem with rational screening is that many cultural or response differences related to race or ethnicity may be subtle. In addition, the rational screening is often done only by members of one or another subgroup.

In this study, we developed a pool of items that we judged would be good indicators of several constructs thought to be of importance in performing the job duties of a group of professional-level federal employees. Rational scoring keys were also developed for the items. Evidence from a validity study indicated disappointing results for the total sample and stimulated a closer examination of the validity of these scales for different subgroups. This chapter reports the results of the validity analyses and analyses of response options to each item. Of most interest, however, is our attempt to provide some interpretation of the differential response patterns.

METHOD

Sample

The sample consisted of 467 incumbents in a large federal agency who participated in a concurrent criterion-related validation of several selection procedures. Of these individuals, 335 were male, 129 female. One hundred were African American; 259, White; and 97, Hispanic. Ethnicity, race, and gender data were unavailable for four individuals. All participants had between 1 and 6 years of tenure; the average tenure was 3.4 years. All examinees were college graduates, and 115 had advanced professional or graduate degrees.

Procedure

Job analyses proceeded through the usual steps of task generation, development of knowledge, skill, and ability statements (KSAs), questionnaire development and administration to provide ratings of tasks, KSAs, and their linkages (Goldstein, Zedeck, & Schneider, 1993). These job analyses indicated the importance of seven KSA dimensions for which we developed biodata measures. These seven included Adaptability, Physical Requirements, Ability to Plan, Prioritize, and Organize, Ability to Maintain a Positive Image, Ability to Evaluate Information and Make Decisions, Initiative and Motivation, and Ability to Relate Effectively With Others. Brief definitions of each of these abilities are contained in Table 10.1.

TABLE 10.1
Definitions of Abilities for Which Biodata Items Were Written

Adaptability: Ability to adapt to unanticipated events or change; remaining calm and levelheaded under stress.

Physical requirements: Willingness and ability to maintain physical conditioning required to perform job tasks.

Ability to plan, prioritize, and organize: Managing competing tasks simultaneously, planning and pursuing activities in a logical fashion, developing and organizing information.

Ability to relate effectively with others: Dealing self-confidently and sensitively with people of differing backgrounds to gain their cooperation.

Ability to maintain a positive image: Maintaining professional demeanor and appearance in interaction with public and colleagues; maintaining high level of honesty and ethics in all behavior.

Ability to evaluate information and make decisions: Recognizing important information; critically questioning assumptions and logic; willingness and ability to make decisions and use good judgment.

Initiative and motivation: Searching out information and ways to do a task or developing one's own capability while following agency procedures and/or directions.

Biodata Item Development. To ensure reliable measurement of each construct, we wrote or selected 25 to 30 items for each of the seven KSA categories previously listed. Items were generated by the authors and selected from pre-existing biodata item banks (Mumford, 1993; Owens, Glennon, & Albright, 1966). Items taken from pre-existing inventories of biodata were altered in some cases by changing the item stem from *you* to *I*, creating additional response options, substituting the generic phrase *your job* for a particular occupation, and making more substantive revisions when the selection situation warranted such change. After we had written or selected 25 to 30 items for each dimension, all items were reviewed by three judges who considered the following questions in deciding whether to retain, revise, or eliminate the item: Does the item fit the construct for which it was written? (Two of three judges had to agree for retention of the item.); Are applicants likely to respond honestly to the item? Is the item likely to be objectionable or perceived to be an invasion of privacy? Is the item likely to be a proxy for ethnic or gender status?

Of the 160 items surviving this screening, rational weights were derived for each item by using the definition of the construct for which the item was written, the item stem and the options. This weighting process involved a series of weightings and discussions by four judges. Feedback on the items was also solicited from a sample of 34 incumbents who responded to the whole set of items. This sample provided an opportunity to assess the intrusiveness and the judged appropriateness of the scoring key, but the sample was not large enough to assess any of the psychometric characteristics of the scales or assess the likelihood of subgroup differences. The total pool of 160 remaining items was piloted with a sample of 230 incumbents. Their responses were used as the basis for a further trimming of the biodata scales which resulted in the final 137 items whose characteristics are the subject of the analyses next described. All biodata measures were administered to subjects in groups of 20 to 25 over the course of 1½ days testing.

Criterion Development. Behaviorally anchored rating scales were constructed to assess 10 performance dimensions: Recording and Writing; Making Oral Presentations; Gathering Information; Analyzing Information; Planning and Organizing; Monitoring Work—Attention to Detail; Working in Dangerous Situations; Developing Constructive Relationships; Effort and Initiative; and Professionalism and Positive Image, as well as an Overall Effectiveness Measure.

For purposes of the analyses reported in this paper, the 10 dimensional ratings were summed to form an overall performance index. A principal factors analysis of the ratings indicated that the first factor accounted for 54% of the variance. Loading on this factor, roughly interpretable as Core Technical Proficiency (Campbell, McCloy, Oppler, & Sager, 1993), were the first six of the rating variables. A second factor, accounting for only 11% of the variance, was labeled Effort and Professionalism. Because a unit-weighted composite of the items loading on these two factors was highly correlated (.54) and the second factor accounted for substantially less variance than did the first factor, the ratings were combined in a single index. Ratings from a relief supervisor were available for a subset ($N = 349$) of the entire sample; inter-rater reliabilities based on this sample indicated that single rater reliability was .60.

Ratings were collected in meetings of 5 to 20 supervisors and relief supervisors at a time. These meetings included a brief training session in which the importance of the validation project and the supervisor's role in the project was stressed. Supervisors were also informed that all ratings were confidential and would not be made available to organizational personnel. The session also included information and training about common rating errors and how to avoid them.

Data Analyses

The original data analysis consisted of the computation of the validities of the rational biodata scales. As these correlations were unexpectedly low and largely nonsignificant, we proceeded to evaluate various possible reasons and carried out a subgroup analysis. This subgroup analysis revealed that for many of the items, the validities were positive and likely practically useful for the White subgroup but validities for the same scale or item were zero or even negative for the minority subgroups. These findings prompted further analyses of the item responses of the various subgroups, which are the major focus of this paper.

The log-linear analyses of item responses we used is described in detail by Green, Crone, and Folk (1989) who used it to analyze subgroup responses to the verbal portion of the Scholastic Aptitute Test. Participants in the study were separated into three performance levels. The frequency of each option choice was then tabulated separately for each subgroup at each performance level, yielding a three-way contingency table. Subgroup comparisons were assessed through an application of the log-linear analysis of contingency tables (Kok, Mellenbergh, & van der Flier, 1985; Mellenbergh, 1982; SPSSX, 1983). This analysis allowed for the separation of subgroup, option, and performance main effects as well as the three two-way interactions and the three-way interaction among these variables. Each effect in this analysis represents a difference in proportions. The main effects in this model are of little interest—the main effects of subgroup and performance group indicate the difference in the sizes of the groups, and the main effect of option indicates differences in the popularity of the options available to the respondent. The interaction of performance group by option indicates the validity of the item (we hope that the proportion of high-performing people who chose the scored option is greater than the proportion of low-performing people). The key question is whether examinees of different subgroups chose the various options more or less frequently than would be expected by their performance level. This likelihood is reflected in the subgroup by option interaction.

Thus, we performed two log-linear analyses for each of the 137 biodata items. In the first analysis, we sought to explain the item responses on the basis of the three main effects and the interactions of performance by option choice and subgroup by performance, but *not* the interaction of option choice by subgroup. This model of item responses was compared to a model that included the main effects, the two interactions in the first model *plus* the interaction of option choice by subgroup. We were looking for items in which the addition of the interaction of interest better explained item responses than did a model without this interaction. To illustrate the type of data we generated for each item, we present a summary of responses to one hypothetical item in Table 10.2; the summary of the log-linear analyses for this item is provided in Table 10.3. An illustration of the response patterns for the three subgroups in our study is depicted in Figure 10.1.

Like the analysis of variance, the log-linear model includes factors for the main effects of performance, race or ethnic subgroup, and option chosen as well as for the various interactions, but the analysis does not partition sums of squares. Each statistical test is a test of a particular model's fit to the data. Each line of Table 10.3 indicates the effects included in the model, the chi-square associated with the model, and its degrees of freedom. For example, a model that includes all three main effects (line 4), which indicate that the responses in Table 10.1 can be accounted for by consideration of performance level, race or

TABLE 10.2
Proportion of Responses to Representative Item Displaying an Option by Subgroup Interaction

Performance Group	Racial or Ethnic Group	High Familiarity with Work	Somewhat Familiar with Work	Familiarity Not Necessary but Preferred	No Familiarity Preferred
		Option Chosen			
Low	White	04	28	46	22
	African Am.	25	21	25	29
	Hispanic Am.	11	28	39	22
Moderate	White	07	24	44	24
	African Am.	08	39	22	31
	Hispanic Am.	06	21	40	33
High	White	03	25	50	22
	African Am.	06	15	27	52
	Hispanic Am.	04	11	41	44

Note: Item stem was "If you were looking for a new job, how familiar would you like to be with the work required in this new position?"

TABLE 10.3
Log-linear Analysis for Table 10.2 Example

Effect	Chi-Square	Degrees of Freedom
1. Performance (PF)	275.24*	33
2. Subgroup (Race)	169.83*	33
3. Option (Opt)	155.67*	32
4. PF, race, & opt	45.93*	28
S. PF, race, opt, & pf x race	41.16*	24
6. PF, race, opt, & pf x opt	37.02*	22
7. PF, race, opt, & race x opt	24.42	22
8. PF, race, opt, pf x race, pf x opt	32.25	18
9. PF, race, opt, pf x opt, race x opt	15.51	16
10. PF, race, opt, pf x race, race x opt	19.65	18
11. PF, race, opt, pf x race, pf x opt, race x opt	10.58	12

*p . < 05.

Option 1: High Familiarity With Work

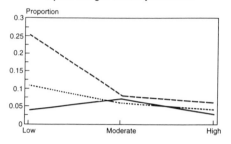

Option 2: Somewhat Familiar With Work

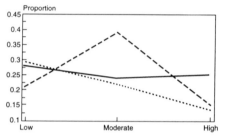

Option 3: Familiarity Unnecessary but Preferred

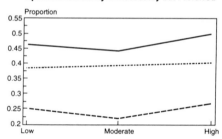

Option 4: No Familiarity Preferred

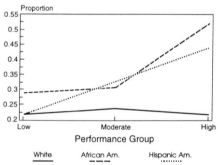

FIG. 10.1. Proportion of race and ethnic subgroup members rated low-, moderate-, and high-performers who endorsed options to example item.

ethnicity, and option chosen, did not fit the data (i.e., chi-square is significant). We mentioned earlier that the key effect for purposes of the discussion in this paper is the interaction of race by option chosen. In this set of analyses, all four models that include this interaction (lines 7, 9, 10, and 11) are not statistically significant, an indication of the model's good fit to the data. A test of the significance of this interaction, however, involves a comparison of two models—the model tested in line 8, which includes the main effects and all two-way interactions except the race by options interaction, and the model in line 11, which includes all three two-way interactions and the main effects. The difference in chi-squares associated with these two models (i.e., 21.67) is itself distributed as a chi-square with degrees of freedom equal to the difference in degrees of freedom associated with the two models being compared (i.e., 6). The chi-square difference in this case is statistically significant ($p < .001$). As already mentioned, the test comparing these two models was the one we employed to test the extent to which subgroups were responding differentially to the biodata options.

As is evident by examining the proportions in Table 10.2 and Figure 10.1, the chi-square difference test given the sample sizes we had available is not unduly powerful. The differences in proportions endorsed are quite large across options. For this hypothetical item, it appears that African Americans in the low-performance group appreciated moving to a job in which they were highly familiar with the work they were doing. The White group appeared to prefer work of intermediate levels of familiarity, and there appeared to be little or no difference across performance levels. African Americans and Hispanic Americans in the high-performance group were more likely than were Whites to choose No Familiarity Preferred.

These analyses of the responses to individual items and item options by different groups were followed by an analysis of the content of the items showing a race by option interaction. Specifically, we compared the number of items for which we obtained a significant interaction in each of the a priori rational scales we developed before the administration of the scales.

RESULTS

Before detailing the results of subgroup analyses of item responses, we want to stress that we identified 29 biodata items whose correlations with the criterion were significant for one of the three subgroups and at least positive for the other two subgroups. This scale yielded a cross-validated r of approximately .20 in a holdout group comprised of about one third of the total sample of 467. There were also minimal differences (i.e., .05 SD or less) in the means of the three subgroups. Minority subgroups' performance was slightly overpredicted by this biodata scale. As a result, this empirically developed scoring key was an effective complement to measures of other constructs used in the final test battery recommended for use by the sponsoring organization.

In Tables 10.4A and B, we present the means, standard deviations, and reliabilities for the biodata scales for the total group as well as the same data for each of the three race or ethic groups. In view of the dichotomous nature of the scoring of many of these items, the reliabilities are reasonable for most scales, but the reliabilities of the Relates With Others and the Image scales are very low. The observed intercorrelations of the scales are presented in the bottom diagonal half of Table 10.4B, and these correlations corrected for attenuation because of unreliability are contained in the upper diagonal half of the same table. As can be seen, these measures are intercorrelated, but the corrected correlations indicate discriminant validity as well. Adaptability seems to be the most highly and uniformly correlated with the other scales. The means and standard deviations of the scales for the different subgroups indicate very small differences and in over one half of the cases the minority mean score is actually slightly higher than that of the majority group.

The validities of the biodata scales for the total group and for each of the subgroups are presented in the first four columns of Table 10.5. Two of the seven scales were significantly related to the performance measure for the total group, but the disappointingly low size of these correlations stimulated further examination of subgroup validities, which are displayed in the second, third, and fourth columns of the table. Validities for the White subgroup were larger, and even with the smaller sample size, they were statistically significant. The multiple correlation of these seven scales for the White group was .25; the Wherry estimate of cross-validated R was .18. Although not as large as some biodata validities (Rothstein et al., 1990, reported an average observed validity of .28), the validity for the White group could be practically useful, especially if used in combination with other predictors uncorrelated with the biodata. Single-scale validities for the two minority subgroups were low and nonsignificant, and over one half were actually negative. Neither multiple R was significant and estimates of cross-validated R for the combination of the seven scales were less than zero.

As already indicated, these results stimulated a closer look at subgroup responses to individual items. Tests of the crucial race by option interaction for all 137 biodata items indicated that, for 42 items, the interaction added significantly ($p < .05$) to the modeling of participant responses. Obviously, 42 is much larger than the 7 or so significant interactions that would be expected by chance alone, but the more formidable task was to provide an explanation of the differences in response patterns across groups.

One attempt to provide this understanding is displayed in the last column of Table 10.5. Here, we indicate the number of items out of the total number of items on each scale for which we obtained evidence of a significant difference in responses across members of different subgroups. Overall, about one third of the items exhibited some differential subgroup response, but for the items

TABLE 10.4A

Means, Standard Deviations, Reliabilities for Total Group and Race and Ethnic Subgroups

	Total			White			Afr. Am.			His. Am.		
	m	SD	rxx	m	SD	rxx	m	SD	rxx	m	SD	rxx
Planning	1.36	.21	.72	1.36	.21	.72	1.39	.20	.66	1.35	.23	.75
Relate with others	1.15	.20	.36	1.16	.20	.37.	1.16	.20	.37	1.14	.20	.36
Image	1.41	.23	.42	1.39	.21	.34	1.48	.24	.47	1.41	.24	.49
Initiative, motivation	1.45	.22	.71	1.46	.23	.74	1.46	.20	.63	1.42	.22	.72
Adaptability	1.48	.20	.61	1.47	.22	.67	1.50	.16	.36	1.49	.20	.61
Physical requirements	2.34	.36	.70	2.32	.35	.69	2.40	.35	.70	2.31	.38	.74
Evaluate, judge	1.77	.19	.50	1.76	.19	.50	1.78	.17	.39	1.80	.20	.57
Performance	4.60	.87		4.68	.86		4.61	.89		4.41	.82	

TABLE 10.4B

Observed and Corrected Intercorrelations Among Biodata Measures for Total Group

	1	2	3	4	5	6	7
Planning (1)	.72	.57	.40	.42	.71	.42	.25
Relate with others (2)	.29	.36	.38	.20	.53	.60	.24
Image (3)	.22	.15	.42	.53	.80	.67	.37
Initiative, motivation (4)	.30	.10	.29	.71	.61	.24	.17
Adaptability (5)	.47	.25	.41	.40	.61	.77	.64
Physical requirements (6)	.30	.30	.36	.20	.50	.70	.44
Evaluate, judge (7)	.15	.10	.17	.10	.35	.26	.50

Note: Correlations above the diagonal are corrected for attenuation due to unreliability. Diagonal values are reliabilities computed using the Total Group's responses.

TABLE 10.5

Validities of Biodata Scales for Total Group and Race and Ethnic Subgroups and Number of Items in Which Race by Option Interaction Was Significant

	Total	White	Af.Am.	His. Am.	Number of Items Indicating Differential Response
Planning	.09*	.16*	−.06	.04	7/26
Relate with others	.05	.09	−.01	.00	9/15
Image	.02	.10	−.02	−.07	5/14
Initiative, motivation	.09*	.11*	−.03	.14	10/30
Adaptability	−.02	−.02	−.02	.02	3/19
Physical requirements	.01	.10	−.09	−.06	2/13
Evaluate, judge	.08	.13*	.16	−.10	6/20
R	.16(.09)	.25* (.18)	.21(−.02)	.27(−.04)	

*p . < 05.

that were supposed to measure the ability to Relate With Others, this proportion was .60. For the Adaptability and Physical Requirements scales, only about 15% of the items were significant.

There is certainly a tendency to overinterpret data such as these, but the following represents our sense as to the differences in the ways members of these three subgroups relate to others. Members of the two minority groups (especially the high-performing members of these groups) are less likely to prefer a supervisor whose primary strength is working with other people. Whites are less likely to want to moderate conflict or to negotiate than are minorities, especially African Americans. Whites seem more likely to be willing to engage in projects by themselves than are minority group members. Hispanic Americans are more likely to want to "order others" and less likely to say that they would not try to influence others than are members of other groups. African Americans are more apt to say that others confide in them "quite often" than are members of the other two groups. This is especially true of high-performing African Americans. Whites are less likely to indicate that they "don't know" their neighbors than are minority individuals, but they are also less likely to indicate they would borrow from each other. Whites are more likely to indicate something of an intermediate type of relationship with neighbors. Majority group respondents are less likely to report that they have held student offices, but somewhat more likely to say that they have had arguments often or occasionally than are minority respondents. Especially low- and moderate-performing members of the White group are less likely than are minority individuals to indicate that they would decide what to do in social situations. Again, generalizations from this summary are difficult, but it appears that minority respondents, especially African Americans, are more relationship oriented, more outgoing, and less confrontational (but more capable of dealing with conflict when it occurs) in interpersonal situations than are majority group people.

Examination of the items in other scales for which there were significant race by options interactions were also undertaken. Perhaps the most interesting of these sets of items were those from the Image scale. The five significant interactions for this scale indicated more of a concern on the part of minorities to maintain an appropriate physical and professional appearance at all times rather than to "be themselves." They were also less likely to be involved in civic organizations or to have received recognition from these organizations.

A third area in which results were seemingly consistent across items was the measure we called Planning—the ability to plan, prioritize, and organize. Models of 7 of the 26 items included a significant race by option interaction. These interactions seemed to indicate a tendency on the part of minorities, especially African Americans, to report that they plan more carefully and compulsively than was true of White respondents. For example, few Whites reported making precise and detailed plans about present and future plans, but minorities, especially low-performing people did. African Americans were more likely to report having regular study times in college than were members of the other groups, and Whites were more likely to report that they studied sporadically. These findings were inconsistent with remarks of minority supervisors and incumbents with whom we discussed these findings. They were generally not favorably disposed to "overplanning" or "overorganizing" activities, but they did report that they were often forced to be more "task-oriented" in their high school and college days because they needed to work to help support their education. When working on simple tasks, Whites were more likely to report daydreaming than were minorities, and the latter groups were more likely to concentrate on the task or on other job-related activities. Minority individuals, especially African Americans, were more likely to report that they kept their homes generally or extremely neat than were White respondents; African Americans, especially low-performing individuals, were much more likely to make careful vacation plans than were members of Hispanic and White groups.

SUMMARY AND CONCLUSIONS

Research on differential validity of biographical data for racial and ethnic groups has generally indicated little evidence that biographical information has different performance implications across groups. We found a lack of validity for biodata for Hispanic and African American subgroups for rational biodata scales. Biodata predictions of White performance were lower than has sometimes been reported, but they were statistically and, we think, practically significant as well.

Examination of the options chosen in response to each item by different subgroups indicated a large number of significantly different response patterns. Differential response patterns were particularly characteristic of the way in which subgroups reported interacting with other people. In addition, consistent and interpretable differences were found for the Planning and Image dimensions of the biographical data. Relatively few significant differences were observed for Adaptability and Physical Requirements dimensions.

We believe these results indicate the need for further research into the meaning of biodata constructs (or items) across racial and ethnic groups whose culture, experiences, and characteristic manner of approaching life and work may differ from those of the majority group. These differences may have different meaning when applied to the measurement of a hypothetical construct. This research, we believe, should include the help of "subject matter experts" from minority groups and should be based on a priori hypotheses that reflect the nature of the constructs measured and the hypothesized cultural differences related to these constructs.

Finally, in some previous research, investigators (e.g., Lefkowitz, 1972) developed separate empirical scoring keys for use with different racial and ethnic subgroups. Most of these studies have proven unsuccessful as scoring keys have not cross-validated. Although these studies might provide hints about the likelihood of differential response patterns, we believe that these efforts must be guided by a priori consideration of constructs and rational scoring keys that are linked to hypotheses about significant background and cultural differences. Without a priori theorizing or planning, investigators' options for interpretating any differential response patterns are limited and perhaps arbitrary. In this study, we had the advantage of having rationally grouped the biodata items, but we had not considered that items thought to measure different constructs might produce differential subgroup response patterns. In this sense, our data are exploratory, but they do suggest caution in the use of biodata or other measures that index experience, interpersonal style, or values constructs.

REFERENCES

Campbell, J. P., McCloy, R. A., Oppler, S. H., & Sager, C. E. (1993). A theory of performance. In N. Schmitt, W. C. Borman & Associates (Eds.), *Personnel selection in organizations.* San Francisco: Jossey-Bass.

Goldstein, I. L., Zedeck, S., & Schneider, B. (1993). An exploration of the job analysis–content validity process. In N. Schmitt, W. C. Borman & Associates (Eds.), *Personnel selection in organizations.* San Francisco: Jossey-Bass.

Green, B. F., Crone, C. R., & Folk, V. G. (1989). A method for studying differential distractor functioning. *Journal of Educational Measurement, 26,* 147–160.

Hogan, J. B. (1994). Empirical keying of background data measures. In G. S. Stokes, M. D. Mumford, & W. A. Owens (Eds.), *Biodata handbook: Theory, research, and use of biographical information in selection and performance prediction.* Palo Alto, CA: Consulting Psychologists Press.

Kok, F. G., Mellenbergh, G. J., & van der Flier, H. (1985). Detecting experimentally induced item bias using the iterative logit method. *Journal of Educational Measurement, 22,* 295–303.

Lefkowitz, J. (1972). Differential validity: Ethnic group as a moderator in predicting tenure. *Personnel Psychology, 25,* 223–240.

Mellenbergh, G. J. (1982). Contingency table models for assessing item bias. *Journal of Educational Statistics, 7,* 105–118.

Mumford, M. D. (1993). *Rationally-keyed biographical data items for constructs related to sales performance.* Unpublished manuscript. Fairfax, VA: George Mason University.

Mumford, M. D., & Stokes, G. S. (1992). Developmental determinants of individual action: Theory and practice in applying background measures. In M. D. Dunnette & L. M. Hough (Eds.), *Handbook of industrial and organizational psychology* (2nd ed., Vol. 3, pp. 61–138). Palo Alto, CA: Consulting Psychologists Press.

Owens, W. A. (1976). Background data. In M. D. Dunnette (Ed.), *Handbook of industrial and organizational psychology* (pp. 609–644). New York: Rand-McNally.

Owens, W. A., Glennon, J. R., & Albright, L. E. (1966). *A catalog of life history items.* Greensboro, NC: Center for Creative Leadership.

Pace, L. A., & Schoenfeldt, L. F. (1977). Legal concerns in the use of weighted applications. *Personnel Psychology, 30,* 159–166.

Reilly, R. R., & Chao, G. T. (1982). Validity and fairness of some alternative employee selection procedures. *Personnel Psychology, 25,* 1–63.

Rothstein, H. R., Schmidt, F. L., Erwin, F. W., Owens, W. A., & Sparks, C. P. (1990). Biographical data in employment selection: Can validities be made generalizable? *Journal of Applied Psychology, 75,* 175–184.

Sackett, P. R., & Wilks, S. L. (1994). Within-group norming and other forms of score adjustment in preemployment testing. *American Psychologist, 49,* 929–954.

Sharf, J. (undated). *The supervisory profile record: Differential validity-test fairness.* Unpublished manuscript. Richardson, Bellows and Co., Inc. Washington, DC.

SPSSX (1983). *User's guide.* New York: McGraw-Hill.

Stokes, G. S., Mumford, M. D., & Owens, W. A. (1994). *Biodata handbook: Theory, research and use of biographical information in selection and performance prediction.* Palo Alto, CA: Consulting Psychologists Press.

Toole, D. L., Gavin, J. F., Murdy, L. B., & Sells, S. B. (1972). The differential validity of personality, personal history, and aptitude data for minority and nonminority employees. *Personnel Psychology, 25,* 661–672.

11

Life Is Not Multiple Choice: Reactions to the Alternatives

Ann Marie Ryan
Michigan State Univerisity

Gary J. Greguras
Bowling Green State University

When one of the us first started teaching, a decision was made not to give any multiple-choice tests because "life is not multiple choice" and students should not be assessed in a way that is incompatible with reality. Practicality, reliability concerns, and other issues have led to deviations from this policy, but in this chapter we focus on this issue: How much does realism in assessment matter? The movement in the educational arena toward replacing multiple-choice testing with performance assessments stems partly from a concern that typical tests are dissociated from the real-world skills supposedly assessed.

What are performance assessments? Linn (1993) described performance assessments as tasks that require performing an activity or constructing a response. As Stiggins (1987) noted, these demonstrations can be in response to structured exercises, or they may take place during normal everyday events. Others (e.g., Frechtling, 1991; Kennedy, 1992) have noted that the term *performance assessment* is often used to encompass any means of assessment other than multiple-choice, paper-and-pencil tests. Baker, O'Neil, and Linn (1993) indicated that the most common elements of performance-based assessment are the use of open-ended tasks; a focus on higher order skills; the use of

context-sensitive strategies; the requirement of several types of performance
and significant amounts of time; and a significant degree of respondent choice.
Peformance assessments have also been termed *direct assessments, alternative
assessments,* and *authentic assessments* (Baker et al., 1993).

A primary criticism offered by those advocating the use of performance
assessments in education is that multiple-choice testing does not reflect reality.
Critics have argued that real-world tasks allow multiple approaches and solutions (e.g., Davey, 1991; McGaghie, 1991). For example, Bridgeman (1992)
noted that engineers and chemists are not confronted with five choices where
there is only one correct answer. Wiggins (1989) argued that authentic assessments should be replications of tasks that face people. The assumption behind
these statements is that life (including work life) is not multiple choice, so why
assess people in this fashion?

Although we might want to quibble about this assumption—perhaps some
of us are limited in the choice of actions we can take in our work life—let us
assume that most workers can, on a day-to-day basis, choose from many
potential responses in completing their work. This chapter is a series of
reminders about the implications of this idea for the process of assessment,
particularly for employee selection.

Specifically, we address two major areas: First, what are the implications of
test format (or testing mode) for content validity evidence? How does the use
of multiple-choice formats or more "realistic" performance assessments relate
to validation evidence? We purposely focus narrowly on content validity evidence because the realism argument is most often brought to bear on it, and
this validation strategy has been used increasingly in recent years (Gatewood
& Feild, 1994). Second, how does test format relate to face validity? Do test
takers view multiple choice tests more negatively than they view performance
assessments?

TEST FORMAT AND CONTENT VALIDITY

Content–Format Confusion

In arguing for changing assessment methods, advocates often mix discussions of content and format. Although cognitive ability, biodata, and personality tests typically are given in multiple-choice format, assessment of
the underlying constructs tapped by these measures is not limited to this
format. This situation is content—format confusion: criticisms are leveled
at format, but the criticisms actually apply to content, and conversely,
criticisms leveled at content really refer to format. We can illustrate this
point with many statements from the performance assessment debate in
educational literature.

Multiple-Choice Tests Do Not Measure Higher-Order Thinking (Bennett, Rock, & Wang, 1991; Brown, 1994; Frederiksen & Collins, 1989; Haney & Madaus, 1989; Linn, Baker, & Dunbar, 1991; Norris, 1990; Wiggins, 1991). Perhaps many multiple-choice cognitive ability tests on the market today do not measure higher-order thinking, but this is not necessarily due to a constraint of the format (Frechtling, 1991; Mehrens, 1992). Baker, Freeman, and Clayton (1991) correctly noted that the problem is not that test developers cannot assess higher-level skills with multiple-choice items, but that, because items assessing lower-level skills are easier to conceive and construct, such items are likely to occur with greater frequency on typical multiple-choice tests.

Multiple-Choice Tests Measure Only Declarative, Not Procedural Knowledge (i.e., Facts, Not Process; Mehrens, 1992). Collis and Romberg (1991) concluded that mathematics tests typically focus on solutions and facts, rather than on strategies or procedural skills. Although multiple-choice formats are often used to get at memory of facts, these formats can also assess procedural knowledge. For example, there has been a recent growth in paper-and-pencil and video situational judgment tests, which use multiple choice as a response format.

Multiple-Choice Tests Are Measures of What People Know, Not What They Use (i.e., They Do Not Tell Much about What a Person Does on a Day-To-Day Basis; e.g., Aschbacher, 1992; Davey 1991; Wiggins, 1991). This criticism can be leveled against any measure of maximal performance, including many forms of performance assessment. Evidence to date suggests that objective measures of typical and maximal performance may not be highly correlated (DuBois, Sackett, Zedeck, & Fogli, 1993; Sackett, Zedeck, & Fogli, 1988).

Multiple-Choice Tests Do Not Adequately Cover the Domain to Be Assessed, Assess Irrelevant Content, or Both (Mehrens, 1992; Wiggins, 1991). This criticism refers to the content validity of many multiple-choice tests developed for classroom use or on the market today, but it is not necessarily a constraint of the multiple-choice format.

The content–format confusion is not limited to one side of the debate, as the following assertions illustrate.

Performance Assessments Have Task Sampling Problems (Petrosko, 1992; Shavelson, 1993; Shavelson, Baxter, & Gao, 1993). Shavelson et al. summarized evidence to show that task-sampling variability (i.e., inconsistent performance across tasks) is a problem with many performance assessments, but they also noted that it need not be a problem in a well-designed measure.

Performance Assessments Contain Correlated Errors (i.e., Have Greater Local Item Dependence). Yen (1993) noted that for performance assessments, a setting is established and then an examinee provides multiple responses to the setting, a process likely resulting in greater local item dependence than would a traditional multiple choice test. As Yen noted, however, there are ways to design and score performance assessments to limit local item dependence effects.

The usefulness of different formats is often illustrated by a comparison of paper-and-pencil versus video tests. This is problematic, however, because a change from paper and pencil to video often involves a change in both format and content. Many people think that computerization and multimedia technology can move testing away from the traditional multiple-choice format (e.g., Haney & Madaus, 1989), yet the typical video and computerized assessment tools on the market today are in a multiple-choice format.

Although the criticisms most frequently voiced in the literature are issues of content and construction and not format per se, this does not mean that a consideration of format has nothing to do with establishing content validity. We next discuss how test format relates to content validation evidence.

Content Validity and Test Format

Guion (1977), in discussing his discontent, noted that "a defined content domain necessarily includes both stimulus content and response content" (p. 3). Sackett (1987) argued that people cannot judge content validity without knowing the nature of responses and how they are to be scored. Murphy and Davidshofer (1994) stated that "validation efforts should be concerned more with the extent to which responses to items provided are a representative sample of the domain of responses than with the extent to which stimuli are representative" (p. 112). When pursuing a content validation strategy, test developers must be concerned with response format, because response format affects the ability to sample from the response content domain.

To illustrate, the following item appeared in Sanchez, Fraser, Fernandez, and DeLaTorre (1993):

An angry customer comes into your office demanding your attention. What course of action would be most typical of you?

a) calm the customer down, then attend to him/her

b) calm the customer down, then ask him/her to wait their turn

c) ignore the customer, s/he is being rude

d) inform the customer that you will not tolerate that type of behavior

This question could also be presented as an open-ended interview question or used as a role-play stem. The same stimulus is used but the response format (and potentially the response content) is different. It is not sufficient to say that the "test" content is the same simply because the same thing is asked.

Figures 11.1, 11.2, and 11.3 illustrate how we can consider both stimulus and response domains in discussing test format. We restrict our discussion to the typical test.

Performance assessments typically provide a narrow but deep coverage of the stimulus domain (this need not always be true; it depends on the extent of sampling). In multiple-choice testing, each item is usually a very narrow sample, and the representativeness of the test depends on the sampling of the whole. For example, the customer-service item just presented is one of many in a multiple-choice test or an interview. In contrast, there are fewer stimuli in a role play (perhaps the equivalent of one interview question).

Thus, one criticism of performance assessment methods is that inadequate sampling of the stimulus domain is typical and that multiple-choice tests do a better job in this regard. Figure 11.1 illustrates what is assumed to be the typical state of affairs, with each box representing the entire stimulus domain to be tapped. Such generalizations are inappropriate: People must review the ade-

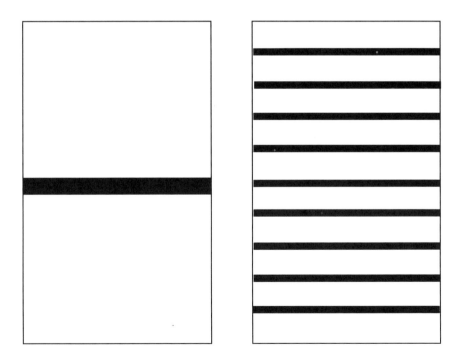

Performance   Multiple
Assessment   Choice

FIG. 11.1. Stimulus domain.

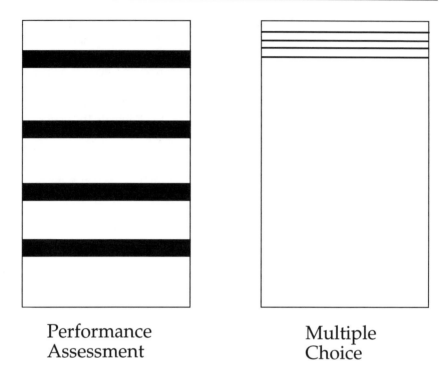

Performance   Multiple
Assessment   Choice

FIG. 11.2. Stimulus domain.

quacy of the stimulus domain sampling as a regular step in test development. For example, Linn (1993) illustrated that increasing the number of tasks in a performance assessment increases its generalizability. Some performance assessments may in fact sample the stimulus domain adequately, and some multiple-choice tests may not cover what they purport to measure (Fig. 11.2). This issue must be attended to in the development of assessment tools.

With respect to the response domain, performance assessment is typically viewed as providing a sampling of the entire response domain (Fig. 11.3b). This view is probably untrue (e.g., in-baskets do not allow test takers to call or to see colleagues about information; artificial time constraints limit potential responses). Typical multiple-choice questions provide only four or five narrow responses from the possible response domain (Fig. 11.3a). Critics have charged that multiple-choice testing inadequately samples the response domain, but the adequacy of multiple-choice response sampling depends on the representativeness of the responses. In the customer-service illustration, are these four choices a representative sample of the response domain, or are there more likely responses?

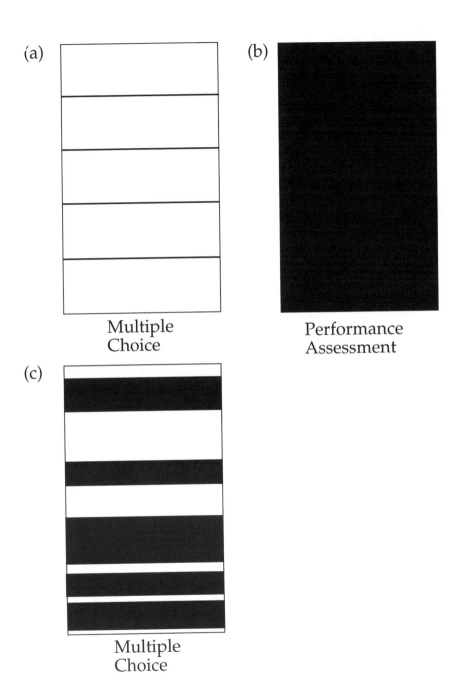

(a) Multiple Choice

(b) Performance Assessment

(c) Multiple Choice

FIG. 11.3. Response domain.

This point is illustrated well by Bridgeman (1992), in work with Graduate Record Examination (GRE) quantitative items, using both multiple-choice and free-response formats. He found that item response theory (IRT) curves from multiple choice and free response questions were similar for some items but different for others. Changes in format did not have uniform effects. The format effects were larger when the multiple-choice options were not an accurate reflection of the types of errors actually made by students (i.e., they were not representative of the response domain). If the response options in a multiple-choice question are the more likely responses, the sampling of the response domain is probably adequate (Fig. 11.3c). As Guion (1977) pointed out, the response content domain cannot be understood independently of the stimulus content domain.

Response domains are often neglected in test constructions. Although computerization and verbal versus written responses (e.g., Saklofske & Kowalchuk, 1992) are seen as having effects on test properties and test scores, little systematic research of these effects has occurred in a framework that provides guidance on the effects of response format across content domains. Perhaps this situation occurs because those developing tests often approach the question from a standpoint that confuses content and format. For example, in our consulting work with civil service selection system design the question of why there is adverse impact on written tests and not on interviews often arises. The answers need to clarify differences because of the skills assessed versus the format of the testing. Yet, even in the published literature in I/O psychology, reference is made to which "methods" have the least adverse impact, rather than explicating what is due to changes in method versus what is due to assessing very different skills.

Exceptions to the neglect of response domain can be found with many biodata and situational judgment tests, where developing the key (both choosing response options and deciding how to score them) involves much effort. Experienced biodata developers would agree that attending to the response domain is time consuming and involves many judgment points.

In sum, many of the criticisms of multiple-choice testing are criticisms of the inadequacy of stimuli and, in particular, inadequate response domain sampling. Proposed alternatives may appear to totally sample the response domain, but often suffer from limited stimulus domain sampling. Care must be taken not to equate test format or mode with content. Nevertheless, this discussion is not a dismissal of the criticisms of multiple-choice tests; the psychological fidelity of many multiple-choice tests used in selection contexts is indeed limited.

Psychological Fidelity

Goldstein, Zedeck, and Schneider (1993) noted that three important factors contribute to psychological fidelity: (a) the degree to which knowledge, skills, and abilities (KSAs) required are tapped by a test; (b) whether a testing mode represents the way tasks are accomplished on the job; and (c) the degree to which a test taps KSAs that are *not* job-related.

Point (a), although seemingly obvious, has been a constant criticism of all forms of assessment. For example, Sternberg (1991) noted that tests typically state problems and ask a test taker to solve them, rather than ask a test taker to recognize and define problems. He also noted that timed tests focus on resource use, where real-life problems typically involve resource allocation (i.e., deciding priorities). There are many examples of assessment tools that do not get at the KSAs they purport to measure.

Point (b)—whether mode represents the way tasks are accomplished on the job—is at the heart of education reformers' criticisms of multiple choice testing. Although this point is often downplayed in establishing content validity evidence for measures, the lack of a semblance of job relatedness in tests (e.g., multiple-choice math problems about train travel versus those set in a manufacturing plant context) has led to reasonable criticisms. Linn et al. (1991) noted, however, that "simply because the measures are derived from actual performance or relatively high-fidelity simulations of performance, it is too often assumed that they are more valid than multiple choice tests" (p. 16). Further, Linn et al. noted that although directness of assessment and transparency (i.e., test takers' ability to understand the basis on which performance is judged) may seem to be desirable, there is no evidence that these criteria do not have other unintended effects. For example, transparency may increase understanding about the task to be performed and increase perceptions of job relevance, but it may also increase faking behavior.

Goldstein et al. (1993) noted that point (c)—ensuring that nonrelevant KSAs are not being assessed—is often a problem with multiple-choice tests. This concern is often addressed in practice, through such things as reading analyses of test materials and job materials. Examples of improving testing procedures to remove nonrelevant KSAs include removing time restrictions and allowing the use of tools such as calculators in test situations (Collis & Romberg, 1991). However, point (c) may also be a problem with "more realistic" tests like videos, where increased context may introduce construct irrelevant variance (e. g., assessment of visual and auditory acuity). Davey (1991) argued that abilities do not occur without context in the real world, and, therefore, they should not be measured out of context. The question is whether the context introduces irrelevant variance in what is supposedly measured. Sometimes, it may simply be a matter of redefining measures as addressing skills in context.

Some readers may not be fans of content validation strategies and may agree with Norman et al. (1987): "Since nearly all forms of assessment represent an abstraction or simulation of reality, it is not essential that a test yields identical results to the 'real world,' only that the results of the test are highly correlated with criterion performance" (p. 298). Whether the role of format in content validity evidence is considered, or one simply looks for criterion-related evidence, the issue of how format affects test performance is still worthy of pursuit. Robustness, we believe, is a useful concept for pursuing format or mode changes further in research and practice.

Robustness

Klimoski and Palmer (1993) defined robustness as the extent to which an assessment device can be administered using a variety of forms or modalities and still retain its ability to produce correct inferences about a candidate's suitability for a position. With the enactment of the Americans with Disabilities Act (ADA), concern has been expressed about how changes to tests lead to differences in the constructs assessed (e.g., reading aloud a written test) and therefore to changes in the inferences we can make about people based on their scores (Arnold & Theimann, 1992; Fischer, 1994; Nester, 1993). Klimoski and Palmer's notion of robustness, presented in the ADA context, is particularly relevant to the test format issue. When does a change in format result in a change in inferences about a test taker?

Robustness across testing modes has received some attention in the literature comparing computerized to paper and pencil testing. As Moreland (1992) summarized, the typical differences across the two modes, such as presentation of only a few items at a time by computer, allowance of skipping, and ease of making item interconnections, may have effects on both the psychometric properties of the test and the attitudes of test takers. Computerization has also been shown to make a difference in test takers' candor or social desirability, although there is evidence to show both increased and decreased socially desirable responses when comparing computerized to paper and pencil testing (see Booth-Kewley, Edwards, & Rosenfeld, 1992, for a summary). Further, Moreland noted that there may be a content by mode interaction, whereby certain types of items may function differently on the basis of method of presentation (e.g., confession-type questions). In summary, the evidence suggests that equivalence of computerized and paper and pencil versions should be established rather than assumed (Van de Vijver & Harsveld, 1994).

Several other studies have examined the equivalence of constructed response (i.e., free-response) and multiple-choice tests (e.g., Martinez, 1991; Traub & Fisher, 1977). Traub and Fisher found that the attribute measured by tests of mathematical reasoning did not vary with format, but what was measured by tests of verbal comprehension did vary with format. They also were unable to identify clear format factors that spanned tests of the same format with different content. Martinez (1991) outlined the need for research on format effects beyond factor-analytic paradigms, such as exploring format interactions with situational and individual (e.g., test anxiety) variables.

Robustness of many assessment tools is considered only in the extreme—by looking at method convergence in assessment centers, for example, without looking at how small administrative changes to one exercise affect what is assessed (Schmitt, Schneider & Cohen, 1990). Researchers must study variation in method in smaller and subtler ways; however, an atheoretical approach involving the study of trivial variations will not be useful. A set of factors hypothesized to affect robustness, systematically evaluated, would be more useful. For example, the Multiple Resources Model of Attention (e.g., Wickens, 1984) suggests that changing input modality (i .e., auditory, visual, or both), or response execution requirements (e.g., vocal, manual) requires test takers to draw on different resources. An examination of the cognitive literature on these topics could provide guidance about a framework for considering the robustness of assessments to change.

Some readers may be tempted to view the discussion to this point as directed at those with a lack of knowledge of psychometrics and basic test development principles. However, Industrial-Organizational (I/O) psychologists have, in recent years, been concerned with the realism of assessments, as we next demonstrate. Furthermore, most people know that the search in our field for alternatives (or more correctly, for supplements) to traditional multiple-choice ability testing is ongoing. Selection researchers have shifted their attention to measures other than g-loaded tests, although many of these still have paper-and-pencil multiple-choice formats. Interpersonal video tests, computer simulations, and multimedia testing are considered innovative. Yet, test developers mainly adhere to the multiple-choice format for responses, despite a broadening of the stimulus domain captured by these assessments.

Besides discussions of format and content validity, at the heart of the debate over the move away from multiple choice testing is the notion of face validity and the reactions of test takers.

REACTIONS TO MODE OF ASSESSMENT

Much recent research has focused on the topic of applicant reactions to various selection procedures, suggesting that the perceived realism of assessment methods is of interest to our field. The questions for the performance assessment debate are: Do people hold more negative reactions to certain formats? Do people react more negatively to less realistic content?

Research has generally shown mean differences in reactions to typical employment tests. Many studies on work samples in the 1970s and 1980s, as well as recent studies on multiple selection measures, have indicated that people see work samples and other more "realistic" assessments as face valid (e. g., Cascio & Phillips, 1979; Gordon & Kleiman, 1976; Roberston & Kandola 1982; Rynes & Connerly, 1993; Smither, Reilly, Millsap, Pearlman, & Stoffey, 1993). Much of this research, however, was not specifically directed at mode of assessment (e.g., computerized versus multiple choice) but at content (e.g., cognitive ability versus work sample versus personality).

Research in the educational arena on test format has suggested a preference for multiple choice tests over essay examinations. Zeidner (1987) found that multiple-choice tests were judged more favorably than were essay examinations by junior high-school students. In particular, multiple-choice tests were seen as fairer, less anxiety provoking, and easier. Essay examinations were seen as fair by 53% of the sample, but about 70% of the sample thought that essay examinations were more reflective of students' knowledge than were multiple choice exams. Thus, face validity may not be the primary basis for perceptions of fairness; expectancy of success may dictate what individuals desire in assessment formats. Nield and Wintre (1986) found that college students preferred short answer or multiple choice with an option to comment on the chosen answer more than they did essay or traditional multiple-choice questions. Although students liked the commenting option, they rarely used it and it had little impact on grades. Thus, the benefits of allowing individuals to use their preferred method of assessment may be largely perceptual rather than behavioral. Bridgeman (1992), in a study of the GRE, found that most sudents (81%) preferred multiple choice, but about equal proportions thought multiple-choice or open-ended formats were fairer.

In summary, the research in the educational arena *clearly* shows that students have a preference for multiple choice items, that preference should be equated with fairness, and the correlation between realism and fairness is not high. Many test takers, perhaps from self-interest, may prefer methods that they see as less fair, less realistic, or both.

To address whether this finding from the educational arena carried over to employment settings, we collected data from 159 job seekers at employment services in northwest Ohio (mean age of 34.28 [SD = 11.06], 60.4% male; 67.3% White; 22.6% African American). We phrased the questions in terms of format preference rather than content, although this fact perhaps affected what people reacted to. The observations from this research include the following:

• There was no preference for a particular format: 18.5% preferred multiple choice, 26.1% preferred hands on, 28.0% had no preference, and 27.4% said their preference would depend on the test content.

• Not all test takers had experience with all formats in a selection content: 58.5% had experience in taking a multiple-choice test for hiring purposes, and 56.1% had taken a hands-on test for hiring purposes. These results imply a need to be careful in assessing reactions without some measure of experience. Most research on applicant reactions to selection procedures mentioned on the following pages did not assess respondent test-taking experience.

• Responses to a series of agree–disagree items (a few of which are presented in Table 11.1), showed considerable variability in reactions.

• Responses for minority group members differed from those of the majority. Minorities were significantly more likely to agree with the first three statements presented in Table 11.1.

TABLE 11.1

Reactions to Test Format

	% Agree	% Disagree
There are no real connections between multiple choice tests and ability to do the job	37.6	30.5
Multiple choice tests cannot determine if I am a good employee	15.7	55.5
I would rather take a hands-on test even if it takes a lot more of my time in applying for a job	19.4	47.7
Multiple choice tests are fairer than hands-on tests because everyone is treated the same	22.3	45.2

[a] Responses were given on a 5-point scale, ranging from 1 = *strongly disagree* to 5 = *strongly agree*. Percentages were created from collapsing across agree and disagree categories.

Smither et al. (1993) found differences between minority and majority group members, males and females, and older and younger applicants on several different reaction measures. Some studies, however, have shown that demographic characteristics were not strongly associated with reactions to selection procedures or with response tendencies (Macan, Avedon, Paese, & Smith, 1994; Rynes & Connerly, 1993). An implicit assumption of the focus on performance assessments as a replacement for multiple-choice testing is that the change in testing mode results in a reduction in adverse impact or at least in more positive attitudes and less anxiety for minority candidates. Little evidence suggests that this assumption is either correct or incorrect (particularly because of the format–content confusion often present in comparisons of the adverse impact of selection devices).

Although these data are for demonstration purposes only, they indicate reactions to format vary; fairness is different from preference; and many individuals may not have well-formulated opinions because they have not taken many tests for employment purposes.

Much research on applicant reactions can be criticized on several other bases (Rosse, Miller, & Stecher, 1994, present many such crititisms). Studies often use college students whose experience with the devices being evaluated poses a problem in generalizability: They are familiar with such tests and have more experience being assessed than do those long removed from the educational system or those with lower levels of education. It is no surprise that most studies show at least neutral responses to all methods (Rynes & Connerly, 1993). Judgments of face validity by subjects in these studies are made with a particular job (often that of manager) in mind, but conclusions are made about face validity of a method for any job. Just as researchers would not evaluate a test's validity apart from the test's intended use, so they should not evaluate face validity apart from the context of test use. With only a few exceptions

(Rosse, Miller, & Stecher, 1994), these studies are artificial: Subjects read scenarios (Kluger & Rothstein, 1993; Rynes & Connerly, 1993) rather than actually participated in the selection process.

Another concern about this area of research is that the variance across individuals in reactions to specific selection procedures is large (e.g., Rosse et al., 1994), yet the conclusions refer to which methods are preferred by applicants in general. In 1950, Adams concluded, "Wide differences often exist between the judgments made by different individuals as to which tests possess face validity" (p. 328). Rynes and Connerly (1993) found that individual response tendencies explained a considerable amount of variance in attitudes toward specific devices. The key is that the face validity and fairness of measures are not universally shared perceptions, as models of procedural justice clearly predict (see the following), yet realism seems to be equated with the desires of test takers in the debate over format.

The most comprehensive model of reactions to selection procedures is Gilliland's (1993). The full model shows that person and situation characteristics influence whether a test taker feels that procedural and distributive justice rules are violated. We present only a small portion of the model in Fig. 11.4 to focus attention on test type and reactions to selection procedures. The model holds that the extent of perceived violation of these rules influences perceptions of the fairness of the procedures, and the fairness of the outcomes of the selection process, or both. The model is idiosyncratic: Perceptions of rule violation and fairness vary across individuals. The question relevant to this discussion is whether simply changing test mode (not content) or increasing the realism of procedures affects perceptions of these procedural rules. Al-

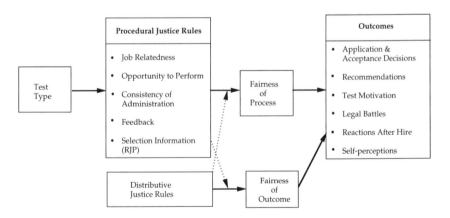

FIG. 11.4. Gilliland's (1993) model of applicant reactions (modified). Adapted from "The perceived fairness of selection systems: An organizational justice perspective," by S. W. Gilliland, 1993, *Academy of Management Review, 18*, pp. 697–734. Reprinted with permission.

though Gilliland's model has test type as a factor, for our purposes we focus on test format besides test content, although both are clearly a part of test type.

For example, Thibaut and Walker (1975) suggested process control, or the ability to control the evidence presented on a person's behalf, influences perceptions of procedural fairness. Changes in the mode of assessment could influence this factor without any change in content. For example, many students who prefer multiple choice to essay tests indicate that they cannot control whether their handwriting and grammatical skills are evaluated in an essay. Another dimension of procedural fairness is correctability (Leventhal, 1980). Performance assessments may not be seen as correctable as multiple-choice tests, on which test takers can simply erase a response without having to begin a task again (which may not even be possible). Another rule of interest is consistency, which the typical multiple-choice test certainly possesses. Some educational reformers and advocates of authentic assessment, however, see consistency as an unnecessary component of an assessment process, and have questioned why all students must be tested in the same way at the same time (Wiggins, 1989). Still another example of the relevance of justice literature to this discussion is that interpersonal treatment has been seen as important to perceptions of fairness (Tyler & Bies, 1989). The administrator in a performance assessment is likely to have greater individual contact with test takers; thus, the importance of this dimension for typical test takers may be enhanced in this situation.

As Gilliland (1993) indicated, the model focuses on predicting fairness perceptions. Another focus worth considering is how perceived violations of these rules affect such reactions as preference. As noted earlier in the discussion of research on student testing, perceptions of fairness may not coincide with preference.

A final shortcoming of the research on perceptions of tests is that although researchers have placed much emphasis on negative effects of disliked testing procedures, they have established little connection to actual behavioral outcomes. Gilliland's model suggests several potential outcomes, but research that links behaviors to reactions has been sparse. Macan et al. (1994) found that applicants' reactions to cognitive ability tests and to assessment centers did affect their intentions to take a job; but other factors (such as job and organizational attractiveness) contributed considerably more to the prediction of intentions. Further, applicant reactions did not appear related to intentions to purchase company products or services. Gilliland (1994) showed that perceived job-relatedness of a selection procedure influenced post-hire job performance. Several researchers (e.g., Macan et al., 1994; Smither et al., 1993) discovered that attitudes were related to performance on some selection procedures, although the causality of these relations has not been addressed, nor is this finding well established or consistent.

How can it be determined if face validity perceptions are really important? They do connect to other perceptions and feelings, but the causal link to behavior has not been convincingly established. For those who say that realism in assessment matters, a demonstration of a link between applicant perceptions of face valildity and behavior would prove the point.

The theoretical basis for this line of research is predicated on fairness as the primary reaction of interest, with face validity (i.e., perceived job-relatedness) as a precursor. Although we doubt that anyone would say that perceptions of fairness are unimportant, we would like to suggest that perhaps a focus on this issue in research on reactions is too narrow. We have concluded that face validity is a determinant of fairness, but we have not thoroughly pursued the factors lead to perceptions of face validity. For example, how are the three aspects that Goldstein et al. (1993) put forth as indicators of psychological fidelity considered in determining face validity? Is one more important than another in influencing test taker perceptions? How does the transparency of a test (i.e., the ability of test takers to assess how well they did; Fredricksen & Collins, 1989) relate to perceptions of face validity?

Fiske (1967) noted that although personality factors may be a source of variance in reactions to tests, there is little research on what types of people react in predictable ways. Several studies have looked at how personality, background characteristics, and current job performance predict reactions to tests (e.g., Brutus, 1993; Ryan, Gregwas, & Ployhart, 1996). Such research is vital to defining the causes of variation in individual reactions, and whether a selection system designers should or could concern themselves with these causes.

Improving models of face validity and reactions to selection procedures by sorting out exactly what applicant reactions mean is important. Are people reacting to the content or the manner in which the content is evaluated, or are they reacting to being evaluated? As Fiske (1967) pointed out, reactions to tests are not just reactions to the test; they are reactions to being evaluated. The current research enthusiasm for face validity does not consider these distinctions.

Who Cares?

Cizek (1991) wrote, "My fear is that we have begun a search for genuine-*looking*, authentic-*looking*, real-*looking* assessments and have eschewed more rigorous standards of validity" (p. 699). Both are important. "Reflecting reality" may be a criterion to evaluate assessment devices against, but it is only one of many. Face validity should not be assumed to be important until researchers provide more concrete demonstrations of its relation to applicant *behavior* and other outcomes. Wiggins (1991), a prime advocate of performance assessments, noted that the aim is not a semblance of realism but rather educational improvement, and researchers must demonstrate, not assume, that realism leads to this end.

Further, many people may not want reality in assessments. Our own observation of individuals taking well-developed video tests suggests that once the novelty of the situation wears off and there is a recognition that one is in an evaluation situation, subject reactions are not as positive. Lind and Tyler (1988) noted that there are two ways of viewing the interaction between distributive and procedural justice. The self-interest model posits that people's interest in the process occurs because of their concern with their personal outcomes. Thus, realism in assessment would be important to an individual only in so much as it was perceived to add to the likelihood of obtaining a job offer. The group value model holds that relationships with others on a societal level are important, and thus the procedures themselves are more important than the outcomes. For this model, realism in assessment would be important if it was thought to increase the fairness of the assessment process regardless of outcome. Blanket statements such as "Everyone wants more realistic assessment," are likely incorrect. Some individuals probably favor more realistic assessment, and the reasons for their attitudes probably differ substantially. Further, the situational context of the assessment, for instance, when highly valued outcomes are at stake, in many ways is likely to affect whether an individual cares.

Assessments do not reflect reality:

Life is not multiple choice.
Life is not lived at maximal performance.
Life involves correlated error (i.e., there is local item dependence).
Life is not administered consistently.
Life is not fair.
Life is like a box of chocolates.

Not everyone wants reality in assessments. Perhaps realism is not always best for maximizing psychometric quality—it can introduce construct irrelevance. The primary question to address is: When is a nonreflection of reality in assessment a cause for concern—psychometrically or in terms of applicant behavior? There still is much research to do to decide if, and how, realism counts.

REFERENCES

Adams, S. (1950). Does face validity exist? *Educational and Psychological Measurement, 10,* 320–328.

Arnold, D. W., & Thiemann, A. J. (1992). To test or not to test: The status of psychological testing under the Americans with Disabilities Act (ADA). *Journal of Business and Psychology, 6,* 503–506.

Aschbacher, P. R. (1992). Issues in performance assessment staff development. *New Directions for Education Reform, 1,* 51–62.

Baker, E. L., Freeman, M., & Clayton, S. (1991). Cognitive assessment of history for large-scale testing. In M.C. Wittrock & E.L. Baker (Eds.), *Testing and cognition* (pp. 131–165). Englewood Cliffs, NJ: Prentice Hall.

Baker, E. L., O'Neil, H. F., & Linn, R. L. (1993). Policy and validity prospects for performance-based assessment. *American Psychologist, 48,* 1210–1218.

Bennett, R. E., Rock, D. A., Wang, M. (1991). Equivalence of free-response and multiple-choice items. *Journal of Educational Measurement, 28*, 77–92.

Booth-Kewley, S., Edwards, J. E., & Rosenfeld, P. (1992). Impression management, social desirability, and computer administration of attitude questionnaires: Does the computer make a difference? *Journal of Applied Psychology, 77*, 562–566.

Bridgeman, B. (1992). A comparison of quantitative questions in open-ended and multiple-choice formats. *Journal of Educational Measurement, 29*, 253–271.

Brown, D. C. (1994). What's new for the 1990's standards? *The Industrial-Organizational Psychologist, 31*, 97–98.

Brutus, S. (1993). *An investigation of determinants of perceived job relatedness.* Unpublished dissertation. Bowling Green State Univeristy.

Cascio, W. F., & Phillips, N. F. (1979). Performance testing: A rose among thorns? *Personnel Psychology, 32*, 751–766.

Cizek, G. J. (1991, May). Innovation or enervation? Performance assessment in perspective. *Phi Delta Kappan, 72*(9), 695–699.

Collis, K., & Romberg, T. A. (1991). Assessment of mathematical performance: An analysis of open-ended test items. In M. C. Wittrock & E. L. Baker (Eds). *Testing and cognition* (pp. 82–130). Englewood Cliffs, NJ: Prentice Hall.

Davey, B. (1991). Evaluating teacher competence through the use of performance assessment tasks: An overview. *Journal of Personnel Evaluation in Education, 5*, 121–132.

DuBois, C. L. Z., Sackett, P. R., Zedeck, S., & Fogli, L. (1993). Further exploration of typical and maximum performance criteria: Definitional issues, prediction, and white–black differences. *Journal of Applied Psychology, 78*, 205–211.

Fischer, R. J. (1994). The Americans with Disabilities Act: Implications for measurement. *Educational Measurement: Issues & Practice, 13*, 17–26, 37.

Fiske, D. W. (1967). The subject reacts to tests. *American Psychologist, 22*, 287–296.

Frechtling, J. A. (1991). Performance assessment: Moonstruck or the real thing? *Educational Measurement: Issues and Practice,* pp. 23–25.

Frederiksen, J. R., & Collins, A. (1989). A systems approach to educational testing. *Educational Researcher, 2*, 27–32.

Gatewood, R. D., & Feild, H. S. (1994). *Human resource selection.* Fort Worth, TX: Dryden Press.

Gilliland, S. W. (1993). The perceived fairness of selection systems: An organizational justice perspective. *Academy of Management Journal, 18*, 694–734.

Gilliland, S. W. (1994). Effects of procedural and distributive justice on reactions to a selection system. *Journal of Applied Psychology, 79*, 691–701.

Goldstein, I. L., Zedeck, S., & Schneider, B. (1993). An exploration of the job analysis— content validity process. In N. Schmitt & W. C. Borman & Associates (Eds.), *Personnel selection in organizations* (pp. 3–34). San Francisco: Jossey-Bass.

Gordon, M. E., & Kleiman, L. S. (1976). The prediction of trainability using a work sample test and an aptitude test: A direct comparison. *Personnel Psychology, 29*, 243–253.

Guion, R. M. (1977). Content validity—the source of my discontent. *Applied Psychological Measurement, 1*, 1–10.

Haney, W., & Madaus, G. (1989, May). Searching for alternatives to standardized tests: Whys, whats, and whithers. *Phi Delta Kappan, 70*(9), 683–687.

Kennedy, R. (1992). What is performance assessment? *New Directions for Education Reform, 1*, 21–27.

Klimoski, R., & Palmer, S. (1993). The ADA and the hiring process in organizations. *Consulting Psychology Journal: Practice and Research, 45*, 10–36.

Kluger, A. N., & Rothstein, H.R. (1993). The influence of selection test type on applicant reactions to employment testing. *Journal of Business and Psychology, 8*, 3–25.

Leventhal, G. (1980). What should be done with equity theory? New approaches to the study of fairness in social relationships. In K. Gergen, M. Greenberg, & R. Willis (Eds.), *Social exchange: Advances in theory and research* (pp. 27–55). New York: Plenum.

Lind, E. A., & Tyler, T. (1988). *The social psychology of procedural justice.* New York: Plenum.

Linn, R. L. (1993). Educational assessment: Expanded expectations and challenges. *Educational Evaluation and Policy Analysis, 15,* 1–16.

Linn, R. L., Baker, E. L., & Dunbar, S. B. (1991). Complex, performance-based assessment: Expectations and validation criteria. *Educational Researcher, 15*(1), 15–21.

Macan, T. H., Avedon, M .J., Paese, M., & Smith, D. E. (1994). The effects of applicants' reactions to cognitive ability tests and an assessment center. *Personnel Psychology, 47,* 715–738.

Martinez, M. E. (1991). A comparison of multiple choice and constructed figural response items. *Journal of Educational Measurement, 28,* 131–145.

McGaghie, W. C. (1991). Professional competence evaluation. *Educational Researcher, 20,* 3–9.

Mehrens, W. A. (1992). Using performance assessment for accountability purposes. *Educational Measurement: Issues and Practice, 11*(1), 3–20.

Moreland, K. L. (1992). Computer-assisted psychological assessment. In M. Zeidner & R. Most (Eds.), *Psychological testing: An inside view* (pp. 343–376). Palo Alto, CA: Consulting Psychologists Press.

Murphy, K. R., & Davidshofer, C. O. (1994). *Psychological testing: Principles and applications.* Englewood Cliffs, NJ: Prentice-Hall.

Nester, M. A. (1993). Psychometric testing and reasonable accommodation for persons with disabilities. *Rehabilitation Psychology, 38,* 75–85.

Nield, A. F., & Wintre, M. G. (1986). Multiple-choice questions with an option to comment: Student attitudes and use. *Teaching of Psychology, 13,* 196–199.

Norman, G. R., Smith, E. K. M., Powles, A. C. P., Rooney, P. J., Henry, N. L., & Dodd, P. E. (1987). Factors underlying performance on written tests of knowledge. *Medical Education, 21,* 297–304.

Norris, S. P. (1990). Effect of eliciting verbal reports of thinking on critical thinking test performance. *Journal of Educational Measurement, 27,* 41–58.

Petrosko, J. M. (1992). The role of quantitative methods in performance assessment. *New Directions for Education Reform, 1,* 28–36.

Robertson, I. T., & Kandola, R. S. (1982). Work sample tests: Validity, adverse impact and applicant reactions. *Journal of Occupational Psychology, 55,* 171–183.

Rosse, J. G., Miller, J. L., & Stecher, M. D. (1994). A field study of job applicants' reactions to personality and cognitive ability testing. *Journal of Applied Psychology, 79,* 987–992.

Ryan, A. M., Greguras, G., & Ployhart, R. (1996). Perceived job relatedness of physical ability testing for firefighters: Exploring variations in reactions. *Human Performance 9,* 219–240.

Rynes, S. L., & Connerly, M. L. (1993). Applicant reactions to alternative selection procedures. *Journal of Business and Psychology, 7,* 261–277.

Sackett, P. R. (1987). Assessment centers and content validity: Some neglected issues. *Personnel Psychology, 40,* 13–26.

Sackett, P. R., Zedeck. S., & Fogli, L. (1988). Relations between typical and maximum job performance. *Journal of Applied Psychology, 73,* 482–486.

Saklofske, D. H., & Kowalchuk, V. L. S. (1992). Influences on testing and test results. In M. Zeidner & R. Most (Eds.), *Psychological testing: An inside view,* (pp. 89–118). Palo Alto, CA: Consulting Psychologists Press.

Sanchez, J. I., Fraser, S. L., Fernandez, D. M., & DeLaTorre, P. (1993, April). *Development and validation of the Customer Service Skills Inventory.* Presented at the eighth annual conference of the Society for Industrial and Organizational Psychology, San Francisco.

Schmitt, N., Schneider, J. R., & Cohen, S. A. (1990). Factors affecting validity of a regionally administered assessment center. *Personnel Psychology, 43,* 1–12.

Shavelson, R. J. (1993). *Sampling variability of performance assessments*. Los Angeles: National Center for Research on Evaluation, Standards, and Student Testing.

Shavelson, R. J., Baxter, G. P., & Gao, X. (1993). Sampling variability of performance assessments. *Journal of Educational Measurement, 30*, 215–232.

Smither, J. W., Reilly, R. R., Millsap, R. E., Pearlman, K., & Stoffey, R. W. (1993). Applicant reactions to selection procedures. *Personnel Psychology, 46*, 49–76.

Sternberg, R. J. (1991). Toward better intelligence tests. In M. C. Wittrock & E. L. Baker (Eds.), *Testing and cognition* (pp. 31–39). Englewood Cliffs, NJ: Prentice Hall.

Stiggins, R. J. (1987). Design and development of performance assessments. *Educational Measurement: Issues and Practice*, pp. 33–42.

Thibaut, J., & Walker, L. (1975). *Procedural justice: A psychological analysis*. Hillsdale, NJ: Lawrence Erlbaum Associates.

Traub, R. E., & Fisher, C. W. (1977). On the equivalence of constructed-response and multiple-choice tests. *Applied Psychological Measurement, 1*, 355–369.

Tyler, T., & Bies, R. (1989). Beyond formal procedures: The interpersonal context of procedural justice. In J. S. Carrell (Ed.), *Advances in applied social psychology: Business settings* (pp. 107–143). Hillsdale, NJ: Lawrence Erlbaum Associates.

Van de Vijver, F. J. R., & Harsveld, M. (1994). The incomplete equivalence of the paper-and-pencil and computerized versions of the General Aptitude Test Battery. *Journal of Applied Psychology, 79*, 852–859.

Wickens, C. D. (1984). *Engineering psychology and human performance*. Columbus, OH: Merrill.

Wiggins, G. (1989). A true test: Toward more authentic and equitable assessment. *Phi Delta Kappan, 70*, 703–713.

Wiggins, G. (1991). A response to Cizek. *Phi Delta Kappan, 72*, 700–703.

Yen, W. M. (1993). Scaling performance assessments: strategies for managing local item dependence. *Journal of Educational Measurement, 30*, 187–213.

Zeidner, M. (1987). Essay versus multiple choice type classroom exams: The student's perspective. *Journal of Educational Research, 80*, 352–358.

12

A Practitioner's Response and Call for Help

David J. Kleinke
Edison Electric Institute

Commenting on the chapters in this book is a truly daunting task that was made easier by Milt Hakel, who said, "Well, you are the practical presenter." Milt suggested that I simply react to the book from my point of view.

I work with investor-owned electric utilities, directing large-scale consortium employee-selection testing projects. At present there are 10 such projects, most based on paper-and-pencil, multiple-choice tests. Significantly, Edison Electric Institute's (EEI) latest project, which selects customer service representatives, uses the consortium's first computer-administered tests.

Many authors in this book have recalled their own experiences as test takers. I continue that tradition briefly. In elementary school and high school, I took several multiple-choice tests and made most of the marks in the right places on them, so much so that I won a college scholarship on the basis of my Scholastic Aptitude Test (SAT) scores. All this happened so long ago that I never knew what those SAT scores were. This comment is relevant to how college admissions testing in particular, and testing in general, have evolved. Back in the Dark Ages, when I took the SAT, nobody seemed to think that test candidates needed to know their scores. After all, these kids were taking the test for the convenience of the colleges making admission decisions. Candidates did not make these decisions so why should they know their scores?

Of course, this view has changed: It would be unthinkable not to release American College Testing (ACT) or SAT scores to college admissions candidates. Even the examinees who take my employee selection tests, as well as their potential supervisors, are uncomfortable when we decline to release their scores to them. I believe that this reaction reflects a shift from seeing a test score as a predictor to seeing it as a label.

I have worked with many multiple choice tests, and have done so long enough to have lived through many attacks on testing. Critics have often concentrated on the sample items published in candidate handbooks. For example, one handbook with which I was associated had the sample verbal analogy, "*Wine* is to *vintage* as *furniture* is to *period*." As you might imagine, this item drew fire as reflecting middle-class White culture. We quickly kicked it out of the handbook.

Lloyd Bond has said that test developers should conduct a sensitivity review of test items early in the test development process to ferret out sources of potential bias in tests. My guess is that "*Wine* is to *vintage* as *furniture* is to *period*" would not pass through such a sensitivity review. My question to Bond would be, "What empirical evidence shows that items that are rejected by such a sensitivity review would in fact result in greater adverse impact?" What do we know? Perhaps members of minority groups might be even better versed in these middle-class, White values.

In addition to adverse impact concerns, those of us in testing often have more qualified applicants than there are slots available. There are more college graduates than there are jobs for college graduates. In many of the companies I work with, reductions in force have cut the number of craft jobs available. For example, the testing executive in one company talked to me about the fate of a junior accountant who was going to be notified that his job had been eliminated. The question the executive was asked me was "Can this person go to a clerical job without taking the required keyboarding test?" The answer was, "No."

There has been a resurgence of interest in standardized testing in the companies with which I work. This resurgence has come about through downsizing, re-engineering, reductions in force (RIFs), or whatever name is used. Layoffs and early retirements have affected people in power plants; many power plant operators and maintenance workers have taken early retirement and must be replaced. Managers can operate an electric company without a junior accountant, but they need power plant operators and line workers to function.

In addition, companies have instituted or have increased testing of employees who are seeking to "bump" others. For example, a company might decide to outsource meter reading. Meter readers with a lot of seniority might be permitted to bid on an apprentice electrician job. But to get the job, they must pass the test required for selection as an apprentice electrician.

There also are demands for new media. My association is currently developing customer service representative tests whose impetus came essentially from line departments. Managers said:

> We know your clerical aptitude battery. We know that this battery of paper and pencil objective tests is very good for selecting people. But customer service

representatives work at keyboards. So we want you to test them at a keyboard. Further, these people work under great strain. They are the people who get the phone calls: 'My power is out. My bill's too high. My cat is lost.'

These line managers are thus saying that they need some measure of typical behavior as well. I have been looking for new media, new ways to test, new alternatives to multiple-choice testing.

A paper and pencil battery of the customary skills and abilities would surely produce the highest criterion-related validity per examinee hour or per testing dollar. But the message is clear: Line management wants the selection procedure to look like the job. They are also strongly disposed toward new ideas—everyone's work life has been changed over the past decade by advances in technology. Line managers expect this technological shift to be reflected in changes in testing.

In some of the papers at the conference that inspired this book, researchers compared apples and oranges or multiple-choice cognitive tests to alternate-mode noncognitive tests. Ryan and Greguras articulated my problem in chapter 11: Are comparisons being made between multiple choice and an alternative format, between content or process or cognitive and noncognitive? Or are comparisons being made across categories?

I agree with Guion's remark in chapter 2 that people who criticize multiple choice tests have not seen the multiple choice tests that he has. For about the past 5 years, colleagues on the education side of the house have been talking more and more about high stakes tests. These are tests for college admission, for professional licensure, for employment. Like Mrs. Malaprop, who was surprised to discover that she had been speaking prose all her life, I have worked with high stakes tests all my working life. Therefore, I am used to seeing well-constructed, closely reviewed test items. I am used to tests where four questions are required to pretest two, to use one. These tests are edited by sharp-eyed former English-teacher editors. These tests have no grammatical inconsistencies and no absence of problems in the stems. I suspect that far too often criticism in the high stakes business comes from somebody's pique over poorly written midterm examinations. I have seen poorly written, really poorly written questions in teachers' handbooks that come with textbooks. Because I have spent more time teaching introductory measurement than anything else, the introductory measurement textbook with the poor questions are most familiar to me.

Guion also reminded me about a kind of validity people talked about sneeringly in graduate school, called *fiat validity*. Fiat validity was defined as the validity that accrues to an instrument on the basis of the claims of its author or publisher. Much of the validity of constructed response or other alternatives is of the fiat validity nature: I claim it is valid, therefore it is. By the same token, I can remember when *face validity* was a bad term. People believed that building face validity was changing "Two plus two equals what?" to "Two joists plus two joists equals how many joists?" for carpenters or "Two invoices plus two invoices equals how many invoices?" for clerks. In attempting to make the item more palatable, test developers unnecessarily added to the reading load and potentially reduced the item's construct validity. Now Guion and Tenopyr (chap. 3) state that adding these constructs may in some ways be helpful. Perhaps these new constructs ought to be included to improve the overall construct validity of tests.

Tenopyr's discussion of the self-esteem movement is also relevant to employment testing. People want to feel good about themselves; they want to pass tests; people want their subordinates to pass tests. I have had problems with supervisors who feel that all subordinates should pass selection or promotion tests. In one case, people in an operating department had demanded two actions of their testing people. The training department complained that new candidates did not have enough mathematics. "We want them to come through with more mathematics. So toughen the mathematics on the test. And, oh, by the way, we want you to pass more people." This remark came from an engineer. Never trust anybody who takes notes on graph paper!

McBride's remarks (chap. 4) were very interesting. About 20 years ago, I sat on Mark Reckase's dissertation committee. Mark did pioneering work in computerized adaptive testing. And for the next 18 years, I was able to say, "In 1972 I was on his dissertation committee. He did great work, and nothing has ever come of computerized adaptive testing." Well, now computerized adaptive testing is here—for the Graduate Record Examination, for Nurse Licensing Examination, and for the Armed Services Vocational Aptitude Battery (AS-VAB).

I work with companies that generate about 75% of the electric power in the United States. One hundred companies use our tests, but we are small potatoes compared to the ASVAB. My company cannot do the item equating that I believe necessary for computerized adaptive testing. We use a test form for several years; we cannot produce a new form every year or every 6 months as the GRE can. We cannot embed items in our tests to pretest them. To get the estimate of an item's difficulty index or the item response curve, the item must be given to a large number of people; test developers must know the item's values or else items and testlets will not be scaled properly or defensibly. And defensibility is, in fact, the name of the game.

Outtz (chap. 5) made an incontrovertible point. He said that we need more research. In testing people always say we need more research. Outtz said that we especially need more research into the underlying constructs, into what is going on. I recall the early reaction to *Pygmalion in the Classroom* (Rosenthal & Jacobson, 1968). Rosenthal and Jacobson's point was that second graders who were expected to improve did so. But Rosenthal and Jacobson never explained what teachers did differently to lead to the improvement. If I were a second-grade teacher and I wanted to see my pupils improve, what should I do? Show me that the tests are different, but most important, tell me what the difference is. Tell me why there is a difference. Bond's scatterplots, where there were mean differences in both the predictor and the criterion, why is the difference in the criterion? We testing types work principally with predictors, but please tell me about the criterion some day. We have a suspicion it may not be supervisor bias.

Nearly 20 years ago, Marv Dunnette was working for my association and did a wonderful job on power plant operator tests. Even then, there were enough minority operators and supervisors to look at possible interaction between race of supervisor and race of subordinate in ratings. Subsequently, HRStrategies has examined this situation in other craft jobs for us and has found no interaction. Minority subordinates were rated essentially the same by minority as by majority supervisors. Why? Why were there differences in the criterion? Someone must address this critical area.

Bond has made a noteworthy distinction between adverse impact and bias. Hough (chap. 9) has described rugged individualism as the measure of what used to be masculinity/femininity. A pronounced male/female difference on such a scale might reflect adverse impact, but not bias, at least in a situation where rugged individualism is, in fact, desirable. In physical ability testing, male-female differences might reflect huge adverse impact, but no bias due from the testing method, because these differences reflect anatomical differences.

Sackett (chap. 8) drew attention to the National Board for Professional Teaching Standards. "What did we do when we wanted an outhouse?" Here in a careful selection procedure, selection in the broadest sense, the result is adverse impact we can walk across. I have no answers.

Hough (chap. 9) frustratingly gave the right statistics with the wrong data. For faking, she showed correlations. As evidence for or against faking, I want to see means. I want to see mean scores because I have experience in having tests that are normed on incumbents, where my cut scores are set on incumbents. And the applicants come in, and something strange has happened. The applicants do not do as well as the incumbents on the cognitive portion, but their personalities and backgrounds are wonderful. They have been to Lourdes. The scores are inflated by almost a full standard deviation. Both biodata and traditional personality scale-type items produce this reversal of fortune. So, for data on faking, I want to see means.

In a reversal, for adverse impact information, I want to see correlations, not means. It has not been fashionable in academe to talk about differential validity. It is passé. But when dealing with an investigator from a government agency or a representative of a union, having demonstrated differential validity is a security blanket.

I want to make two points about Ryan and Greguras's ideas (chap. 11), points that come from dealing with job candidates and their representatives, from having tests reviewed by labor union officials and government investigators. The first point is that the testing mode does not matter; test content does. The notion that multiple-choice format stifles creativity is just not an issue in my world. But I have reviewed a lot of biodata and personality measures with union people who hate them.

The second point is that there is no research into the most important unanswered question in testing. What research would help me to answer a candidate who said, "I want to improve my performance on your aptitude test." I cannot tell this person about standard errors of the difference between measures. I cannot tell this person about the relative stability of aptitude and achievement in adults. I can only say, "Try your best." I have nothing to say to the person who says, "How should I improve? Should I work on math because I did poorly? Or reading because I did well? How can I improve myself so I pass the test the next time?"

REFERENCE

Rosenthal, R., & Jacobson, L. (1968). *Pygmalion in the classroom: Teacher expectation and pupils' intellectual development*. New York: Holt, Rinehart & Winston.

13

Been There, Done That!

Milton D. Hakel
Bowling Green State University

Those of us who have prospered as a consequence of our relative success in answering multiple choice paper and pencil ability test items do not see much of a problem. We have been there and done that. Traditional tests are obviously fair—every examinee gets presented with the identical set of tasks, scoring is objective, cheating is discouraged, time limits are enforced, every step can be verified in public. Oh sure, it would be nice to score at the 95th (or 99th) percentile, rather than just at the 90th. And if tests could be improved so that my true performance would be revealed, well, I would support that effort—I have always tested below my true ability, I just know it. The day I took the Miller Analogies Test I had a cold. The American College Test (ACT) was so long ago, and anyway, I was just a high school kid—doing OK but not *really* trying. Never did have to take the Graduate Record Examination (GRE), thank goodness. And I have yet to encounter personally any pre-employment screening tests for holders of PhD's. With the same sigh of relief I felt when I was no longer eligible for induction via draft into the U.S. military, I can at last safely say that I am beyond multiple choice. The system worked for me—long live the system.

What! That is not good enough? More is wanted? Both merit *and* fairness?

What should researchers conclude about alternatives to traditional testing for selection? I feel disappointed. I was looking for a silver bullet. It seems to me that the alternatives leave plenty to be desired. And the critics are right: Traditional testing leaves plenty to be desired, too.

Despite the missing silver bullet, I would like to single out several key contributions in the preceding chapters and present them as punch lines for emphasis:

- It is not just the testing medium or a matter of face validity. People like tests that they pass.
- Personality constructs can predict *targeted* performance criteria.
- Biodata constructs may show differential response patterns among ethnic groups.
- Complex thinking skills can be measured.
- Multimedia tests can decrease mean differences between ethnic groups on tests, but they can also increase these differences.
- Computerized versions of paper and pencil tests may measure the wrong things.
- Constructed responses have biases, too, and they can also measure the wrong things.
- Authentic performance a$$e$$ment$ co$t lot$.
- There are six facets of validity, but validity is unitary.
- Why are there group differences on criteria?
- What can I do to raise my score on your test?

Everyone knows that there is more to a person than can be conveyed by a single score. This fact is obvious on the criterion side of the equation, even to the general public. Job performance bears a stronger similarity to the decathlon (a series of performances) than it does, for example, to either the 100-meter dash (a single, simple performance) or a chess game (a single, complex performance). There is no general factor in job performance, and although one undoubtedly could be found, it would lose so much detail as to be misleading. Indeed, there are multiple job performance factors (McCloy, Campbell, & Cudeck, 1994). Closer to the public consciousness, think about baseball statistics as a domain in which job performance is routinely quantified and clearly multifaceted and multidimensional. Would any major league club pick only right-handed hitters?

Or, if sports information is too gendercentric, consider this exchange, from the comic strip *Dilbert* (Adams, 1996):

Manager: Alice, I'd like you to meet the newest member of my management team. Keith is highly qualified. He has a Masters in Business Administration.

Alice: Very impressive. They must have taught you a lot about motivating employees.

Keith: No, not really.

Alice: Well… you probably learned how to identify and hire good people, right?

Keith:	That might have been optional reading.
Alice:	Did you learn negotiation skills?
Keith:	No.
Alice:	Strategic thinking?
Keith:	No.
Alice:	Business writing?
Keith:	No. It was mostly finance and accounting. And economics.
Alice:	So, you're a highly qualified leader because... you're good at math?

If *Dilbert* can be taken as evidence, the general public does not have high regard for the use of a single credential on the predictor side of the equation. Deficient predictors are no more desirable than deficient criteria.

Until 1925, even the best scientists were sure that our galaxy comprised the entire universe. Then astronomers grew keener, and what had been thought to be distant, fuzzy stars turned out to be additional galaxies, now estimated to number 50 billion. Meta-analysis has recently been added to our toolkit, and it has vastly expanded our observational power. It is a methodological advance that I regard as being no less important than Galileo's telescope. Our data are frightfully noisy, and meta-analysis helps us to detect signal among the noise.

To the general public, the results of meta-analyses seem to say that *g* is all that matters on the predictor side of the equation. *g* appears to be the whole universe of human ability. Can a simple linear sum tell us enough about a person's probable job (or educational) performance to warrant abandoning the search for better prediction? Why not award PhDs to 10-year-olds who score above a cut point on a general intelligence test?

Should researchers abandon Dunnette's modified model? In 1963, Dunnette published "A modified model for test validation and selection research" in the *Journal of Applied Psychology*. The model not only identified links between predictor constructs, individuals, and job behaviors, but also included situational variance among the determinants of organizational consequences. Recently, Dunette said, "That's about the most thoroughly discredited hypothesis I've ever seen" (Dunnette, June 12, 1996, personal communication). He was referring to the vanquished variance, seen as situational main effects. Meta-analyses of selection test validity correlations have shown that essentially *all* variance in these correlations can be accounted for, explained by, a handful of "artifacts": sampling error, and so on. There is, therefore, no apparent need to invoke other constructs or more complex explanations, such as unspecified situational differences.

Maybe the *g*-ocentrists are right, but then again maybe not. All the data are not in yet. And remember:

While meta-analysis may be a step toward an "objective" summarization of the state of the art in a given scientific area, I get the impression that at least some folks think the method somehow will facilitate arriving at scientific "truth." At its very best, meta-analysis cannot determine what is *true*, it only can attempt to measure what *is*. If we constantly keep in mind that, had meta-analysis been around at the time, it would have confirmed that planet Earth was flat and the center of the universe, we'll be all right. (Fine, 1990, p. 494)

There is a national quest for a level playing field for employee selection, and I cannot imagine that a model based on *g* alone will turn out to be sufficient. Both merit *and* fairness are needed: The whole person is hired for the job. What are the options? Traditional testing, the paper-and-pencil multiple choice cognitive ability test, appears to be unbeatable, although it suffers from many shortcomings, most notably adverse impact roughly double the size of criterion differences. The alternatives examined in these pages do not seem to be sufficiently attractive to offset their own shortcomings. More research is needed, and the punch lines show the promising directions.

There is no silver bullet. But no doubt this book is not the last visit to traditional testing or its alternatives. We, and certainly our successors, are bound to make telling observations and supply conceptual insights to expand the known universe.

REFERENCES

Adams, Scott. (October 27, 1996). Dilbert, *Toledo Blade*.

Dunnette, M. D. (1963). A modified model for test validation and selection research. *Journal of Applied Psychology, 47,* 317–323.

Fine, Bernard J. (1990). Letter to the Editor. *Science, 250,* 494.

McCloy, R. A., Campbell, J. P., & Cudeck, R. (1994). A confirmatory test of a model of performance determinants. *Journal of Applied Psychology, 79,* 493–505.

Author Index

Subject Index

219